The Mekong

Also by Milton Osborne

BOOKS

The French Presence in Cochinchina and Cambodia: Rule and Response (1859–1905), 1969; reprinted 1997

Region of Revolt: Focus on Southeast Asia, 1970; revised and expanded edition 1971

Politics and Power in Cambodia: The Sihanouk Years, 1973

River Road to China: The Mekong River Expedition, 1866–1973, 1975; new edition 1996; US edition 1999

Before Kampuchea: Preludes to Tragedy, 1979

Sihanouk: Prince of light, prince of darkness, 1994; Japanese edition 1996

Southeast Asia: An introductory history, 1979; 2nd edition 1983; 3rd edition 1985; Japanese edition 1987; 4th edition 1988; 5th edition 1990; 6th edition 1995; 7th edition 1997

RESEARCH MONOGRAPHS

Singapore and Malaysia, 1964

Strategic Hamlets in South Viet-Nam: A Survey and a Comparison, 1965

The Mekong

Turbulent past, uncertain future

Milton Osborne

GROVE PRESS
New York

Maps on pages x, 145, 230 by MAPgraphics, Brisbane, Australia

Originally published in 2000 by Allen & Unwin, St. Leonards, Australia

Published simultaneously in Canada
Printed in the United States of America

FIRST GROVE PRESS PAPERBACK EDITION

Library of Congress Cataloging-in-Publication Data

Osborne, Milton E.
    The Mekong, turbulent past, uncertain future / Milton Osborne.
        p.   cm.
    Includes bibliographical references and index.
    ISBN 0-8021-3802-0 (pbk.)
    1. Indochina—Civilization. 2. Mekong River Valley—Civilization. I. Title.

DS537 .O83 2000
959.7—dc21

99-086337

Grove Press
841 Broadway
New York, NY 10003

01 02 03 04   10 9 8 7 6 5 4 3 2 1

Contents

Maps and Illustrations

Colour illlustrations

For Dinah

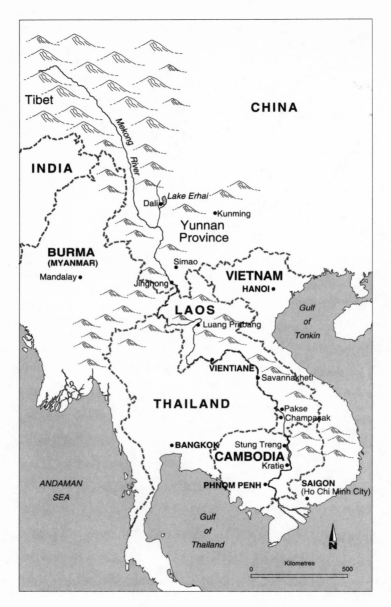

The course of the Mekong

Preface

The book that follows deals with one of the world's great rivers, the Mekong. The twelfth largest in size it is, for reasons that I examine in the text, still surprisingly little known by comparison with other great rivers such as the Nile or the Amazon. Yet the Mekong and the lands that lie beside it possess a rich if turbulent history, face major contemporary political and economic problems and, as I spell out in the following pages, an uncertain future. While I never planned to do so, I have spent forty fascinated years in close association with the Mekong— living beside it, travelling on it, and studying its history. The present book is very much a reflection of this personal experience. Those forty years of personal association have yielded friendships and intellectual debts that I have tried to acknowledge in full in the 'Sources, Notes and Acknowledgements' provided at the end of the text. Writing about two thousand years of history is a task that can only be undertaken with the help of others, but as must always be the case, the judgments made in this book and the choice of issues discussed are mine alone.

In writing about a large geographical region I have tried to follow a simple rule in the choice of spellings I have adopted for the many place names that are cited. In short, I have used the most common contemporary spelling, even though this means that current usage can differ considerably from that of, say, the nineteenth century. So what was commonly known as 'Keng Hung' in the nineteenth century is now identified as 'Jinghong'. In other cases the difference between earlier and current usage is not great. The change from 'Tali' to 'Dali' in western Yunnan is a case in point. I should note that I have found no need to change the identification of the Chinese capital from 'Peking' to 'Beijing'. In this I find myself in the admirable company of Simon Leys and Jonathan Spence. Widely known Vietnamese toponyms such as 'Saigon' and 'Danang' are recorded as one word, but less well-known names are cited in their common Vietnamese form as, for instance, 'My Tho'. Where there are references to the Mekong in quotations from earlier periods which use different spellings, I have preserved the contemporary usage.

In the case of Chinese personal names, and while I have adopted the modern spelling of 'Mao Zedong' (formerly 'Mao Tse-tung'), I have continued to use the older, and much better known spelling of 'Chou Ta-kuan' when writing about the Chinese imperial envoy who visited Cambodia in the thirteenth century and has left us with the only eye-witness account of the great city of Angkor in its prime. Anyone wishing to read this account in translation would be hard pressed to find it by looking for 'Zhou Daguan' as the author in a catalogue or book index.

Illustrations and maps not otherwise acknowledged are my own material.

Milton Osborne
Sydney, 1999

The Mekong River and Region: An Outline Chronology

1st century AD	Archeology covering this period has revealed the existence of a seaport at Oc Eo on the edge of the Mekong Delta that had links with China and the Mediterranean world.
2nd–6th centuries	Chinese records speak of 'Funan', a state established in the Mekong Delta region. Modern scholarship judges Funan to have been a collection of petty states rather than a single polity.
c. 3rd century	The Chinese build a bridge across the Mekong in western Yunnan.
6th–9th centuries	Chinese records no longer speak of Funan but of 'Chenla', a state in two parts, one around the territory of modern Cambodia, the other possibly centred on Wat Phu in southern Laos.
9th–15th centuries	Period of the great Cambodian empire based at Angkor.
c. 1278	Marco Polo presumed to have crossed the Mekong in western Yunnan when travelling out of China on his way to Bengal.
1296–97	Chinese envoy Chou Ta-kuan visits Angkor

and writes a detailed description of the city and its inhabitants.

post-1431   The Cambodian king leaves Angkor; henceforth the Cambodian capital is located at or near the site of modern Phnom Penh.

1511   The Portuguese capture Malacca and shortly afterwards references to the Mekong appear in their records.

1555   First recorded visit to Cambodia by a European, the Portuguese priest, Father da Cruz. He leaves in 1557.

1563   Publication of the first map showing the Mekong running through Cambodia.

1580s   After an absence of decades, Portuguese and Spanish missionaries return to Cambodia.

1593–99   Portuguese and Spanish freebooters, led by Blas Ruiz and Diego Veloso, play an active role in Cambodia's royal politics.

1603   First reference to Angkor in a European publication.

1641–42   A Dutch trader, Gerritt van Wuysthoff, travels up the Mekong to Vientiane.

1778   The Siamese sack Vientiane and carry off the Emerald Buddha.

1783   After many decades during which there is no firm record of any visits to Angkor by Europeans, a French priest, Father Langenois, travels to the temples.

1828   The Siamese sack Vientiane again.

1850   Father Bouillevaux visits Angkor.

1858	France begins its invasion of Vietnam, capturing Saigon in 1861.
1860	Henri Mouhot visits Angkor (he later dies near Luang Prabang in 1861).
1863	France establishes a protectorate over Cambodia.
1866–68	The French Mekong Expedition explores the river from Vietnam to Yunnan.
1886	Auguste Pavie appointed French vice-consul in Luang Prabang.
1893	France begins to assert control over Laos, with Pavie at the forefront of exploration of the Lao territories. The French construct a railway across the Khone Falls and launch gunboats on the Falls' northern (upriver) side.
post-1900	France extends control over Cambodia, Laos and Vietnam as 'French Indochina'. European powers recognise China's sovereignty over the Sip Song Panna (Xishuangbanna) region in the far south of Yunnan Province.
1914–18	First World War.
1930s	The Great Depression has major effects in Vietnam. Emergence of the Indochinese Communist Party.
1941	Outbreak of the Pacific War. By this stage Japan has effective military control of the countries of Indochina.
1946–54	First Indochina War.
1957	Establishment of the Mekong Committee.
1963	Major renewal of hostilities in Vietnam, signalled by the Battle of Ap Bac.

1965–75	The Second Indochina War (the Vietnam War) involves Cambodia and Laos as well as Vietnam, and leads to the defeat of the American forces and also of their South Vietnamese, Cambodian and Lao allies.
1975	Communist governments come to power in the whole of Vietnam, in Laos and in Cambodia. In Cambodia, the Pol Pot regime embarks on a reign of terror.
1978–79	Vietnam invades Cambodia and overthrows the Pol Pot regime.
late 1980s	Renewed discussion about possibilities for economic development of the Mekong and its surrounding region.
1991	Arrangements to settle the Cambodia problem give added impetus to planning for development of the Mekong and its region.
1993	The Chinese complete the first dam built on the Upper Mekong, at Manwan, after starting work in 1984.
1994	Pak Mun Dam on the Mun River, a tributary of the Mekong in Thailand, is completed. The 'Friendship Bridge' linking Thailand and Laos, the first bridge built over the Lower Mekong, is completed.
1995	The Mekong Committee is reconstituted as the Mekong River Commission.
1996	The Chinese commence construction of a second dam on the Upper Mekong, at Dachaoshan.
1998	Theun Hinboun Dam is completed in Laos.

Prologue

Between 1969 and 1997 Cambodia's total forest cover has been reduced by 30 per cent. If the present rate of logging continues, the country's forest reserves will be exhausted by 2003.

From a report funded by the World Bank and released in May 1998

The first mouthful of chilled Beer Lao tasted delicious as we sat, hot, sweaty and a little tired in the 40 degree heat. This was not a time to think about comparisons with Foster's or some other international brand. For the moment, the local product more than met our needs. I had been thinking about it longingly for hours as Boun, my Lao guide, and I spent a long morning cycling back and forth on Don Khon (Khon Island) in the far south of Laos, where the Mekong River reaches the great natural barrier of the Khone Falls.

It had been a companionable time as the cheerfully rotund Boun spoke wistfully in French—a language seldom heard in Laos these days—of his years of teacher training in Montpellier nearly three decades before, and of the changes he had witnessed since the communists came to power in 1975. Now back in Khinak, one of the last settlements on the way south to Laos's border with Cambodia, I savoured another mouthful and was about to ask him about contemporary political events. But before I could do so the sleepy midday scene was transformed by the noisy arrival of two large new four-wheel-drive vehicles, which pulled to a sudden halt outside the eating house in a flurry of dust.

A dozen men got out, their jovial faces and back-slapping camaraderie testifying to their good spirits. The newcomers' evident good humour became even more apparent as they settled in for a long lunch washed down with copious quantities of local beer and Thai whisky—appropriately for the setting, they were drinking the ubiquitous Mekong brand. My curiosity was piqued. Who were these men whose bellies, hanging like pelmets over their sagging trouser belts, gave clear evidence of their having dined well many times before? And what could explain an evident celebration in this out-of-the-way location? By any standard it seemed an odd place for such an event. Khinak, after all, is just another unremarkable riverside settlement. A flyspeck on the map of Laos, it seemed not much more than that on the ground in May 1998. Wooden buildings straggled along a dusty road, with the more favoured looking out over a quiet arm of the Mekong River. In the blanket heat of midday, with the river gunmetal grey under a sky washed almost clear of colour, the energy of the new arrivals contrasted with the absence of any other move- ment, either along Khinak's single street or on the river itself.

I had visited Khinak once before, in 1960, driving up into Laos through Cambodia's sparsely settled northeast border regions. Nearly forty years later, nothing much in its appearance seemed to have changed. It was a little larger than I remembered, but otherwise it seemed very much the same, except that Route 13 leading to the Cambodian border, some twenty kilometres further south, now bypassed Khinak a little to the east. On this visit I had not wanted to venture to that border, for to have done so would have been to risk an encounter with renegade Cambodian soldiers who had turned to banditry in this lawless frontier area. Only a few weeks before my visit armed men in uniform had held up, beaten and robbed a convoy of aid workers as they travelled along Route 13 just above the Cambodian border. And Boun had made quite clear that he shared my caution.

Now, with the arrival of these newcomers, I had a different question to put to Boun. Enquiries about political developments in the Lao People's Democratic Republic could wait. Could he answer the more immediate question of what was going on before us? He could and did, though it was apparent from his initial hesitation that he felt some embarrassment about the answer. The men who sat nearby, Boun explained to me, were Sino-Thai businessmen who had come from Thailand to southern Laos to buy timber growing in the regions of northeastern Cambodia still controlled by remnants of the Khmer Rouge. He knew this since the men who were so heartily enjoying their lunch had stopped in Pakse—the last major town in southern Laos, located about one hundred and twenty kilometres further north—two days before. While there, they had talked openly about their plans in front of one of his friends. Now they were celebrating the successful conclusion of a deal that would see illegally logged timber shipped out of Cambodia, through Laos and into Thailand. And would no one intervene to stop this transaction? I asked naively. But who could? Boun asked in turn. The government in Phnom Penh did not control the area where the timber would be felled. As for Laos—and here was the cause of his embarrassment—well, 'arrangements' would be made for the timber's transit. Just how and where he did not know, or was reluctant to say. We returned to talking about his student days.

The encounter put a dampener on the pleasure of the day. It had started so well, and I had been able to laugh at, if not entirely disregard, the problems of manoeuvring a poorly maintained bicycle with a broken pedal and loose handlebars over the rough tracks of Khon Island. Even Boun's temporarily losing his way did not seem to matter much, for in a single morning I was once again witnessing some of the almost numberless moods of the Mekong. It had been wide and calm, sparkling in the early morning light, as we crossed from our overnight accommodation to the left bank to load our bikes into a van for the short trip further south. Then, once more in a boat, we had glided through narrow waterways bordered by stands of bright green reeds before landing to ride to the western end of Khon Island. Once there we gazed on the majestic power of the river tumbling over the Somphamit Falls. This achieved, we had returned upstream to spend another hour in a small boat, motionless in the middle of a wide, brown reach of the river hoping to catch a glimpse of the remaining freshwater dolphins which live above the falls. While the sun grew ever hotter and the narrowness of the boat meant movement was almost impossible, the effort seemed worthwhile, even though the dolphins never appeared. This was not a time for talk but rather an opportunity to reflect on the extraordinary variations in the Mekong's character even over a very short distance. Now, in the Khinak eating house, the problems that afflict the Mekong and the environment of the countries through which it flows were before me in an unexpected fashion.

Four days later, as I passed through Bangkok's airport on my way to Phnom Penh, I bought a copy of *The Sunday Nation*, and the implications of what I had seen in Khinak were given sharp emphasis. The local newspaper carried a report of a study funded by the World Bank that told of the ongoing rape of Cambodia's forest reserves. Forest cover had been dramatically reduced since 1969, and it was estimated that in 1997 alone the Phnom Penh government had lost US$90 million of revenue as the result of illegal logging.

Just what this meant for the Mekong and its tributaries was given further point once I reached Phnom Penh and talked with knowledgeable friends. They spoke of how the clear-felling of trees in recent years had left huge areas of Cambodia stripped bare, so that each wet season topsoil is washed away and into the country's river system. Some of the worst results of this process involved the rapid increase in sedimentation in Cambodia's Great Lake, which is linked to the Mekong by the Tonle Sap River. Less well known, but just as worrying, were developments that were being reported from Prey Veng and Svay Rieng provinces south of Phnom Penh. With the flooding accompanying each wet season, villagers are now finding that, instead of benefiting as they once did from the deposit of rich silt brought by the river, their fields are now left carpeted with mud. This has caused such problems that villages have had to send their young men to the capital in the hope that they will be able to earn enough as day labourers to compensate for the loss of previously productive land that has now been rendered infertile. The situation does not yet match the devastation wreaked by logging in Thailand, where disastrous floods have followed unrestricted clear-felling of timber, but there is every reason to be concerned at what has happened already.

I shall never know the size or the exact consequences of the deal I saw being celebrated in Khinak. But I recognised that it was one more destructive event to be added to a growing catalogue of concerns associated with developments along the Mekong's course, from its source in Tibet to its delta in southern Vietnam. By comparison with the dams being built or planned on the Mekong and its tributaries, or the proposal from China to blast an all-season navigation channel along the river's course in northern Laos, what I had witnessed was probably only a minor contribution to the river's actual and potential troubles. But it would be a contribution nonetheless. Here was further evidence that the Mekong is not only a great river with a turbulent, if largely unknown, past. Increasingly, there seems every reason to fear that it is a river with an endangered future.

I

Beginnings, Discovery and the Colonial Years

1

Monuments, Tombs and a Great River

The first view of the Mekong fairly took one's breath away . . .

H. Warington Smyth, Notes of a Journey on the Upper Mekong, Siam, *London, 1895*

Seen on a fine winter's day, the Angkorian temple tower standing on a hillside above a valley in eastern France looks inescapably incongruous. No matter that this is a monument to Doudart de Lagrée, one of France's most distinguished, if largely forgotten, nineteenth century explorers, a man who served his country in Cambodia. No matter, either, that the tower is located in his birthplace, Saint-Vincent-de-Mercuze, a village twenty-seven kilometres from Grenoble and so small that its name does not appear in full on a large-scale road atlas. The ultimate impression is bizarre as a visitor views the monument beneath the towering cliffs of the Grande-Chartreuse mountains and sees, beyond, the distant Alps capped with snow. It would be hard to imagine a more striking contrast than that between the fecund tropical world close to the mighty Mekong River, which the monument's architecture seeks to summon up, and the austere mountains and valleys of the Dauphiné.

Yet to dwell on the bizarre would be unfair to the man whom the monument commemorates. Saint-Vincent-de-Mercuze was not only the ancestral home of Ernest Marc Louis de Gonzague Doudart de Lagrée, French naval officer and leader of the French expedition up the Mekong River in 1866–68. It was also, after

9

many vicissitudes, the final burial place for his mortal remains. Today, Lagrée's name is hardly known outside France, except among the ranks of those who share a fascination with the history of exploration in Southeast Asia. And even in his natal village his monument seems scarcely to command the interest and respect that might be expected.

Before reaching Saint-Vincent-de-Mercuze, I knew that this unusual monument had originally been located in Grenoble, only to be removed by the civic authorities in the dead of night from its place of honour in the city's post office square in 1961 as part of a program of 'modernisation'. And I knew that another, French, writer who had sought information about the monument from Saint-Vincent's mayor had never received a reply to his letter of enquiry. It was as if the commune of Saint-Vincent-de-Mercuze felt vaguely ashamed of this exotic monument, just as the councillors of Grenoble had felt it necessary to remove the tower from their city under cover of darkness.

So I was not entirely surprised when enquiries about the monument made at the *mairie* led to my being directed not to the mock Angkorian tower but to the Lagrée family mausoleum, located high above the village in a deconsecrated church. Here, indeed, there is a more conventional tribute to the explorer's memory, with a bust of the man and a fine, black marble slab inscribed in gold with the words that Lagrée is supposed to have uttered while still a schoolboy in the Jesuit college at Chambéry: 'France is my homeland. I would prefer to be a nonentity here than a great lord in a foreign country.' The best evidence suggests that these words are nothing more than a posthumous exercise in secular hagiography. Only afterwards, and without any indication of its location on the map of the village which the staff at the *mairie* had given me, did I find the temple tower, with the panels around its base depicting scenes from Lagrée's life. All were defaced, with the explorer's head knocked off in every case. There seemed a sad symmetry between this fact and the contemporary rape of the statuary and carvings found in Cambodia's Angkor temple ruins—ruins that are also depicted on this extraordinary monument.

The late twentieth century has been less than kind to the memory of men who were once hailed as heroes, and Doudart de Lagrée is not the only one whose monument has been treated with disdain, and worse. Francis Garnier, the man who led the Mekong Expedition to its conclusion after Lagrée died a tragic death in China, is honoured with a statue in Paris; a statue which has been mocked by those who abhor the imperialist values it enshrined when it was erected in 1896. In truth, it is an extraordinary confection. Garnier stands in a classically heroic pose, with half-naked women and wild animals drawn from an Indochinese bestiary draped about his legs and feet. When I last saw it, Garnier's nose bore what looked at first like a partially inflated condom. It was a relief, at least, to realise that it was only a faded plastic 'red nose' of the kind sold for charity.

Rather closer to the Mekong River itself, on its tributary the Nam Khan, not far from Luang Prabang, the former royal capital of Laos, is another monument, a tomb built over the remains of the French naturalist and explorer, Henri Mouhot. Often mistakenly identified as the 'discoverer' of the ruins of the great Cambodian temple complex at Angkor, Mouhot more accurately was their first important Western publicist. He, like Lagrée and Garnier, had led a life in the Indochinese region that was closely linked to the Mekong River. When I saw his tomb in 1996, only a few years after it had been reclaimed from the jungle, there were already signs that some recent visitors had tried to vandalise a plaque attached to its side.

This recital of monuments and tombs, of neglect and deface-ment, has a common theme—the Mekong River. Francis Garnier once wrote that he was obsessed by the river. He had, in his words, *une monomanie du Mékong*. I hope my own interest in the river can more kindly be described as a deep and abiding fascination. It is a fascination that began when I first caught sight of the Mekong in 1959 through the windows of a noisily vibrating Royal Air Cambodge DC3 flying from Saigon to Phnom Penh.

At the time I knew little more than the river's name and the fact that it flowed through Cambodia, the country in which I was about to begin a posting as a junior foreign service officer. Even though this was in April, and so at the height of the dry season when the Mekong was at its lowest level, what I saw through the thick, dusty haze was a river of enormous size stretching in great serpentine bends into the far distance. My experience of large rivers was limited to having seen the Murray River in Australia and it was immediately apparent that what lay beneath the aircraft was something of a quite different order. I knew nothing of this great river's history. In this, I found, I was part of a large majority, even among those who knew of the river's existence and far more about Southeast Asia than I did in 1959. Neither did I realise that the first major expedition to chart the Mekong's course had set out from Saigon in southern Vietnam less than one hundred years before I had my first aerial view of the river's grandeur. Amazingly enough, and despite all the exploration that took place in the intervening years, it was not until 1994 that the source of the Mekong was finally pinpointed in eastern Tibet. At last there was an end to the debate that had raged over centuries as to just where the river began its long journey to the South China Sea.

Living in Phnom Penh meant being constantly aware of the Mekong. Ocean-going ships came up the river to unload at the city's docks and carry away their cargoes of rubber and rice. Local wood-fired ferries brought passengers downstream from distant provinces. And the river formed the stage for the annual Water Festival which, when I first saw it, was still graced by the presence of the Cambodian king. Taking place over several days, the festival was a mix of bacchanalian excess, gratitude for the end of the rainy season and days filled with boat races whose finishing line lay at the point where the Mekong joins its major Cambodian tributary, the Tonle Sap.

But it was not just this range of human activity that captured my attention, for the Mekong has its own life marked by rises and falls in height according to the seasons—the difference between low and high water in Phnom Penh is as much as ten metres. And, most strikingly of all, as the flow of the water in the Mekong grows ever greater in the rainy season, with the river's size swollen not just by the rains but also by the melting of the distant snows in Tibet, an amazing natural phenomenon occurs. With its bed unable to accommodate all of the water flowing down the river, part of the Mekong's volume backs up into the Tonle Sap so that this tributary ceases to flow south and instead reverses to run backwards into Cambodia's Great Lake. For a brief moment at the end of the rainy season the waters of the Tonle Sap stabilise, ceasing to flow in either direction. Then, suddenly, the flow reverses and rushes towards Phnom Penh. And as it does, the river carries with it a huge quantity of fish which are harvested for weeks and then carried away in ox carts to be dried to form the protein base for Cambodia's rural population living distant from the river system.

It is impossible to overestimate the importance of this natural phenomenon and thus the importance of the Great Lake. It is the largest freshwater lake in Southeast Asia and the fish that are so readily harvested from its waters and from the river that flows out of it contribute more than 60 per cent of the Cambodian population's protein intake. The distinctive pungent smell of drying fish that greets a visitor entering a Cambodian village in late November or early December is testimony enough to this fact. Even a brief review of the Great Lake's dimensions and its variation in size from wet to dry season underline how remarkable is its transition from one period of the year to another. At its lowest level the lake covers approximately 2700 square kilometres, but this coverage swells to no less than 16 000 square kilometres at its highest level, with depths reaching as much as nine metres. At low water, large areas of the lake are little more than one metre deep.

Living in Phnom Penh in the early 1960s meant coming to know the river and its tributaries in peaceful times. It was a focus for water sports, for sailing and water skiing, and even, if you were far enough away from Phnom Penh's pollution, for swimming. But I soon came to know the Mekong as something more than a setting for sport and relaxation. As plans slowly developed to tap the river's potential for irrigation and hydro-electricity, I travelled with the first Australian engineer to carry out a preliminary reconnaissance of the Mekong between the isolated provincial settlement of Kratie and the major waterfalls located at the border between Cambodia and Laos. I saw a very different river from the wide channel, unimpeded by rapids, that flows past the Cambodian capital. A little to the north of Kratie are the Sambor rapids, the first major barrier to all-season navigation. Then, beyond the even more isolated settlement of Stung Treng, lie the Khone Falls, a series of interlocking falls and cataracts spread across some eleven kilometres. Seeing them for the first time in 1960, I was staggered by their power. At that time I knew nothing of the efforts that had been made over the years to find a passage through them so that uninterrupted navigation could continue from Cambodia into Laos. I hardly imagined that anyone could try to overcome this formidable obstacle.

In the years after I made my first acquaintance with the Mekong, I slowly gained a knowledge of its history and of the way in which kingdoms had risen and fallen along its course and its major tributaries. I learned that the river had been a central part of Southeast Asia's history before its existence was known to the Western world, and that later its lower reaches had been the setting for European rivalry both commercial and religious; that it had been the site for extraordinary but ultimately futile Iberian derring-do in the sixteenth and seventeenth centuries; and that its existence was then almost forgotten by the world away from Asia. The more I learned, the more I became aware that war, treachery and massacre were no strangers to the Mekong's banks, a condition that tragically continued to the recent past.

Once my interest focused on the nineteenth century, three facts became strikingly clear. The first was that up to the 1860s no European knew the full nature of the Mekong's course to its many mouths, where the Mekong Delta meets the South China Sea, from its passage through China's Yunnan Province. As for its source, while there was general acceptance that the river rose in eastern Tibet, no one knew exactly where. Secondly, once I had started reading the documents in the French archives and published records, I realised that the French Mekong Expedition, which began in 1866 and came to an end two years later, was an epic endeavour in an age of heroic exploration. And, thirdly, it became clear that this was an expedition that had largely been forgotten outside France. This was despite the admiration the expedition and its members earned in England in the years immediately following its completion. It was striking to think that, as an Australian in 1959, I had known about the exploration of the rivers of Africa by men such as John Speke and Richard Burton, and even had some sense of the importance of the Amazon, yet I knew nothing of the exploration of the Mekong. So impressed was I by this expedition that I tried to capture my admiration for its members in a book recording their progress, achievements and failures: *River Road to China: The Search for the Source of the Mekong, 1866–73* (see Sources, Notes and Acknowledgements at the end of the present book). Even now, the fact that the Mekong was explored by Frenchmen seems to weigh against the expedition's receiving the credit it deserves. *The Oxford Book of Exploration*, published as recently as 1993, for instance, makes no mention of the expedition led by Doudart de Lagrée. It is a curious, even extraordinary, omission.

But while I was looking at the past, the Mekong was very much part of a war-torn contemporary world as the Second Indochina War, the American war in Vietnam that spread into Laos and Cambodia, raged ever more fiercely. The hostilities ensured that there could be no possibility of the development plans so confidently proposed in the 1950s and early 1960s coming to fruition. As a regular visitor to Cambodia and Vietnam in the 1960s and early 1970s, I became used to travelling by fixed-wing aircraft and military helicopters above the river and to helter-skelter road trips along Mekong Delta roads through territory which passed into Vietcong control once darkness fell.

When the Vietnam War ended, the Mekong again slipped from general consciousness. As a reviewer wrote about my book describing the French Mekong Expedition, 'Americans discovered the Mekong in 1965 and forgot about it in 1975'. Not that the river vanished from the minds of those who had fought on and around it—American Vietnam veterans could speak of 'being up the Mekong' as a metaphor for risk and danger. And while not explicit, it is difficult to think that Francis Ford Coppola had any other river in mind when, in *Apocalypse Now*, he had his protagonist travel up a river to find Marlon Brando's Kurtz in surroundings reminiscent of the Angkor ruins. But as the countries of Indochina, Cambodia, Laos and Vietnam began their new lives under unchallenged communist control after 1975, the Mekong became inaccessible to almost all Western foreigners. Nowhere was more inaccessible than Cambodia under the terrible tyranny of Pol Pot, but Laos and Vietnam too were essentially closed societies in these immediate post–Vietnam War years, except for a few officials and aid organisations, or those who through ideology were ready to ignore the human rights abuses of these regimes. These were not people for whom the Mekong had an immediate importance.

Even with the changes in international politics that occurred during the 1990s, plans to develop the Mekong remained on hold and travel along its course was restricted. Then, as the 1980s drew to a close, there was renewed interest in the possibilities of exploiting the Mekong's economic potential. Finally, the Mekong Committee, originally established in 1957, was transformed into the Mekong River Commission in 1995 with four member states, Cambodia, Laos, Thailand and Vietnam. Talk began once again of dams along the Lower Mekong, the region below its course through China and, as economic liberalisation slowly gained a grip over the former communist states of Indochina, travel on and near the river by tourists became possible. Not that this last activity was without occasional complications, as I found when a two-day boat trip north from Luang Prabang to Huay Xai in early 1996 had to be aborted after one day because bandits who were active further up the river had shown themselves quite ready to shoot anyone who resisted their demands.

Complications of a quite different order were looming further upstream. In the 1980s China decided it needed dams to generate hydro-electricity to service a growing industrial capacity in Yunnan Province. It completed its first dam on the Mekong at Manwan in 1993, has begun construction of a second, and is planning at least a further five and possibly as many as thirteen more. Occasional placatory statements to the contrary, there seems little reason to believe Chinese planners have much concern for the consequences of this dam-building program on the downstream countries through which the Mekong flows. Suggestions that the dams will provide improved water flow during the dry season are a subject of controversy. And talk by Chinese officials of the desirability of blasting an all-season channel along the Mekong, where it runs through the gorges of northern Laos, do nothing to ameliorate worries about the dams' impact. With problems of pollution already taking their toll on the river, resulting in diminished fishing hauls in the Mekong Delta, the future health of the Mekong is, by any measure, a matter for serious concern.

This, then, is a book about the Mekong's past and present, its uncertain future, and the lands through which it flows. It is a book about a river whose course has now been charted in detail but whose character is still little known to those who do not live by its banks. In terms of length, the Mekong is the twelfth largest river in the world, measuring more than 4350 kilometres from source to sea—some experts say it's as many as 4800 kilometres, though I have never been able to find the basis for this discrepancy. When measured by volume, the Mekong moves up the league table of great rivers. With an annual discharge of 475 billion cubic metres into the South China Sea, it can be counted as the tenth largest in the world. Its drainage basin covers no less than 795 000 square kilometres.

The topography of the territory through which the Mekong flows gives the river its paradoxical character, since unlike many of the world's other mighty rivers it has served to divide rather than unite the countries which lie along it. This is particularly so in the contrast that exists between the upper and lower sections of the river, and as a result of the almost endless succession of rapids that lie along its course in Laos. So it is not surprising that the river is known by different names along its length. While its best known name comes from a contraction of the Thai name for the river, Mae Nam Khong, or 'Mother of the Waters', it is called by many other local names. For part of its upper course in China it is called the Dza Chu, 'River of Rocks', while more generally in that country it is known as the Lancang Jiang, 'Turbulent River'. In Cambodia it is sometimes known as the Tonle Thom, 'Great River'. In Vietnam it is both the Song Lon, again meaning 'Great River' and the Song Cuu Long, or 'Nine Dragons River', a name stemming from the number of channels into which it divides as it flows through the Mekong Delta. In reality, the number of channels, large and small, can scarcely be numbered, but nine is a propitious number and dragons were powerful symbols of royal authority for the Vietnamese emperors as the delta region came under their control.

The contrast between the agriculturally rich delta region and the Mekong's source at the head of the Rupsa-la Pass at 5100 metres in the bleak, high plateaux of eastern Tibet is profound. After flowing roughly eastwards from its source for about 85 kilometres, the Mekong turns south, falling about 2000 metres to Qando, a stop on the ancient yak route from Chengdu in China to Lhasa. It then flows through deep gorges that remain hostile to settlement to the present day before emerging at Baoshan on the Burma road. From this point the river still has

1200 kilometres of Chinese territory through which to pass, much of it inhospitable territory characterised by malaria-ridden valleys.

By the time the Mekong passes out of Chinese territory it has dropped a dramatic 4500 metres from its altitude at source. It continues for 200 kilometres as the boundary between Burma and Laos before reaching a minor tributary, the Ruak River, where the territories of Burma, Laos and Thailand come together. This is a region that has long been associated with the cultivation and sale of opium and its derivatives and has been known for decades as the 'Golden Triangle'. The term describes the rugged hinterland surrounding the confluence of the Mekong and the Ruak—not the point at which the borders of the three countries meet. Despite the efforts of governments to restrict the commerce in opium, and because those efforts are often undercut by corrupt officials, large quantities of opium are still grown, processed into heroin and then smuggled out to an ever-expanding international market from this area. Knowing the world's fascination with drugs and responding to the upsurge in tourism, Thai tourist operators have transformed the meaning of the term 'The Golden Triangle', and have erected a sign to prove it. So, if you wish, your tourist bus will stop and you may be photographed standing beneath the sign with the Mekong in the background.

From this point onward, the river is usually described as the 'Lower Mekong' and has only a further 500 metres to fall before it reaches the sea. But that point is still 2000 kilometres away. For a time the Mekong marks the boundary between Laos and Thailand before turning eastward to run through Laos alone, passing between steeply rising gorge walls and over repeated rapids that impede navigation during much of the year. In the dry season the depth of the water in sections of the river above the ancient royal capital of Luang Prabang can be as little as half a metre. Even when the waters are relatively high, shortly after the end of the rainy season, the navigable course for a boat of any size can narrow to a width of thirty metres or even less as it runs between jagged rocks.

Downstream from Luang Prabang, and as it continues past the modern Lao capital of Vientiane, the Mekong widens as the mountains give way to riverine plains. But its course continues to be interrupted by rapids and groups of islands. The remarkable variations in the width and depth of the river continue here. At flood time, some sections of the river can stretch to a width of more than four kilometres and depths greater than a hundred metres have been recorded. The obstacles in the river's course finally culminate in the Four Thousand Islands (Si Phan Don) above the Khone Falls. Despite their limited height, the amount of water flowing over these falls at high water is greater than that passing over the much better known Niagara Falls. Seen at any time, they provide a sense of enormous power. When the river is at its highest level the noise made by the water rushing over the falls is deafening and spray drenches any observer who has scrambled through the jungle to view them from below.

Once in Cambodia, and steadily increasing in width, the Mekong flows over one further major set of rapids above Kratie. From this point on navigation is unimpeded to the sea. At Phnom Penh, Cambodia's modern capital, the Tonle Sap River flowing out of the Great Lake joins the Mekong, and the two rivers form a vast 'water plain', two kilometres across. It then divides into two main watercourses, one still bearing its name, the other known as the Bassac. Together these flow on finally to form the Mekong Delta. Notorious three decades ago as a bitterly contested battleground in the Vietnam War, the delta is also where the known history of the Mekong begins in the early centuries of the Christian era.

2

A River gives Birth
to an Empire

These are monuments which have caused merchants from
overseas to speak so often of 'Cambodia the rich and noble'.

Chou Ta-kuan, describing Angkor at the time of his going there in 1296

When he visited Cambodia in 1959—his second visit, for he
had been there in 1930—the novelist Somerset Maugham
followed the well-established path that led tourists to the imposing temple ruins of Angkor at their site close to the kingdom's
Great Lake. Returning to Phnom Penh, and before a gathering
of the English-speaking community that hung on his every word,
I heard him hand down his verdict. 'No one,' he said with
trembling jaw, 'no one should die before they see Angkor.' He
had made his visit with time to spare, as he lived on until 1965.
In his enthusiasm he echoed the voices of earlier visitors to the
great temple complex once its existence became widely known to
the Western world in the second half of the nineteenth century.
For the Angkor ruins have cast a spell over a procession of writers,
from Pierre Loti and Sacheverell Sitwell to Han Suyin and a host
of lesser known figures. Like so many others, I have a crystal-clear
memory of my own first sight of the greatest of all the temples,
Angkor Wat, in July 1959. Driving towards it from the south,
along a road that ran through towering trees, the vast building
with its distinctive towers suddenly came into view and seemed
to occupy the whole of the skyline. Below its outer wall Buddhist
monks stood by the temple's moat with the late afternoon sun

illuminating their yellow robes, which were reflected in the still, darkly green waters below them.

I doubt that Maugham knew more about the history of Angkor than could be absorbed from the excellent guide books that already existed at that time. This is no criticism, for part of the wonder of the ruins is that they can be appreciated without a deep knowledge of their history. But even if he had done more and read the already copious academic literature, the knowledge available in 1959 about the Angkor complex, and the empire of which it was the centre, has since been much revised and expanded; and revision continues. In the process scholars have turned not only to the ruins, inscriptions and Chinese texts that have something to say about early Cambodian history, but also to the latest technological aids, including satellite imagery, to advance their understanding. In all of this this there is a vital constant, the Mekong River and its major Cambodian tributary, the Tonle Sap, and the part they played in the rise to glory of the greatest of the land-based states of early Southeast Asian history.

A search for the beginnings of Cambodian history starts in the Mekong Delta at the beginning of the Christian era. Instead of the densely populated region the delta is today, we must imagine a largely waterlogged world of black mud and mangrove trees, bordered by thick tropical forest where the land rose away from the flood plain. Drainage canals had only slowly begun to ensure that some areas were protected from the annual floods that came with the rainy season and the steady rise in the Mekong's level, its volume swollen both by the rains and by the melting of the snows in faraway Tibet. There was so much water that one of the earliest Chinese visitors to the delta wrote of 'sailing through Cambodia'. Even seventeen centuries later, Phan Huy Chu, a Vietnamese scholar–official writing of the same region in the 1820s, gives an impression that not all that much had changed over the years. 'No one goes anywhere on foot,' he observed. 'The rich people use big boats, and the little people use small boats to go down to the sea.'

Conquering the vast marshy tracts of the Mekong Delta was a necessity for the rise of the earliest settlements in areas that were to become part, many centuries later, of Cambodia and Vietnam. This necessity is captured in one of the Cambodian national birth legends, which tells of the arrival of a prince from India, named Kambu, who married the daughter of the Naga King, or Serpent Spirit of the Waters, who ruled over the land that was to become Cambodia. Approving of the union between Kambu and his daughter, Soma, the Naga King used his magic powers to drink the waters covering the land where the couple were to live. There could be few more graphic affirmations of the importance of the slow but essential battle waged by the delta's earliest inhabitants to transform the environment.

When the Chinese wrote of the delta region and the territory close to it they called it 'Funan'. Scholars are still wrestling with the derivation of the word, and even more importantly with its meaning. Does it derive, as many have argued, from *bnam,* an early version of the Cambodian word for a hill, *phnom,* a word familiar as a result of its forming part of the name for Cambodia's modern capital? The possibility is appealing, for to visit the areas of Cambodia that once formed part of 'Funan' is to understand immediately why hills are so important and should have been chosen as the locations of religious sanctuaries. To stand on top of a hill barely one hundred metres high but which rises from a dead flat plain is to experience a strong sense of power and of separation from all that lies below. In a flat world, even the smallest hills have a fascination for those who live near them, one that is quite disproportionate to their actual height. The psalmist's conviction of help coming from the hills is not a feeling restricted to the ancient Middle Eastern world in which those lines were written.

But what was Funan, and who were the people who lived there? Answers to both these questions, which rely to a large extent on Chinese sources, are either incomplete, in dispute, or both. There is even a debate among scholars as to whether there ever was a *single* Funan, a unified state ruled from one central capital. Perhaps, instead, there were many small states whose power waxed and waned over the decades. As to Funan's inhabitants, there is greater agreement on this point, with the consensus being that the population of what the Chinese called Funan was predominantly of Malay or Indonesian ethnic stock. But if we accept the suggestion that the name Funan is derived from the Cambodian, or Khmer, *bnam,* then this would imply that as early as the third and fourth centuries, when Chinese travellers were reporting on the region, there were already some Khmers—ethnic Cambodians—living in and around the Mekong Delta. Yet it has to be noted that there is no other linguistic evidence for this conclusion. The Vietnamese, who finally came to dominate this region, played no part in this imperfectly understood period of history. Only in the seventeenth century did their advance guard begin a steady migration into the Mekong Delta, and not until the eighteenth were Vietnamese rulers able to claim undisputed control over the region.

A vital element in Funan's population was a limited number of people who had come to the region from India. Probably most had come as merchants or traders, but there were also those who were either members of the priestly Brahmin caste or at least claimed to be so. As such, they brought with them a store of knowledge about Indian religions and skills ranging from writing and astrology to statecraft. A telling indication of the influence that Indian culture exerted over this and other parts of mainland Southeast Asia in early historic times is another Cambodian national birth legend associated with the Funan region. This recounts the arrival of a foreign Brahmin, Kaundinya, whose attempt to land in Cambodia was at first opposed by a local woman named Willow Leaf. Through the power of his magic bow he overcame Willow Leaf's opposition and subsequently married her.

This, at least, is the picture of developments that has generally been accepted by scholars, with the Kaundinya birth legend seemingly giving support to the picture of wisdom imported from India. There is another point of view that gives a much more important role to the inhabitants of Funan, whatever that name describes. This view is advanced by Michael Vickery, a highly qualified student of Cambodian history who revels in his iden-tification as the enfant terrible in this field of studies. He is not only at the forefront of those who argue that there was never a *single* 'Funan'. Additionally he advances a view that places as much importance on travel by early Southeast Asians ('Funanese' included) to India, in order to acquire the knowledge that was available in that country, as on Indians coming to Southeast Asia to impart it. For Vickery, Southeast Asians in the early centuries of the Christian era should be seen as just as capable seafarers as were Indians. Otherwise, how can their culture have reached destinations as far away as Africa? Still, wherever historical truth lies, there is no denying that ideas relating to kingship and the state that had their origins in India were important in this early period of the rise of civilisations in the lower reaches of the Mekong.

There is much that is curious and contradictory in what the Chinese records have to say about Funan. They speak of people who are both 'malicious and cunning' and yet whose character is 'good' and who, although having to contend with invasions from their neighbours, do not like to fight. Despite the advanced state of Chinese civilisation, or perhaps because of it, some of the accounts the Chinese records provide read like dubious travellers' tales. Yet there are unmistakable elements of truth to be found in these accounts. Allowing for the routine disdain of Chinese views of foreigners, the description of the Funanese as 'ugly and black', and having 'curly hair', fits well with the picture of a people who nowadays would be described as Malays or Indonesians. And the report that these people enjoyed cockfights and fights between pigs seems entirely believable. Both these kinds of contests between animals were later depicted on low-relief carvings at Angkor. And if pig fights do not seem to have survived into modern times, cockfights certainly have.

Yet how are we to evaluate some of the other details the Chinese records supply, such as the accounts of justice being decided by ordeal with the accused having to handle red-hot iron or survive after being thrown into a moat full of crocodiles? To emerge uninjured, or alive, from these tests was the proof of innocence, the Chinese commentators tell us. Since some of these tests by ordeal were observed by visitors to Cambodia at a much later time, they are believable. Less believable are the claims that one of Funan's rulers extended his dominions for five to six thousand *li*, the *li* being an elastic measure of distance that has at various times meant as little as 500 metres and as much as a mile.

Amid all the uncertainty surrounding the nature and history of Funan, archeology offers some reassuring material evidence of one aspect of life in the first three or four centuries of the Christian era. During the early years of the Second World War, a French polymath, Louis Mallaret, excavated a site just to the west of the Bassac River in the far south of Vietnam. Today, the site lies a short distance inland from the Vietnamese provincial town of Rach Gia on the Gulf of Thailand. Known as Oc Eo, subsequent research, including aerial photography, has confirmed the picture of this settlement's having once been a seaport, before the steady depositing of silt stretched the coastline further south. And it was not simply a local port, for among the objects found at Oc Eo were coins from as far away as the Mediterranean Roman world, as well as objects that clearly came from the Middle East and the Indian subcontinent.

The excavations at Oc Eo and the accumulation of evidence from Chinese sources make clear that Funan was in touch with a much wider world than the watery regions of the Mekong Delta. Not least, we can suppose that Oc Eo, and perhaps other coastal settlements, were both entrepôts for goods being traded from east to west and centres to which rare forest products, the plumes of exotic birds and semi-precious stones were brought down the Mekong River and sold to the outside world. Above all, these forest products would have included benzoin, the rare resin that was highly regarded in China and the Middle East and Europe and used as a substitute for frankincense. In addition to its use in perfumery, benzoin burnt as incense played an essential role in the rituals of Chinese Taoists who believed that its fumes could cleanse the body of the negative effects of consumption of grain.

Out of this imperfect picture suffused with the aromatic smoke of incense we have to join our imagination to the limited evidence that is available to account for the emergence of the Khmers into Cambodia's early history. In terms of the generally accepted interpretation of Cambodia's early history, we can suppose that the wealth of centres such as Oc Eo and Angkor Borei, a location inland from Oc Eo, acted as a magnet in attracting the Khmers into the territory of modern Cambodia. According to this view, they came from a homeland somewhere along the Mekong in what is today southern Laos. And it was down the Mekong that they came, slowly but steadily, with Wat Phu, a temple site near the modern Lao settlement of Champassak with structures dating back to before the eighth century, identified as one of their earliest sacred foundations—a location that continued to be regarded as a kind of Khmer 'holy land' through later centuries as the power of the Angkorian empire grew.

After being inaccessible for nearly two decades, as the reclusive Lao socialist government based in Vientiane hesitated to permit foreign tourists to travel in their country, it is again possible to visit Wat Phu and to sense why this site would have been so important to the Khmers. Wat Phu, the 'Mountain Temple', is located on a steeply rising feature that dominates the dead-flat plain running between it and the Mekong. The sides of the mountain are heavily wooded until at its summit there is a distinctive rocky outcrop some eighteen metres high. For the Khmers this could only be a *linga*, a phallus, the source of both supernatural power and earthly regeneration in the Indian religions that had spread into Southeast Asia. And adding to the sense of spiritual power that the early Khmer worshippers found at the mountain, a spring provides a constant flow of pure water which falls onto a natural platform ninety metres above the plain. This was where the Hindu god Siva was honoured, where human sacrifices were possibly offered to the supernatural powers that regulated human existence, and where Buddhist pilgrims still come today.

When, from a boat on the Mekong, I first saw the mountain on which Wat Phu is built, I had to take its phallic identification on trust, for the feature on top of the mountain rising above Wat Phu's sanctuary seemed only barely taller than it was wide. But when, a year later, I saw the feature from the hills rising to the east of the Mekong, it was clear that this was a distinctive feature that could, indeed, be construed as phallic, jutting blue-mauve in colour into the sky above the wooded slopes of its mountain. And when one reaches the mountain, there is no denying that the sanctuary has the air of a magic place, a fact that has inspired a succession of purple passages in the descriptions offered by visitors. Typical is that left by George Groslier, one of the many Frenchmen for whom the study of Indochina was both a vocation and a love affair. When he visited Wat Phu in June 1913, the summit was obscured by the clouds of the rainy season, but this did not mar his pleasure as he looked out, unknowingly echoing A. E. Housman's lines about 'blue remembered hills'.

> Above the temple, the flank of the mountain on which the
> temple is built, rises to be lost in perpetual cloud. From the rocks

that loom over the sanctuary cool water falls, drop by drop. The chant of a Buddhist monk, seated cross-legged in a grotto above drifts down to me. A gentle breeze ruffles the water of the great lake into which the base of the mountain plunges, and from somewhere I cannot identify it carries the scent of citronella and frangipanni. The view extends across the plain, across the valley of the Mekong to the blue horizon of the Bolaven mountains.

We do not how the Khmer newcomers came to dominate the existing population of Funan after they had moved down the Mekong into the lands below the Khone Falls (and in Michael Vickery's view it was a case of Khmer leaders moving *up* the Mekong rather than down the river). What is certain is that from the fifth century onwards there is evidence they ruled over a region that had previously been identified as Funan but which now was identified by the Chinese as 'Chenla', a name whose meaning remains unresolved. The Khmer 'kings' or 'princes' who now held power based themselves in areas far removed from the seacoast setting of Oc Eo. Settlements to the east of the Tonle Sap and Great Lake, as well as by the Mekong close to modern Kratie, became prominent.

Increasingly the evidence which scholars analyse comes from inscriptions in Sanskrit and Khmer incised on stone steles. These provide a daunting set of reign names and claimed royal relationships between rulers such as Bhavavarman, Mahendravarman and Isanavarman. (The Sanskrit suffix 'varman' means 'protected by', so Bhavavarman was 'the ruler protected by Bhava', one of the many names for the Hindu god Siva. It is a usage that has been revived by Cambodia's present king, Sihanouk, when his full name is cited.) The virtues of these rulers are celebrated in panegyrics lauding their military prowess, their religious devotion and their incomparable charismatic attraction. In the case of Isanavarman, who ruled in the seventh century, an inscription boasts that women of his court felt it would have been worth rape by the enemy to be a recipient of his smile.

Strikingly, the Khmers of this early period were already facing a problem that lies behind much of the thinking that has recently been devoted to plans to exploit the Mekong for irrigation. For despite the enormous volume of water that flows down the

Mekong, and the vast amount of rain that accompanies the rainy season between June and November, away from the river's banks Cambodia rapidly dries out when the rains cease to fall. This was not a problem for the important settlement of Sambhupura—the 'City of Siva'—which was established on the east bank of the Mekong, and where its name lives on to the present day in the small village of Sambor and in the nearby rapids. But for other centres, including Isanapura, the city associated with Isanavarman of the dazzling smile, adequate supplies of water could not be drawn directly from a river.

This was no minor matter for, if the Chinese records can be trusted, Isanapura was a city of consequence. According to the material the historian Ma Tuan-lin prepared for the Sui dynasty, in the seventh century it was a city of twenty thousand families at the centre of a kingdom of thirty cities, each with several thousand families. It was a martial society in which men habitually went about armed and the king was protected by more than a thousand bodyguards. But located on a site north and east of the modern provincial capital of Kompong Thom, Sambor Prei Kuk, it was a city well inland from Cambodia's Great Lake. To supply its water needs it had to rely on a series of reservoirs built to trap water during the wet season. If the size of the city was anything like the size claimed by Ma Tuan-lin, prodigious efforts must have been involved in digging and maintaining these water sources.

Yet for all the effort that must have been involved, the centre of Khmer power moved away from Isanapura at the end of the eighth century to become fixed close to the Great Lake near modern Siemreap. This is the area that we know today as the site of the Angkor ruins, and very recent archeological research suggests that it may have been an important area of settlement even earlier than has usually been thought. Even if this proves to be the case, from the beginning of the ninth century the story of Cambodia is the story of the rise to ever-greater power of the Angkorian empire. And an essential part of that story is the Great Lake and its link with the Mekong through the Tonle Sap River.

Just as most visitors to the temples of Angkor are overcome with awe at their first sight of this extraordinary architectural achievement, so it is easy to be overwhelmed by the statistics associated with this vast site. No fewer than forty principal temples were built here between the ninth and fifteenth centuries and they spread over an area of some 320 square kilometres. (Hundreds more were built throughout the territory of modern Cambodia, Thailand and southern Laos.) The best known of these temples is Angkor Wat, 'the City which became a Temple'. It is unquestionably the grandest of all the monuments, and in its entirety the temple covers some 200 hectares within a surrounding moat. As such, it is the largest religious building the world has ever known.

But it is not only the size of the temples that staggers the imagination. For hand in hand with size are the skill and beauty of the carvings with which the temples are decorated, most particularly the bas-reliefs that stretch in some case for kilometres and tell the stories of Hindu epics as well as recording the battles of kings and showing scenes from the daily life of the population. Here is a richness of iconography and symbolism to rival anything to be found in the great cathedrals of Europe. Much of this internal decoration would have been viewed only by royalty and their priests. But even the most humble in the population would have been able to gaze at Angkor Wat and the other temples in their time of glory, to see the temples' towers burnished with gold, and to know that here indeed was an earthly vision of the abodes of the gods.

At first glance the choice of a site near modern Siemreap seems puzzling. Unlike its predecessor states in Funan, the Angkor region was not suited for easy access to the sea, even though the Mekong and then the Tonle Sap were always routes for water craft to reach the city. On the other hand, the Angkor site had the attraction of being well removed from a potential enemy as another powerful kingdom rose to prominence along the coast of what is today modern central Vietnam. This was the state of Champa. Fated to be one of history's losers, it eventually vanished before the advance of the Vietnamese in the seventeenth and eighteenth centuries. Like Angkor, Champa was deeply influenced by Indian culture, though its people spoke an Indonesian language. In its heyday, Champa was able to challenge the Cambodian rulers based at Angkor, its troops travelling up the Mekong and Tonle Sap Rivers in the thirteenth century in their massive war canoes to sack the city and temporarily bring the

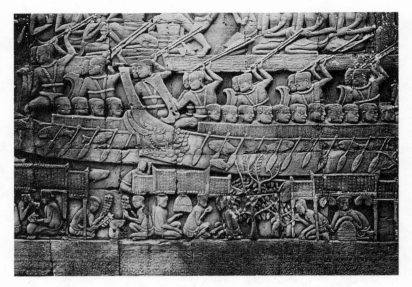

The bas-reliefs decorating the late thirteenth century Bayon temple at Angkor are remarkable for combining narrative descriptions of historical events with scenes from everyday life. In this relief, the central part of the carving shows Cham war canoes on their way to attack Angkor, while below are Cambodians watching a cock fight, playing dice and blowing on a flute.

empire to its knees. Depictions of the savage naval battles between the Khmers and their Cham adversaries on the Great Lake form one of the most vivid sets of bas-reliefs on the great Bayon temple at Angkor.

Surprisingly, much of the land close to where the city of Angkor was built and where it steadily grew to greatness was not particularly suited to intensive agriculture, particularly inland from the Great Lake. And here we enter into one of the much-debated aspects of Angkorian history that has pitted one set of historians' views against another, and has remained a matter in dispute. How did the Cambodians who lived at Angkor feed themselves? All manner of evidence makes clear that Angkor had a large population, almost certainly in excess of one million in the city that was at the heart of an empire stretching into modern Vietnam, Laos and Thailand. At a comparable time, London was a city of less than 35 000 inhabitants.

Inscriptions detailing the numbers of priests, servants and slaves required to maintain the temples great and small testify to the size of the population. So, too, do the monuments themselves, which were often constructed in an amazingly short period of time—only thirty-five years in the case of Angkor Wat—and built to a quite extraordinary degree of architectural accuracy. In the case of Angkor Wat, accuracy in construction was such that variations from a theoretically exact line in the construction of walls running over great distances were less than 0.1 per cent. We do not know how many men were employed to achieve this astonishing feat of labour, but the number must have run into tens of thousands. What is more, by great good fortune we have a detailed Chinese account of Angkor in the thirteenth century which, while it does not offer a figure for the size of Angkor's population, leaves no doubt that even in the closing years of its greatness it was a mighty city with many inhabitants. It is the only eye-witness account that exists for the whole of the Angkorian period.

The author of the account, 'Notes on the Customs of Cambodia', was Chou Ta-kuan, a Chinese envoy who visited Angkor between April 1296 and August 1297. Like so many others before and after him, he came to Cambodia up the Mekong, reaching the river from the sea through one of the few channels not closed by sandbars at the end of the dry season. He left a description of the delta as a landscape dominated by swamps and thick vegetation—so that even experienced sailors had difficulty in finding their way through the maze of large and small channels. Travelling up the Mekong past the site of modern Phnom Penh, he continued along the Tonle Sap until he reached his final landfall on the shores of the Great Lake.

His account of what he saw contains much that is tinged with Sinic disdain: for the population who were a 'coarse people, ugly and deeply sunburnt', and for some Cambodian women who, he observed, preferred to 'urinate standing up'. For Chou this was too much. To act in this way could only be described as 'ridiculous'. Yet his account is full of remarkable detail, some dubious, some invaluable. Indeed, much of his account reads like that of a stereotypical nineteenth century European traveller. So, he mixes near-prurient interest with apparent amazement in his accounts of how priests were commissioned to deflower virgins, using their hands. 'Some also say,' he observes, 'that the priest has intercourse with the girls; others deny this. As Chinese are not allowed to witness these proceedings, the exact truth is hard to learn.'

There is a genuine tone of amazement in Chou Ta-kuan's account of the reportedly vigorous sexual appetites of Cambodian women almost immediately after giving birth to a child. One or two days after they have given birth, he reports, they demand that their husbands make love to them. If the husband fails to do so he is put aside. Chou's tone is almost resigned when, in summing up, he notes that 'though their sexual impulses are very strong, it is said some of them remain faithful'.

Describing the presence of Chinese traders at Angkor, he sounds genuinely peeved by the increasing ability of local traders to outwit his compatriots in commercial transactions. But even in his scorn for the failings of these 'southern barbarians' Chou Ta-kuan could not hide his admiration for the city they had built and for the the majesty of its ruler. He concludes his account of Angkor with a description of the king going forth in procession, with the sovereign preceded by a female bodyguard and the king himself standing erect on an elephant and holding a sacred sword in his hand. Clearly reluctant to have to make the admission, Chou Ta-kuan is forced to acknowledge that 'it is plain to see that these people, even though they are barbarians, know how to honour a prince'.

Tucked away in the information Chou provides, almost as an afterthought, is an observation which is important for the debate that has been joined as to how the population was fed, and what the role of Cambodia's Great Lake was in this matter. That the Great Lake provided an essential supply of food is quite clear from Chou's record, and this without doubt played a part in the initial decision by the Khmers to establish themselves near its shores. Then, as now, fish bred in vast numbers during the rainy season as part of the cycle that depended on the annual reversal of the Tonle Sap as the Mekong flooded then subsided. But since Chou Ta-kuan makes clear that rice was a vital part of the Angkorian diet, and since, too, he writes of the city's inhabitants harvesting several crops a year, how was it possible to achieve such agricultural success?

For decades scholars thought they had the answer. Over the centuries various rulers at Angkor constructed enormous reservoirs. The largest, known as the Western Baray, was eight kilometres long by two wide and capable of holding up to 70 million cubic metres of water. Just as the temples of Angkor stand today to give a sense of the majesty of the city when it was inhabited, so too does the Western Baray impress a modern visitor by its size. It was rehabilitated in the 1930s and again in the 1950s. I have happy memories of this vast reservoir providing a site for a cooling swim after a day of temple visiting, with little thought given, I must confess, to the enormous amount of labour, forced or voluntary, that must have been expended to build it. Surely, scholars argued, this and other reservoirs and the complex series of moats and canals that surrounded the temples were part of a sophisticated hydraulic system that had both symbolic and practical application. Symbolically, the water that surrounded the temples represented the 'seas' of the Hindu universe, just as the central towers of the temples were evocations of Mount Meru, the sacred mountain at the centre of that universe. Practically, it was thought, the water system enabled the population to irrigate their rice fields and so to produce three, or even more, crops each year.

Sadly, for these intellectually elegant ideas were refined by a much-loved French scholar, Bernard-Philippe Groslier, this attractive explanation of Angkor's capacity to feed itself is increasingly discounted. Detailed analysis of the capacity of Angkor's reservoirs and of aerial photographs of the region about the city have led to very different conclusions. Now, it is thought, the reservoirs and their linked system of canals probably were used for some domestic purposes, such as providing drinking water. But they were not used for large-scale irrigation. The fact that Angkor's population was able to grow three rice crops annually was, more prosaically, partly the result of using the natural pattern of irrigation stemming from the rise and fall of the waters of the nearby Great Lake—a system of water exploitation described as 'retreat irrigation'. And this is where Chou Ta-kuan provides a telling clue.

Recounting the extent to which the Great Lake rose and fell according to the seasons, with a difference of more than twelve metres between low and high water, Chou speaks of the population coming down to the retreating waters, once the dry season had arrived, to plant their rice crop. So the Great Lake, an essential for the supply of fish for Angkor, is now seen as having had a vital accompanying role in the production of rice. And that role would have been supplemented by conventionally irrigated rice grown away from the lake and by another variety of rice which Chou describes as growing in pace with rising flood waters. Perhaps this was a form of wild rice, since the topography around Angkor does not seem to have been suited to another remarkable variety of rice still to be seen in Cambodia. This is a variety known as 'floating rice'. It can be planted in areas subject to flooding as with its rapidly growing and immensely long stalks it is able to keep pace with rising waters so that the ripening heads of grain are not submerged.

When, in the fifteenth century, the power of the Angkorian state began to erode, the lake's role in agriculture faded away. Yet its central importance as a breeding ground for fish never ceased. It is only now, at the end of the twentieth century, that serious questions have begun to be raised about the long-term viability of the lake as a rich source for fish. For the first time, planned and already constructed dams on the Mekong's upper reaches and tributaries, combined with increased upstream irrigation usage and deforestation, have made answers to those questions worryingly uncertain. Already, for multiple reasons, but most importantly because of the Mekong's carrying increasing amounts of topsoil washed off during the rainy season, the floor of the Great Lake is rising, a fact that seems certain to affect its essential role as a source of fish for Cambodia's population.

B y the middle of the fifteenth century, a Cambodian empire ruled from Angkor had ceased to exist. No single, overriding cause for this event can be identified, nor would it be sensible to try and find one. Great events of history, as the end of the Angkorian empire certainly was, are the result of many causes. Clearly, the rise of new and powerful Thai states to the west of Angkor played a major part in the empire's decline. The Siamese, as the Cambodians of Angkor called them, had once been Angkor's subjects, then they became its enemies. Emphasising the importance of the Mekong for the history of mainland

Southeast Asia, the slow rise to power of Thai kingdoms independent of Angkor was linked to rulers who emerged from the small state of Chiang Saen, which was located on the river close to the modern tripartite border of Thailand, Burma and Laos.

At Angkor itself the population may have reached a point of national exhaustion after centuries of intense building activity and wars of conquest, so that the effort to maintain the city's economic system at a time of foreign threat was simply too great. Possibly, too, malaria played a part as poorly maintained canals became breeding grounds for mosquitoes. And, for reasons we simply do not understand, even before the city grouped about its magnificent temples was abandoned by the royal court, the Cambodian state was increasingly looking outwards to assure its existence through trade.

In whatever combination, these and other causes brought an end to the greatest land empire Southeast Asia has ever known. Just when this happened is the subject of an all-too-familiar controversy among scholars. According to some, in the final decades of the fourteenth century, and after repeated challenges from the newly powerful Thai states to the west, a Cambodian king temporarily moved the court to Basan, a location on the east bank of the Mekong a little to the north of its confluence with the Tonle Sap. But this proved to be an area vulnerable to flooding and the court returned once more to Angkor. Others argue that the move to Basan, if indeed it took place, occurred later. What matters, and is beyond dispute, is the fact that shortly after a particularly vigorous Thai attack in 1431, the Cambodian court left Angkor for the last time, moving south down the Tonle Sap to establish a capital at the site of modern Phnom Penh. Chou Ta-kuan's detailed descriptions of the pomp and circumstance associated with the Cambodian court, the pictorial evidence of the bas-reliefs at Angkor, and descriptions enshrined in Cambodian chronicles leave no doubt that this departure would have been a grand affair, with the king setting out in a great royal barge, surrounded by a convoy of his troops and followers, and according to legend with specially prepared vessels bearing Angkor's most sacred statues to be re-erected in the new capital. Drums and conch-shell trumpets would have sounded as the colourfully dressed court sailed away with banners raised above the gilded hulls of their boats.

Only once, for a very brief time around 1551, were the great temples of Angkor again home to the Cambodian court. From obscure Portuguese documents and the record provided by fragmentary inscriptions and new bas-reliefs at Angkor Wat, we know that the Cambodian king of the time returned to Angkor and set some thousands of men to work clearing the jungle from the ruins of Angkor Thom. When they had done so, he was said to have been mightily impressed, but within a short time, perhaps no more than weeks, he too abandoned the temples to the steady invasion of the forest.

The location we now know as Phnom Penh was a 'natural' site for a new capital, set as it was at the meeting of the Mekong and the Tonle Sap. Even before the court moved there it had become an important trade centre for goods coming up and down the Mekong, and for the rest of Cambodian history the kingdom's capital was maintained either at Phnom Penh or close by. With trade the increasing preoccupation of Cambodia's rulers, this was a location that suited merchants coming from several directions. This fact was reflected in the name by which the new capital was first known. It was called Chatomuk, or place of the 'four faces'. It is a name that takes its meaning from the four arms of the rivers that meet at Phnom Penh and then move apart, but it also has the wider resonance of a place open to the four quarters of the compass. It is a name that has survived in usage to the present day.

Sadly, for those who cherish romance, it seems certain that the Cambodian ruler's new capital did not acquire the name Phnom Penh until some time after the court moved there. But at least the Mekong river system has a central place in the legend that explains the adoption of the new name. Some time before the Cambodian court left Angkor, the legend recounts, a woman named Penh lived beside a small, conical hillock not far from the river bank and near the confluence of the Mekong and the Tonle Sap. One day, when the rivers were in flood, Penh saw a huge tree floating with the current and pulled it to shore, hoping to use it for firewood. To her amazement, she found wedged among the branches of the tree four statues of the Buddha and one of the Hindu god Vishnu. Penh recognised this as a sign that the gods had decided to leave the holy city of Angkor and to give their blessing to the area about her home as the new capital of Cambodia.

Penh, like so many of her modern descendants, was a woman of energy and determination. She called on the people who lived nearby to carry the images to her home, where they were placed in a temporary shelter. Then she organised her compatriots to pile earth onto the hillock located by her home so as to transform it into a feature that could legitimately be called a hill, a *phnom*. When this was done, she built a temple on top of the hill to house the images of the Buddha, while a separate chapel was constructed to house the image of Vishnu. In memory of these events, the city that grew up after the court left Angkor was called Phnom Penh, the 'Hill of Lady Penh'.

Whatever the historical facts lying behind this legend, Phnom Penh, or locations not far removed from it, now formed the centre of the Cambodian world. It was a world about which distant Europe knew nothing, just as nothing, or next to nothing, was known by any European about the Mekong. The reason for this qualified comment lies in the often obscure accounts provided by Marco Polo of his travels. At a time when there is debate about whether he ever journeyed to China, let alone the degree of accuracy of the information contained in his famous book, we can note that if the Venetian traveller did indeed travel from Peking to Bengal around 1278 as he claimed, Polo would have crossed the Mekong in Yunnan. But for Polo, as for the Chinese in the imperial capital at this time, the Mekong was of no great importance in itself, and he does not single it out for mention. By contrast, Polo makes a clear reference to Erhai Lake located close to the city of Dali, and which eventually drains into the Mekong. This lake, he asserted, contained fish that were 'the best in the world'. As for the people who lived in the region, they were partial, according to Polo, to a local version of what we might call steak tartar, mixing finely minced raw meat with garlic and spices.

In contrast to a lake that provided bountiful supplies of fish, the Mekong was simply a barrier to be crossed along the Southern Silk Route that led through regions inhabited by barbarians; descriptions of their distinctive sexual mores are a pervasive theme throughout Polo's book. Writing of the regions of western

Yunnan near Lake Erhai and the upper reaches of the Mekong, Polo dwells on the readiness of the local men to offer their wives to passing travellers for sexual enjoyment. Some men in these regions, he claims, would never dream of marrying a virgin, so that a woman seeking to marry must be able to show at least a score of tokens given to her by previous lovers. 'Obviously,' Polo observes, 'the country is a fine one for a lad from sixteen to twenty-four.' He would have crossed the river by a bridge, for bridges had been built to facilitate a crossing as early as the third century of the Christian era. What was important was what lay beyond, rather than anything to be found in the malarial valleys of this desolate region inhabited by people who did not form part of the Han Chinese world. This view of the Mekong and of the lands about it in western Yunnan province was to last into the twentieth century. It is a very different view from that held by the modern mandarins of contemporary China. As for the next Europeans to see the Mekong—more than a century after Polo passed over the river—the details of the river's passage through Southwestern China were unknown. For Europeans, knowledge even of the Mekong's lower reaches came slowly and painfully.

3

Priests, Freebooters and Merchants: Europeans Discover the Mekong

The land of Cambodia possesses many rivers.

Tomé Pires, a Portuguese apothecary turned trader, writing in Malacca between 1512 and 1515

Late on a July afternoon in 1511, Don Affonse de Albuquerque, Portugal's proconsul in the East and governor of the recently conquered territory of Goa, sailed his small armada of eighteen ships into the port of Malacca. Today a prosperous backwater on the west coast of Peninsular Malaysia, Malacca in the early sixteenth century was the greatest of Southeast Asia's ports, the entrepôt for trade throughout the Indonesian archipelago and for that passing between China and India. Although the city itself was relatively small in area, and lacking in any of the great temple buildings so characteristic of Angkor, it was home to thriving communities of traders from many parts of Asia. Some estimates put its population as high as 100 000. As it was a vital link in the rich spice trade, the Portuguese had eyed Malacca ever since Vasco da Gama had rounded the Cape and brought Portuguese ships to the Eastern Seas thirteen years earlier.

With flags streaming and trumpets sounding, the alien vessels sailed into Malacca's roads and dropped their anchors a few cable lengths from the shore. At an order from the commander, the ships' cannons roared a salute that was also a harbinger of doom for the city's inhabitants who had thronged the seashore to watch this unsettling sight. Here were new and dangerous enemies

whom their rulers were ill-equipped to confront. The cosmopol-
itan population of Malacca would have been all too aware of the
way in which the Portuguese treated those whom they regarded
both as infidels and as opponents of their determination to gain
control of trade in the East. Albuquerque's name was already
synonymous with savage ferocity following his seizure of Goa the
year before, when his forces had killed, raped and pillaged for
four days after they entered that city. Albuquerque himself had
reported to the Portuguese king: 'No matter where we found
them, we did not spare the life of a single Muslim; we filled the
mosques with them and set them on fire'.

Laudatory contemporary Portuguese accounts of his arrival
claim that Albuquerque had come to Malacca to gain the release
of some compatriots who had earlier been seized and were now
held by the city's sultan. While he sought trade, the admiring
chroniclers insist, he had no hostile intent. This was nonsense.
No doubt he did hope to free his compatriots, some of whom
had been forcibly converted to Islam and circumcised to boot.
But there was never any doubt about Albuquerque's true aim.
He wanted to seize Malacca and so gain for Portugal control of
the trade that flowed through the city.

After negotiations that led nowhere, the Portuguese commander decided to attack. Before dawn on 25 July, the Feast of
St James, 800 Portuguese, aided by 200 Indian auxiliaries,
stormed ashore shouting the saint's name. To their surprise they
were met by solid resistance, so much so that by the end of the
day they had failed to take the city and were forced to retreat
to their boats. For nine days Albuquerque enforced a strict
blockade of Malacca before again attacking. And this time the
assault was successful. Portugal had a base in Southeast Asia and
soon after its freebooters, traders and missionaries were spreading
throughout the region. It is from the activities of these three
groups, their interests intimately linked, that detailed knowledge
of the Mekong first enters European knowledge.

In a world that now abhors colonial conquest, there is no way
in which a case can be made to glorify the aims of the
Portuguese who established themselves at Malacca and spread
their activities through so much of Southeast Asia. Even among

their own contemporaries there were a few who did not share the admiration for the exploits of men such as Albuquerque, let alone for his compatriots who were pirates in all but name. In the eyes of the great Jesuit, St Francis Xavier, these were men whose learning scarcely extended beyond knowing how to conjugate the verb *rapio*. Yet the story of these men is remarkable nonetheless, and central to that story is a need to recognise that a passionate belief in the Christian doctrine went hand in hand with the burning desire for wealth that had driven so many of Portugal's impoverished nobles and rootless younger sons to seek their fortune in the East. Central, too, is the fact that traders, priests and freebooters alike showed great courage as they pursued their goals, living and surviving in conditions that are almost unimaginable today. To survive and overcome tropical heat and humidity, dressed in unsuitable clothing and often racked by tropical diseases or afflicted by dysentery, speaks of men who were grittily determined if nothing else. Not least, all who survived did so with an almost daily awareness of the tariff of sudden deaths among their contemporaries in this distant outpost of Iberian endeavour.

Albuquerque's aim was to control the trade of Southeast Asia, not to seek territorial gain. With this goal, he and his successors sought, through both treaties and ruthless force, to ensure that Malacca should be the port to which all important commerce flowed. This meant sending vessels to points as diverse as the nutmeg-rich islands of the Moluccas and the Siamese court, located at Ayuthia on the Menam or Chao Phraya River. It did not mean, in these early years, making contact with the Cambodian court, for that country's capital was initially counted as unimportant and there was no first-hand knowledge of what lay beyond the many mouths of the Mekong where the river reached the South China Sea. Not until 1540 was a determined effort made to explore the coast of what is today southern Vietnam. We know of this exploration from the writings of Ferdinand Mendez Pinto. But well before this time, Tomé Pires, apothecary turned trader in Malacca, and an assiduous compiler of geographical information, was recording his understanding of the nature of the Cambodian kingdom and of the Mekong.

According to Pires, Cambodia's king and his people were warlike and, he noted, the kingdom had hostile relations with its neighbours. While his account of the products traded out of Cambodia was largely accurate, although overly optimistic in terms of the value he ascribed to them, his understanding of the Mekong was less so. Probably reflecting some knowledge of the many mouths of the Mekong along the coast of the delta, he wrote that 'Cambodia possesses many rivers'. Pires believed that the principal river, which he left unnamed, was a branch of the River Ganges. In this belief he was the first of many who speculated that the great rivers of South and Southeast Asia all sprang from a single source deep in the interior of the Asian continent.

Not much more knowledge emerged as the result of the explorations of Antonio de Faria, a man who combined the courage of sailing into the unknown and a fervent Catholic faith with a vicious readiness to torture Asian captives to death. The results of de Faria's voyage carried out in 1540–41 would have become rapidly available to the authorities in Malacca, although Ferdinand Pinto's account of the voyage was not published until many years later. He tells us that, coasting along the Gulf of Thailand, de Faria took note of the 'bar of the Cambodia', following the common practice of the time of naming a river from the country through which it flowed. We can presume he was referring to one of the many outlets of the river in the Mekong Delta that debouch into the South China Sea. The river had its origins, local informants told him, in an inland lake, near to gold and diamond mines. Later in his voyage he heard, again from local sources, that the Cambodia River was the boundary between the country of that name and the now-decaying Kingdom of Champa. As the century progressed, the number of references to the Mekong grew, with the proposition that it rose in some vast, distant lake an increasingly common assertion. The river was even immortalised in a verse of the *Lusiads*, the epic poem by Camoens, Portugal's most honoured poet, in which he recounts his adventures in the East, and in particular his survival following a shipwreck which left him on the banks of the Mekong.

As the sixteenth century progressed, so, too, did maps published in Europe slowly come to show an area identified as 'Cambodia', and then, later, a river designated the 'Mekong' or 'Cambodia'. In his detailed examination of the Portuguese and

Spanish association with Cambodia and Angkor in the sixteenth century, Bernard-Philippe Groslier notes that it was not until 1563 that a map was published showing Cambodia with a river running through it and with the river given the name 'Mecon'. In an echo of the early references to the river having its origin in a great lake, this first depiction of the river showed the river forming a lake before reaching the sea. By the end of the century the Mekong was firmly fixed as a feature of maps of mainland Southeast Asia, but marked with any accuracy only for a relatively short distance from the sea. Its upper course, let alone its source, was quite unknown, and confusion was present about its relationship to other Asian rivers, including the Menam or Chao Phraya River, which meets the sea just below modern Bangkok.

This lack of information was to last for many years. For despite European contacts with both Cambodia and Laos during the sixteenth and particularly the seventeenth centuries, including travel on large sections of the Mekong itself, it was not until the nineteenth century that anything like a detailed map of the Mekong was finally produced. This state of affairs at first seems puzzling, until one remembers that the Europeans who were the first to see the Mekong and travel on its waters were interested in other things than cartography. They sought souls, trade and power. Provided they survived, charting the river, however essential it was to providing a means for their travel, was a secondary concern.

The first European to record his visit to Cambodia and his travel on the Mekong was the Portuguese Dominican missionary, Father Gaspar da Cruz. He reached the Cambodian capital at Lovek, a little north of Phnom Penh, in 1555 and remained there until 1557. An account of his experiences was published twelve years later in his homeland. Da Cruz makes clear that he was not the first of his countrymen to make this journey, for he notes that a group of Portuguese had earlier been the cause of 'troubles' in the country. This fact had not deterred him from setting out to convert the heathen in a country where 'he had heard that there was a favourable opportunity to preach'. Like so many of the early Europeans who had an association with the river, we can gain little if any sense of his personality.

But we can surely presume that he was dedicated to his task, and we know of his frustration at his inability to gain Christian converts in a country where Buddhism, tinged by Hinduism and entrenched folk beliefs, was the universal religion. Hoping to win over the Cambodian ruler to the Christian religion, da Cruz encountered implacable resistance to his venture from the Brahmin priests, who continued to occupy a position of honour in the court, as well as from the Buddhist clergy.

Yet despite the failure of his evangelising endeavour, da Cruz had many interesting things to say about his sojourn. Of the river itself, his account mixed accurate fact with credulous speculation. So, his description of the course of the river in the area around Phnom Penh was correct and detailed, but his explanation for the annual reversal of the Tonle Sap supposed that great swamps close to the sea filled with water to the point where they forced the current back into Cambodia's Great Lake. Without providing details, he noted that the river was used by traders who came from a kingdom in distant Laos to trade in Lovek. And his descriptions of the country make clear that as he travelled on the river he had observed the mass of wildlife that lived by its banks. Not surprisingly, the subject on which he provided the greatest detail was the practice of religion in Cambodia, and in this he was surprisingly accurate in his observations. In terms of his own hope for converts, this knowledge did nothing to advance his cause.

Following da Cruz's departure from Cambodia in 1557, there was a sustained period during which there are no convincing records of any kind of European activity linked to the Cambodian court or to the Mekong. There may have been occasional Portuguese visitors, and it is possible that freebooters from that country operated along the coast of the Mekong Delta, an activity they would have shared with the well-recorded presence of Chinese pirates in this region. But it is not until the 1580s that there is convincing evidence for a renewed presence, first, of Dominican missionaries and then of Franciscans in Cambodia. The pious histories of their orders provide a roll call of their names. First to return were Fathers Lopo Cardoso and João de Madeira, probably in 1583, followed by Father Sylvestre d'Avezedo, and a little later Fathers Reynaldo de Santa Maria and Gaspar do Salvador in 1584.

Their hope to find converts proved an almost total failure. For his part, all d'Avezedo could do was to minister to a mixed congregation of Portuguese merchants and the small number of Chams, Malays and Japanese who had embraced Christianity and who formed part of the polyglot population living in and near Cambodia's capital. For the rest, the foreign priests had a fluctuating relationship with the Cambodian ruler of the day, King Satha, and continued to be opposed by the Buddhist clergy. By the end of the sixteenth century the efforts of the Portuguese missionaries were almost at an end and it would be of little more than antiquarian interest to refer to them, except for two things. While they pursued their thankless task of trying to convert the unconvertible, these missionaries were among the first Europeans to see the temples of Angkor and to leave detailed descriptions of them.

Although he was not the first European to see the temples of Angkor in the nineteenth century, it was Henri Mouhot, the French explorer and naturalist, who alerted the Western world to their splendour after his visit in 1860. This event and the reason for Mouhot's success in publicising the Angkor complex form a later part of the Mekong's story. But long before this, in 1603, a brief account of the temples appeared in a book written by one Marcello de Ribadeneyra and published in Barcelona. This was rapidly followed by other published accounts mentioning the Angkor complex in the first decade of the seventeenth century.

Relying on reports from Portuguese and Spanish priests who had visited the temples, these accounts, for all of their lack of historical understanding and resort to fantasy, make clear that the Angkor complex was seen as a mighty architectural achievement. It is easy enough to point to the mistakes found in these early commentaries, with one writer placing the temples on the banks of the Mekong, rather than by the Great Lake that feeds the Tonle Sap River. But there is no doubting the wonder the ruins inspired in these first European visitors. They marvelled at the size of the temples and the great wall that encircled the city of Angkor Thom. A striking feature of most of these early accounts is the presumption that there was no way in which the temples could have been built by ancestors of the Cambodians who now formed the country's population. So, in his description Ribadeneyra plumped for the view that the temples had been built 'by Alexander the Great or the Romans', while Gabriel de San Antonio, publishing two years later, suggested that it must have been 'the Jews', who were 'numerous in China', who had built Angkor before later emigrating to the Middle Kingdom.

Why were these accounts largely forgotten, so that Angkor's remarkable complex of temples could be rediscovered two and a half centuries later? In part, the answer lies simply in the obscurity of the books in which these references to Angkor were to be found. Written for a small Iberian audience, these were books that were linked to the brief period of Portuguese and Spanish influence in Cambodia, and when that faded so did memories of the descriptions of a city that had ceased to be part of the daily life of the Cambodians themselves. By the third decade of the seventeenth century the Portuguese and Spanish priests, adventurers and traders who briefly saw their fortunes linked to Cambodia had gone on their way. Portugal was a declining power in Asia, losing control of Malacca to the Dutch in 1641, and Spanish interest was concentrated in the Philippines. But before the Portuguese and Spaniards ended their close involvement in Cambodia they were involved in an extraordinary series of events that prefigure the actual deeds of the White Rajahs of Sarawak and the fictional exploits of Conrad's *Lord Jim*, though scarcely with Jim's hopes for altruistic endeavour combined with personal redemption.

The men who came, briefly, to hold the fate of Cambodia in their hands were Diego Veloso and Blas Ruiz, the former a Portuguese, the latter a Spaniard. We know virtually nothing of Veloso's background, save that he came from Amarante, a small town in the northeast of Portugal, not far inland from Oporto. In 1593 he was thirty-four years old, and had been living in Cambodia for about ten years, becoming fluent in the Cambodian language and apparently providing assistance to his missionary compatriots. He had also successfully gained an entré into the Cambodian court, to the point where he contracted an alliance with a woman of high status, though perhaps not the ruler's 'cousin' as one Iberian chronicler later asserted. Plainly, the Cambodian king of the time, Satha, saw Veloso as providing a means of gaining support from the authorities in Malacca so as to prop up his regime against the ever-present threat of invasion from the ruler of Siam. It was a role that Veloso was eager to play, and he formed a palace guard of his fellow countrymen to protect the king. With their knowledge of what was then modern weaponry, they were valued by Satha even if the Cambodian religious establishment remained hostile to this European presence.

Stretched in their efforts to deal with actual and potential enemies, the authorities at Malacca were unable to respond to the Cambodian king's calls for assistance. But now Blas Ruiz de Hernán Gonzáles entered the scene. His arrival in Cambodia was itself a suitable prelude for the dramas that were to characterise his short life. Born in Peru, by the time he was twenty-two years old he was living in Manila, Spain's colonial capital in the Philippines. In 1592 he sailed from Manila for Cambodia, only to be captured somewhere along the coast of what is today southern Vietnam and enslaved by the ruler of the now declining state of Champa. With one companion, he escaped from bondage and made his way overland to Cambodia where, as had happened with Diego Veloso, the king showed him exceptional favour. This was favour with a purpose, for King Satha now lent an ear to Blas Ruiz's suggestion that without any response to his appeals for help from Malacca the king might usefully seek assistance from the Spanish rulers in Manila. With this in mind, and with Portugal at this time forming part of the Spanish realm, it was quite logical for Satha to select Veloso as the envoy he sent to Manila despite his Portuguese connections.

Armed with a royal letter written on gold leaf and with promises that in return for aid against Siam the King of Cambodia was ready to give free rein to Catholic missionaries and trading advantages to Spanish merchants, Veloso set sail down the Mekong in July 1593. Unable to persuade the Spanish authorities to respond positively to Satha's entreaties, Veloso returned to Cambodia. He was in time to be present when Siam's ruler, King Nareth, invaded Cambodia in April 1594, captured the capital of Lovek and seized a wounded Diego Veloso and an unscathed Blas Ruiz who had fought with the Cambodian forces against the invader.

This was anything but the end for this redoubtable pair. Blas Ruiz was placed as a prisoner on a vessel bound for Siam, while

Veloso was taken away overland in Nareth's train. Soon after the vessel on which he had been placed set sail down the Mekong, Ruiz led his fellow captives in a successful assault against the crew, put them ashore and headed for Manila. There he was joined not long after by Veloso, whose talents for ingratiating himself with Southeast Asian royalty had charmed King Nareth into sending him to seek Spanish aid for Siam.

Together again, and with Veloso apparently untroubled by any commitments he had made to the Siamese ruler, the Portuguese and the Spaniard gathered a group of adventurers and missionaries to go to Cambodia, where they argued there were souls to be won and booty to be gained under the patronage of King Satha. Embarking in three ships, the eager band left Manila in January 1596. Only Ruiz's vessel reached Phnom Penh unscathed. Veloso and his companions were shipwrecked on the edge of the Mekong Delta and had to reach Phnom Penh on foot, while the third vessel of the enterprise, carrying the expedition's leader, General Juan Xuarès Gallinato, was blown off course and ended up in Malacca.

To their dismay, Veloso and Ruiz found that their patron, King Satha, had been deposed, and that he and his family had fled to an increasingly powerful Lao kingdom with its capital at Vientiane. Satha's place had been taken by a royal relative, Chung Prei, who had established himself upriver from Phnom Penh at Srei Santhor. Nothing daunted, the former favourites of Satha entered into negotiations with his successor in the hope of gaining his patronage. The scene was now set for a bloody incident which reflected the jealousies and resentments that were so much a part of this freebooting era. Chung Prei, who was well aware of the close links that Satha had forged with Veloso and his associates, had placed his personal safety in the hands of a mixed bodyguard of Chams and Malays. These were men who had originally been recruited by Satha, but who, arriving after the Siamese forced the Cambodian king from the throne, had readily agreed to serve the new Cambodian ruler. Suspicious of Veloso and Ruiz, Chung Prei told the pair to remain with their followers in Phnom Penh. They were still there when a convoy of Chinese junks sailed up the river in search of trade.

Seeing the Iberians camped in Phnom Penh, and still smarting from high-handed treatment they had received in Manila, the

Chinese prepared to attack what seemed to them an easy target, since they heavily outnumbered the Spanish and Portuguese. It was an unwise decision for, sensing what was afoot, the better armed Europeans took the fight to the Chinese, seizing their vessels and killing not only many of those who had arrived on the junks but also members of the Chinese trading community living in Phnom Penh. And for good measure, they burnt down the houses of these resident Chinese. This was not the first nor the last instance of violence taking place on the banks of the Mekong, but it was the first in which men of Europe were without question culpable.

Realising that their actions could put them at odds with the new ruler of Cambodia—for in attacking the Chinese merchants they were damaging the king's control of trade—Veloso, Ruiz and their followers decided to seek an audience with Chung Prei. Leaving some of their number behind in Phnom Penh they travelled the short distance up the Mekong to Srei Santhor. The new king would not receive them and as weeks passed it became clear that their position was increasingly hazardous. Ever men of action, they saw only one course open to them: an attack against Chung Prei's palace. Blessed by their accompanying missionaries, and led by Veloso and Ruiz, the Spanish band mounted a surprise night assault in May 1596, killing the king, burning down his palace and blowing up his powder magazine. Holding at bay a convoy of enemy vessels which pursued them down the Mekong, they reached Phnom Penh to find that their actions had displeased their nominal leader, Gallinato, who had finally reached Cambodia after his ship had been blown off course and he had ended up in Malacca. Denouncing their actions, and making reparations both to the court at Srei Santhor and to the Chinese merchants in Phnom Penh, Gallinato ordered Veloso, Ruiz and their followers to embark with him and leave Cambodia. This they did in June 1596.

For many, this might have been the end of the story, but not for the singularly intrepid Diego Veloso and Blas Ruiz. When Gallinato sailed into the Vietnamese port of Faifo (the modern Hoi An), Veloso and Ruiz prevailed on him to allow them to disembark so that they could travel overland to Vientiane to make contact with the deposed King Satha. Even though they were accompanied by Vietnamese guides, making this journey across the mountains dividing Vietnam from Laos, through thick jungle, was a remarkable achievement. Yet the records tell us nothing of the difficulties they must have encountered along the way, not least from the weather, for their travels took place at the wettest time of the year and when the daily temperature frequently rose above thirty degrees. Then, when they arrived in October 1596, it was to find that Satha, their former protector, had died. They immediately set about trying to persuade Satha's son and his mother and grandmother to return with them to Cambodia and to claim the throne.

News of Veloso's and Ruiz's presence in Vientiane travelled rapidly down the Mekong to Srei Santhor, where the court was in turmoil, with plots and counterplots among rival Cambodian factions and with the Malay mercenaries playing an increasingly assertive role. Knowing of Veloso's and Ruiz's reputation, and fearing an attack from Spanish ships they believed were waiting to enter the Mekong, the court mandarins sent a messenger up the river to Vientiane to invite Satha's son to mount the Cambodian throne. In May 1597 he did so, under the reign name of Barom Reachea II.

Weak and self-indulgent, Barom Reachea rapidly alienated powerful figures within his court and survived only because of the backing of his Iberian supporters. Indeed, two of his courtiers, one the most senior Cambodian, the other the leader of the Malay mercenaries, were killed by Blas Ruiz when they threatened to attack the ruler. In this fevered atmosphere, which included an attempt by supporters of the earlier usurper Chung Prei to bring down Barom Reachea, Veloso the Portuguese and Ruiz the Spaniard had a partial falling out. Each claimed the right to command, with Veloso asserting the primacy of Malacca's authority over activities in Cambodia and Ruiz claiming the contrary for Manila. It is not clear how the Cambodian ruler interpreted this development, but we know that he now sought aid from both Malacca and Manila, promising assistance to Franciscans, Dominicans and Jesuits alike, and hoping that this favourable attitude towards missionaries would result in an increase in trade and the assurance of security against his enemies. Moreover, in 1598 he showed his gratitude to Veloso and

Ruiz, who were now reconciled with each other, by appointing them governors of two provinces in the south of the country, provinces from which they could control both arms of the Mekong below Phnom Penh.

This was the high point of Iberian influence in Cambodia but a sudden end to Veloso's and Ruiz's remarkable but short-lived career as governors within the kingdom was not far distant. Reinforced by the arrival of priests and soldiers from Manila, and joined in their endeavours by a ship's company of Japanese commanded by an adventurer of mixed Portuguese and Asian ancestry, Veloso and Ruiz entered into new negotiations with the Cambodian court. Now they wanted not just control of two provinces but a dominant role in the affairs of the kingdom as a whole. In taking this step, they crystallised the resentment that the bulk of the Cambodian court officials already felt towards them, a resentment heightened by the fact that these officials blamed Veloso and Ruiz for maintaining the dissolute Barom Reachea on the throne.

As Veloso and Ruiz pursued their goals at Srei Santhor, aided in the best Iberian tradition of the Cross supporting the Crown by the Dominican Father Maldonado, trouble was brewing down-stream in Phnom Penh. True to its character as a Southeast Asian trading city, Phnom Penh had clearly defined quarters for the various foreign communities living there, as was the case with the Chinese community mentioned earlier. So the Spanish and Portuguese grouped in one area, as did the longer established communities of Malays and Japanese in other distinct quarters. When, with preordained inevitability, trouble flared between a Spaniard and a group of Malays, the commander of the Iberians did not hesitate. Aided by members of the Japanese community, the Iberians attacked the Malay quarter. In response the Malays laid siege to the Spaniards. Hearing of these developments, and disregarding the Cambodian king's urgings to go into hiding, Veloso and Ruiz came down the river from Srei Santhor to join their comrades. It was a brave but foolish gesture, for soon after their arrival around the middle of 1599 they, along with almost all their comrades, soldiers, priests and traders, were massacred by a combined force of Cambodians and Malays. The Iberian dream of souls saved for Christ and of riches flowing to their distant homelands was almost at an end.

But if these dreams were at an end, the connection with men from the Iberian peninsula was never totally broken. Spanish and Portuguese priests continued to visit and seek to evangelise through much of the seventeenth century, their efforts unmarked by success. And small numbers of Iberians settled permanently, marrying local women, losing all but the most precarious memory of their language, though preserving a commitment to the Catholic faith. Descendants of these men were still present when the French arrived in the nineteenth century and their names, such as Fernandez and de Monteiro, remained to surprise me when I first came to use the Phnom Penh telephone directory in 1959. For modern historians attuned to the need to place primacy on the 'Asianness' of Asian History, men such as Diego Veloso and Blaz Ruiz are seen, at best, as subjects for only passing mention. Yet, for a brief span of time, they held the fate of kings and a country in their hands. Their story is surely one of the most remarkable linked to the Mekong, and like so many others it was a story that ended in blood.

While Portuguese and Spaniards were pursuing their ultimately unsuccessful goals in Cambodia, an industrious Dutchman, Jan Huygen van Linschoten, had spent five years living in Goa as secretary to that territory's Portuguese archbishop. In this position he was able to accumulate a mass of information about Southeast Asia. Returning to the Netherlands in 1592, he condensed the knowledge he had acquired into two books published in 1595 and 1596. In relation to the Dutch entry into Southeast Asia and the formation of the Dutch East India Company in 1602, van Linschoten's works played a major part in bringing detailed information to the attention of his countrymen. On a more restricted scale, van Linschoten emerges as the first non-Iberian author to identify the Mekong as a river of great importance. In doing so, van Linschoten's book reflected the remarkable advance in knowledge of mainland Southeast Asia that had occurred over the previous fifty years. His work was translated into English in 1598, so the merchants of London who were increasingly eager to share in the profits of the Asian spice trade could read that:

Through this kingdom [Champa] runneth the river Mecon into
the sea, which the Indians name Captain of all the Rivers, for it
hath so much water in the Summer that it covereth and watereth
all the country as the river Nilus does Egypt . . . Upwards in the
land behind Cambaia [Cambodia] are many nations, as Laos,
which are great and mightie people, others named Auas [Avas or
Burmese] and Bramas [inhabitants of Lower Burma] which dwel
in the hilles . . .

Van Linschoten's account, with its strikingly accurate note of
countries bordering the Mekong, was of interest for anyone
concerned with developing knowledge about the river. But for
the Dutch East India Company beginning its remarkable, and
frequently ruthless, military and commercial assault on the spice
trade of Southeast Asia, Cambodia was a secondary backwater.
With a keen sense of where commercial opportunity lay, the
Dutch concentrated their efforts in the Indonesian archipelago.
Realising that Cambodia was increasingly under pressure from
the expanding kingdom of Siam, the Dutch waited until 1636
before establishing a permanent trading post there. They located
their factory at Udong, a little north of Phnom Penh on the
Tonle Sap, from where they purchased rice to send to Batavia
(the Dutch headquarters in Java and predecessor of modern
Jakarta), and deer skins and lac, the resinous substance used in
the manufacture of laquer, for sale in Japan.

Five years later, acting on orders from Governor van Diemen
in Batavia, a party from the Dutch factory set off up the Mekong
with the aim of reaching Vientiane and promoting trade with the
ruler of the Lao kingdom based there. The party was led by
Gerritt van Wuysthoff, accompanied by five of his countrymen,
a Lao merchant to act as a guide, and a 'Malay'. The account
van Wuysthoff left behind, first published in 1669, provides a
brief but fascinating insight into court life in Vientiane at the
time. Just as importantly, it is one of the first to record in some
detail the physical difficulties facing anyone travelling up the
Mekong. Only one earlier printed reference to these difficulties
appears to have existed, in a little-known book by the Jesuit
António Cardim, published in Rome in 1646. Recounting a
journey up the Mekong into Laos by a group of European priests,
Cardim noted that it took eight months to make their journey

because of the strong current of the river and the need to travel overland around a major waterfall.

Like the records left behind by the Portuguese and Spaniards, van Wuysthoff's account of his travels gives little indication of his personality. And as with his Iberian predecessors, we can do little more than conclude that he was a man of determination, for only someone with this attribute could have survived the rigours of the journey he undertook. It is probably fair to assume that, like his countrymen whom John Barrow described when he visited Batavia a century and a half later, he fortified himself each morning with a glass or two of gin. But would he have dressed in the clothes of 'velvet stiffened with buckram' which Barrow also describes and which are depicted in the earlier portraits of Dutch worthies who served in Asia in the seventeenth century? The answer is probably 'yes', for well into the twentieth century Europeans living in Asia have felt compelled to dress in unsuitably hot clothing as a demonstration of their capacity to disregard local climatic conditions. In one brief passage we do gain an insight into van Wuysthoff's austere, Netherlander's worldview. Writing of a festival he witnessed at Lakhon in southern Laos, he noted that after watching a fireworks display he and his companions had walked about the settlement by the light of the moon, 'but we could only move with difficulty because of the horrible fornications that were taking place everywhere'.

At one level of description, van Wuysthoff's record of his journey is notably in error. Setting out from the Cambodian capital at Lovek in July 1641 his party reached the region of the Khone Falls and the maze of islands just above them in the middle of August. Here he concluded that the Mekong was joined by another major watercourse flowing eastward from Burma. But if he was mistaken about this fact, his journal provides abundant evidence of the difficulties that lay in the way of using the Mekong for navigation. It took him no less than twelve days to make his way around the Khone Falls. Writing of the falls, van Wuysthoff tells of how, even half a mile away, he could hear them with a sound 'like the sea crashing against rocks'. Then, further north, fourteen days were required to pass through the complex system of rapids at Khemerat. In a comment on the river's course, van Wuysthoff remarked on the frequent presence of jagged rocks along its banks, a feature that is still striking for a present-day traveller. Finally, in mid-November, four months after setting out and with almost all of their journey accomplished during the wet season, the Dutch party reached Vientiane.

They found a walled city of considerable size, protected by the Mekong and by moats on three sides. The king's palace, which was built of teak and decorated with gilded statues, was of such a size, van Wuysthoff recorded, that it could have been thought a town on its own. They were received with pomp and taken, mounted on elephants, to pay homage to the Lao king. When that monarch eventually arrived to greet the European visitors, he was mounted on a white elephant and accompanied by three hundred bodyguards and sixteen war elephants. Graciously receiving a letter sent to him from Governor van Diemen, the king pondered aloud whether he should reciprocate by sending an envoy to Batavia. In the event, he decided against this course of action because of his country's difficult relations with Cambodia. But potential difficulties or not, the Lao court was able to entertain the Dutchmen with dancing and fireworks and to reward each of the party with a gift. Reserved and sceptical though he may have been, van Wuysthoff was impressed by the apparent prosperity of the Lao court and by the temples of Vientiane which were served by innumerable Buddhist monks.

His mission accomplished, van Wuysthoff left Vientiane in December. For unexplained reasons, his companions were required to remain in the Lao capital for a further eight months. Because of this delay in their departure, they observed the arrival in the city of a Jesuit missionary, Father Giovanni Leria, in 1642. He too had reached Vientiane by travelling on and beside the Mekong. And despite being refused permission to evangelise in Laos, Leria somehow succeeded in remaining in the country for a full five years before finally departing overland to the coast of northern Vietnam. Extracts from the reports he diligently sent back to his order's superiors were eventually published in 1663 by Father Giovanni Filippo de Marini as his *New and Curious History of the Kingdoms of Tunquing and Laos*. Of great interest is the summary Leria provided of the Mekong's origins, for what he described in the mid-seventeenth century remained essentially unamended for nearly two hundred years.

This great river, which has been incorrectly situated by geographers ancient and modern, has its source in a very deep marsh, shaped like a lake, that lies to the north on high mountains in the province of Yunnan, on the frontiers of China; falling from thence it rushes headlong from this valley and, forcing a passage through sheer violence, small and narrow though it be, it does not tarry there long . . .

As it entered Laos, Leria's account continued, now clearly in error, the Mekong split into two, with one course flowing into the Bay of Bengal and the other continuing on to Cambodia. While he judged that navigation was possible on the river through all seasons, Leria, like van Wuysthoff, entered a vital caveat. At all seasons, he wrote, passage of the Khone Falls required a delay of at least ten days of land travel and portage of goods.

With Leria's description of the river we come to the end of substantial European references to the Mekong for many years. Cambodia continued to decline before the growing power of Siam and Vietnam, for by the latter part of the seventeenth century Vietnamese colonists were advancing into the lands once ruled by Champa, including the Mekong Delta. Missionaries had found the Buddhist countries along the river barren ground to till, and the limited prospects for trade led the Dutch to abandon their factory in Cambodia in 1670. The only memory of these men that survived into the twentieth century in Cambodia was a Catholic church on the banks of the Tonle Sap, known as the Eglise Hoalong, the Church of the Hollanders, built on a site that Dutch merchants had briefly occupied in the seventeenth century. It was a church I came to know well in 1966, for it was here that I met Father Paulus Tep Im Sotha, a Cambodian Catholic priest of great intelligence and warmth of personality. In a manner not too different from that of his priestly predecessors, he preached to a small Catholic flock in an overwhelmingly Buddhist country. He, too, was to become a witness to yet another massacre beside the Mekong. And like many of those predecessors, he eventually was faced with the prospect of flight or martyrdom.

Representatives of the English East India Company, who had established their factory in 1651, left after a much shorter period

A map of 'Ancient India' published in Description de l'univers *(Paris, 1715), showing that as late as the 18th century knowledge of the Mekong's course was still very limited. In this case the Chao Phraya or Menam River which flows past Bangkok is depicted as a branch of the Mekong.*

than their Dutch rivals, remaining for only five years. Slowly, but no less surely, European interest in Cambodia and Laos faded, so that only a few priests from various orders struggled to pursue their vocation among the tiny Catholic population grouped near Phnom Penh, with the orders quarrelling among themselves in a thoroughly unchristian fashion as to who had the right to embrace this thankless task.

Yet this early, and in some ways heroic, period of European interest in the countries of Indochina raises an intriguing question in relation to the eventual full-scale effort to explore the Mekong that took place in the 1860s. The second-in-command of the French expedition that set off from Saigon in 1866 to make its way up the Mekong was Francis Garnier, a naval officer of immense enthusiasm and considerable intelligence. We know that Garnier had read a translation into French from the original Flemish of van Wuysthoff's account of his travels on the Mekong. So he had to be aware of the formidable barrier the Khone Falls represented for navigation before the expedition began. Whether he was aware of Leria's similar comments on the falls is not clear. Even though Marini's book had been translated into French, it is quite possible that Garnier had not encountered this obscure publication. Why then did he not take van Wuysthoff's comments into account when, from the moment he arrived in France's new colony of Cochinchina in southern Vietnam in 1863, he became a passionate advocate of the view that the Mekong would provide a navigable route into China?

It is, ultimately, an unanswerable question, but perhaps a clue to his thinking can be found in an engagingly titled book written by Josiah Condor and published in London in 1830. The book was *The Modern Traveller*, in which Condor drew upon every available European source, including van Wuysthof and Marini, to provide a tentative account of the Mekong's course. He concluded that it was possible that the Mekong and the Chao Phraya or Menam Rivers came together at some point between Laos and Yunnan, and recorded van Wuysthof's references to the Khone Falls and the Mekong's rocky banks. Yet, in an almost despairing footnote dealing with the uncertainties of the information available to him, he referred to 'the strange perplexity in which we have found ourselves' as he tried to present a complete picture of a river about which there were so many unresolved issues. Yet this 'perplexity' did not prevent Condor speculating that in the future there could be steamboats 'ascending the unknown course of the Mei-kong'.

Perhaps Francis Garnier, enthusiast that he was, simply would not believe that any river could be impossible of navigation. Possessed of facts little different or improved upon from those available to Condor thirty years before, he must have felt that nineteenth century technology offered the means to surmount any physical barrier the river might offer. As we shall see, he was unambiguously wrong.

4

Filling in the Blanks on the Map: Henri Mouhot and the Rediscovery of Angkor

One of these temples—a rival to that of Solomon, and erected by some ancient Michael Angelo—might take its place beside our most beautiful buildings. It is grander than anything left to us by Greece and Rome.

Henri Mouhot, describing Angkor Wat, which he visited in 1860

With the departure of the Dutch from their trading post close to Phnom Penh, European interest in Cambodia faded to become almost non-existent. For more than a century and a half what little knowledge there was of that country, and of the Mekong flowing through it, came from the dedicated missionary priests who sought, without success, to find converts among an indifferent Buddhist population. Their unrewarded efforts took place at a time when the political map of mainland Southeast Asia was undergoing fundamental change. Both Siam and Vietnam were growing stronger, a fact that boded ill for Cambodia as it was increasingly squeezed between its two much larger neighbours.

Siamese attacks against Cambodia had been a regular occurrence since the fall of Angkor in the fifteenth century. Now, as the Vietnamese steadily advanced southwards into what is today the region around Saigon (Ho Chi Minh City), they too saw that there were still rich pickings to be had in Cambodia. In 1658 a Vietnamese military expedition sailed up the Mekong to the Cambodian capital at Udong and put it to the sack. Cambodia may have been a weakened kingdom, but a fleet of twenty-seven large vessels and seventy smaller boats were needed to carry off the booty the Vietnamese seized. They also captured no fewer than eight hundred elephants and six hundred artillery pieces. It was a blow from which the Cambodian kingdom never fully recovered. Barely surviving as an independent state in the decades before it fell under French control, Cambodia was a vassal of both the Siamese court at Bangkok and the Vietnamese at Hue.

Apart from brief references to the unsettled nature of life in Cambodia by European voyagers, such as the scholarly English buccaneer William Dampier, accounts of developments in Cambodia and Laos are few and far between until the nineteenth century. The maps produced before that era continued to show a course for the Mekong that was unrelated to actual knowledge. Not until the French naturalist and explorer, Henri Mouhot, travelled to Luang Prabang in 1860 was there more than the most limited knowledge of the Mekong's course above Vientiane. Indeed, as the foremost Western historian of Laos, Martin Stuart-Fox, has put it, during the eighteenth century 'no missionary or merchant, traveller or diplomat left any first hand account' of the region. Indeed, it was only when Doudart de Lagrée led his expedition up the river in the 1860s that the Mekong was mapped in a professional fashion for the first time.

Lack of European knowledge of events did not, of course, mean that nothing of importance occurred along the Mekong's long course. In Laos there were several important events that passed largely unnoticed by the outside world, as the Lao kingdoms based in Luang Prabang, Vientiane and Champassak were, like Cambodia, increasingly targets for rivalry between Siam and Vietnam and, additionally, Burma. The tangled nature of this mix of competition and shifting alliances among the royal courts of mainland Southeast Asia provided the opportunity for a bold stroke by the Siamese ruler in Bangkok to enforce his authority over Vientiane in 1778. Acting on the pretext that one of Bangkok's vassals had been wrongly executed by the Lao ruler, the Siamese besieged Vientiane. When the city capitulated after four months, the Siamese followed the time-honoured procedure of putting it to the sack as they looted all that could be carried away and drove many of the inhabitants into slavery.

Of all the booty the Siamese carried off, nothing was more

valuable than the 'Emerald Buddha' image they seized from the Wat Pha Kaew pagoda, the Buddhist temple most closely linked to the Lao royal family. Carved not from emerald but from green jasper, a member of the jade family, legend places the statue's origin in India. Its existence was first noted in chronicles record- ing the history of what is today northeastern Thailand in the sixteenth century. Taken from that region first to Luang Prabang and then to Vientiane, the Emerald Buddha was a prize of the utmost worth for the Siamese to carry away. Initially it was housed in a temple in Thonburi, across the river from the city of Bangkok. Then, as a new Grand Palace was constructed for Thailand's Chakri Dynasty, a special pagoda was built to house the statue that had become the palladium of the Siamese king- dom. Few of the tourists who flock to see the image in its present setting within the Grand Palace in Bangkok realise that it had been an object of devout veneration in Laos for two centuries before it was relocated in Thailand. Barely seventy-five cen- timetres high and lacking the fluid grace of many of Thailand's other famous Buddha images, its sanctity nevertheless is such that contemporary Thai legislators swear their most solemn oaths in its name.

Vientiane was rebuilt, only to be sacked again nearly fifty years later, and as a sign of what was to become the full-scale involvement of European imperialists in mainland Southeast Asian affairs later in the century, this second sack had a link to growing European interest in the region. By the 1820s, Vientiane was ruled by King Anouvong (Chao-Anou in many older accounts), a man of energy and dangerous ambition. Determined to remove his kingdom from its status as a vassal of King Rama III of Siam, Anouvong was inspired to act by a rumour that reached Vientiane to the effect that English warships were poised to attack Bangkok. The rumour was false, but believable in the light of the recent establishment of a British presence in Burma following the Burmese defeat in the First Anglo–Burmese War. Spurred into action by false hope, Anouvong invaded Siamese territory.

After initial successes, he was soon retreating before superior forces which now marched on Vientiane. When the Siamese crossed the Mekong and reached the Lao capital they took terrible revenge for Anouvong's act of supreme lèse-majesté. All secular buildings were destroyed and images were stripped from the pagodas and their surrounding monasteries. Only Wat Si Saket, a recent but particularly holy foundation, was left untouched. The human costs exacted were no less frightful, as those inhabitants who had not been killed or selected for slavery were driven into great bamboo structures and burnt to death. When Anouvong was captured a year later he was sent to Bangkok, where he was displayed in a cage to endure the taunts and abuse of those who came to see him. Within a few years— experts disagree on just how many—Anouvong was dead, though whether through disease or secret assassination is unknown. Vientiane, the city that had so impressed Gerritt van Wuysthoff and Father Giovanni Leria, had ceased to exist.

J ust as we have no knowledge of Europeans visiting Laos during the eighteenth century, so too there is no certain record of the temples at Angkor receiving any Western visitors for more than a century after 1653. In that year, the splendidly named Diego Enriquez de Losada, a Spaniard from Manila who was in Cambodia to build a boat with the excellent timbers available there, visited the temples. He was mightily impressed by the architecture and decoration of Angkor Wat. There is a possibility that, not long after, a French priest from the Société des Missions Etrangères, Father Louis Chevreul, visited Angkor while he lived in the Cambodian capital at Udong between 1665 and 1670. All that can be said with certainty is that he was well informed about the site's existence and of the veneration in which it was held, including by the Siamese ruler in Ayuthia. But the ruins were not, as is often popularly supposed, totally forgotten, and references to the temple complex continued to appear in books published in Europe. It was not, however, until 1783 that we have a description of Angkor Wat that was linked to its author's actually having seen the temples. This brief description was given by another priest from the Missions Etrangères, Father Henri Langenois, and it is of interest chiefly for the confirmation that he gave of the continuing importance of Angkor Wat as a Buddhist devotional site that still attracted pilgrims.

By the middle of the nineteenth century, mainland Southeast Asia was an area of developing imperial rivalry between France and Britain. As a consequence, there was a growing determination to explore regions that still held mysteries for outsiders and which abutted on China, the vast empire that was thought to be a potential source of great commercial opportunity. This was the reason for the attempt made in 1837 by a Captain McLeod, a British army officer, to travel from Burma into China in search of a possible future route for trade between the newly established British colony and the Middle Kingdom. He reached the Mekong at Jinghong, having first travelled up the Salween River and then across country, but was refused entry into Yunnan by Chinese officials. Unlike the French explorers who succeeded him, McLeod did not regard the Mekong as a possible basis for navigating into China. For him, as for Marco Polo centuries before, the Mekong was essentially an obstacle to be crossed.

As an interest in the countries of Indochina was rekindled, so was there renewed attention to the ruined temples at Angkor. Scholarship devoted to Asia went hand in hand with an increase in the number of Europeans, especially missionaries, who were now resident in Siam, and in Vietnam and Cambodia. And some of these missionaries had interests that extended well beyond the search for converts to Catholicism into topics such as history and ethnography. Men such as Monsignor Pallegoix, who worked as a missionary in Siam and published his *Description du royaume Thai ou Siam* in 1854, knew that a translation of Chou Ta-kuan's description of Angkor had been published in France in 1819. And they were also aware that a little later translations into French of seventeenth century works by Spanish and Portuguese writers had appeared which mentioned Angkor. Against this background, a French missionary, Father Emile Bouillevaux, became the first European in the ninteenth century both to visit Angkor (in 1850) and subsequently to publish an account of what he saw.

Born in northeastern France, Bouillevaux was one of the small band of priests who toiled so thanklessly in southern Vietnam and in Cambodia. In Vietnam they were at times at mortal risk from persecution. In Cambodia they were tolerated by the Cambodian court, but as Monsignor Miche, a missionary bishop who served in that country, wrote with a Gallic eye to value in 1861,

'It is certain for anyone who has lived for some years in Cambodia that one can never obtain much success with Cambodians, unless it is through buying the freedom of debt slaves; but that method is long and very costly'. Miche's countryman, Bouillevaux, did not publish his account of Angkor until 1857, and when he did it was an austere and essentially unsympathetic description by a man who was later described as a 'tireless chatterbox'. Not least, it seems, he was affronted by the naked breasts of the carvings of *apsaras*, or heavenly beings, which decorate Angkor Wat in their hundreds. Today these delicately carved low reliefs are recognised as part of the extraordinary artistic richness of the greatest of the Cambodian temples. So, while he could, and did, claim to have been the first modern visitor to Angkor to describe the temples and was increasingly resentful at his lack of recognition, Bouillevaux could not in any sense be regarded as having brought their wonder to the attention of the world. That honour, as noted previously, rests firmly in the hands of Henri Mouhot who, additionally, played a part in advancing knowledge about the Mekong's course in northern Laos.

At first glance, Mouhot seems an unlikely person to have embarked on travels into unexplored areas of Cambodia and Laos, and to have brought the wonder of Angkor to the world. Indeed, he saw himself as a naturalist and ethnographer as much as an explorer, and certainly not as an archeologist. And if cartography and the accurate fixing of geographical positions were the necessary duties of an explorer, these were not talents Mouhot possessed in an unqualified form. Though, to be fair, he made very important contributions which assisted later mapmakers.

The son of a Protestant bourgeois family, Mouhot was born in 1826 in Montbéliard, a gritty industrial city in northeastern France. Known today for its Peugeot car assembly factory, it has little of the charm that some writers ascribed to it in the nineteenth century. Mouhot's early adult life was spent not in Asia but in Russia and Poland, where he worked as a teacher for ten years. Returning to Western Europe in 1854, he shortly after married a relative of the famed Scottish explorer of Africa, Mungo Park, and took up residence on the Channel island of Jersey. Very evidently, Mouhot had a way with words and an ability to win friends. This latter point was of capital importance since it meant

Henri Mouhot, the 'rediscoverer' of Angkor, was responsible for bringing their magnificence to the Western world's attention. (From Le Tour du Monde, *Paris, 1863)*

that when he died an untimely death in Laos in 1861 there was no shortage of supporters in both France and England who were ready to see his carefully kept journals transformed into a book.

The sparse evidence we have suggests that his decision to leave Jersey and set out for Southeast Asia was the result of his having read Sir John Bowring's *The Kingdom and People of Siam*, which was published in 1857. If this is correct, Mouhot would have read the short reference to the Angkor temples in that book. Whatever his motivation for deciding to travel to Asia, we know that he sailed from London in April 1858, finally reaching Bangkok in September.

For the next three years Mouhot was engaged in almost constant travel in Thailand, Cambodia and Laos. By June 1859 he had reached the Cambodian capital at Udong. What had once been a mighty kingdom had now shrunk in size and was wedged between two much stronger neighbours, Siam and Vietnam. Required to pay tribute to both, Cambodians, David Chandler notes, described their country as a 'two-headed bird', a state in decline and forced to show constant concern for the interests of its two suzerains. In Udong, Mouhot struck up a friendly acquaintance with the King of Cambodia's son, Norodom. This young man, who was later to rule from 1860 until 1904, offered Mouhot cognac, using the only two words of English that he knew, 'good brandy', and making clear that he expected to be given a gift of a modern firearm. But he also indicated that he was ready to assist Mouhot in his travels. At first these took Mouhot up the Mekong's main course, so that he could then travel further east to spend time with French missionaries working among hill peoples in a region close to the modern border between Cambodia and southern Vietnam. This experience yielded Mouhot's first comments on the 'Mekon', a river which he found had 'an aspect [that] is less gay than the Menam north of Bangkok; yet there is something very imposing in this expanse of water'.

By December 1859 Mouhot was back near Udong preparing to travel finally to see the temple ruins at Angkor about which he had now heard several reports. Like so many visitors before him, his approach to the temple complex was across the Great Lake. If he had been reserved in his initial comments about the Mekong proper, he did not stint his admiration for the lake.

The entrance to the great lake of Cambodia is grand and beautiful.

The river becomes wider and wider, until at last it is four or five miles in breadth; and then you enter the immense sheet of water called Touli-Sap [Mouhot's transcription of Tonle Sap], as large and full of motion as a sea.

. . .

The shore is low, and thickly covered with trees, which are half submerged . . . the waves glitter in the broad sunshine with a brilliancy which the eye can scarcely support, and, in many parts of the lake, nothing is visible all around but water . . .

Accompanied by a French missionary priest, the Abbé Sylvestre, Mouhot reached the small settlement he called New Ongcor on 22 January 1860, travelling on to the ruins the next day. He was staggered by what he saw, for these were 'of such grandeur, remains of structures which must have been raised at such immense cost of labour, that, at first view, one is filled with profound admiration'. For the next three weeks he worked his way through the thick forest that surrounded most of the temples, recording the dimensions of the buildings he encountered and describing their features with enthusiasm if not always accuracy and understanding. Not surprisingly, for instance, he did not recognise the probable symbolism of the great faces sculpted on the towers of the Bayon temple as representations of a *Bodhisattva*, a holy person not yet having reached the condition of Buddhahood, and in this case apparently incorporating Jayavarman VII, the king who had built the Bayon. Even today there is some doubt about this identification. He also erred both in the relative ages he assigned to the various temples he visited and in his suggested date of their origin, which he thought might be as far back as 2000 years. But these failings pale into insignificance against the detailed and perceptive descriptions he did provide, most particularly of Angkor Wat, the greatest of all the temples and the least affected by the passage of centuries. Surrounded as it is by a wide moat, Angkor Wat had not been invaded by the forest whose trees slowly but steadily had grown up through the other temples, pulling apart the heavy blocks of stone out of which they had been built.

Not the least of Mouhot's contributions was to detail the scenes found in extensive bas-reliefs of Angkor Wat and the Bayon. He described the mix of legend and history that the carvings provide, always writing in terms devoid of the Eurocentric or religiously prejudiced attitudes so obvious in Bouillevaux's account of his visit. Remarkably, given all that has happened in Cambodia since Mouhot's visit to the Angkor ruins, it is still possible to capture not just the excitement that he experienced, for this is an emotion that the site so readily instils, but also the view that he describes from Phnom Bakheng, a temple set on a hundred-metre-high hill to the north of Angkor Wat.

> On the one side you gaze upon the wooded plain and the pyramidal temple of Ongcor [Angkor Wat], with its rich colonnades . . . [in another direction] the new city, the view losing itself in the waters of the great lake on the horizon. On the opposite side stretches the long chain of mountains whose quarries, they say, furnished the beautiful stone used for the temples; and amid thick forests, which extend along the base, is a pretty, small lake which looks like a blue ribbon on a carpet of verdure . . .

To the power of his description, Mouhot added the sketches he made of the temples and some of these were reproduced when his journals were published. As Michael Smithies, who has written extensively on Mouhot's life, has suggested, these pictures, in combination with his vigorous prose, probably played a large part in establishing Mouhot as the man who 'discovered' Angkor.

Returning to Bangkok in April 1860, Mouhot was soon conceiving plans for a new expedition into unknown territory. He had decided to travel through the northeastern regions of the Siamese state, an area that is today northeastern Thailand but which, in the mid-nineteenth century, was still described as Laos. It consisted of small princely states in tributary relationship with the Bangkok court and was a region in which large areas had never been visited by Europeans. Mouhot's goal was to travel to and across the Mekong until he reached the border of northern Vietnam. He would then return to the Mekong and travel down it to Cambodia. He began his journey in September 1860, accompanied by two Siamese servants, Phrai and Deng, and his pet dog, a King Charles spaniel named Tine-Tine.

Seasoned traveller though he was, Mouhot found the going hard, not least because of the difficulty he had in gaining help from local officials. His journals began to reveal an impatience that he had either not shown or had overcome in his previous travels, and his generally depressed mood was reflected in critical comments he now made about those he saw as 'the scum of the Laotian and Siamese races'. Yet he persevered and, still ready to be entranced by his physical surroundings, he reached the Mekong at Pak Lai on 24 June 1861. A month and a day later he reached Luang Prabang, having travelled by ox cart beside the river on a road constructed many decades before when there had been an active trade between parts of northern Thailand and Yunnan.

Like so many visitors since, Mouhot was pleased with what he found at Luang Prabang, calling it 'a delightful little town'. It was much smaller than he had expected, not at all the sizeable settlement that Monsignor Pallegoix had claimed it to be when he published his book and wrote of its having 80 000 inhabitants.

Instead, he estimated the population at '7000 or 8000 only', and continued: 'The situation is very pleasant. The mountains which, above and below this town, enclose the Mekon, form here a kind of circular valley or amphitheatre . . . Were it not for the constant blaze of the tropical sun, or if the mid-day heat were tempered by a gentle breeze, the place would be a little paradise.' And now, beguiled by the landscape through which it ran, Mouhot formed a different view of the Mekong.

> In a letter I wrote from Cambodia I described the Mekon river as imposing but monotonous and unpicturesque; but in this part of the country it presents a very different appearance . . . There is almost an excess of grandeur.
>   . . .
>   At Paklaïe . . . I had the pleasure of again seeing the beautiful stream, which now seems to me like an old friend; I have so long drunk of its waters, it has so long cradled me on its bosom or tried my patience, at one time flowing majestically among the mountains, at another muddy and yellow as the Arno at Florence.

Remarkably, as is the case with the Angkor ruins, a modern visitor to Luang Prabang has no difficulty in sensing why Mouhot found the town so attractive. Not, of course, in the newer sections where the all-too-familiar graceless concrete buildings are devoid of charm, but in the oldest quarters built around Mount Phousi, where Luang Prabang is built on a peninsula bounded by the Mekong on one side and the Nam Khan on the other. Here, in a world of gilded pagodas and wooden buildings, one does not feel far removed from the sleepy settlement of Mouhot's time. Even more strikingly reminiscent of the town that existed in the nineteenth century is the view to be gained of Luang Prabang from the right bank of the Mekong. We know what this view was like in the 1860s because Louis Delaporte, the talented expedition artist who accompanied Doudart de Lagrée and Francis Garnier up the Mekong, recorded it while he was in Luang Prabang in 1867. To climb up the steeply rising hill from the river bank to the ruins of Wat Chom Pet is to be rewarded with a panorama that is only marginally changed from what Delaporte saw with his artist's eye.

On 9 August, Mouhot left Luang Prabang to travel further east. He had been received by local royalty, to whom he offered,

*Mouhot's tomb is located by the Nam Khan River, close to
Luang Prabang. Originally constructed by the French Mekong
Expedition in 1867, it can be seen in its restored form today.
(From Francis Garnier,* Voyage d'exploration en
Indo-Chine, *Paris, 1885)*

as he had done in Cambodia two years earlier, the gift of a rifle,
but now he wanted to press on to complete the outward section
of his travels. Having reached the village of Nam Kane, east of
Luang Prabang, on 15 August, he was once again in Luang
Prabang two weeks later. From this point on his journal is largely
a collection of geographical and meteorological information,
though there is a stirring account of his having shot a man-eating
tiger and of witnessing a rhinoceros hunt. By now he was having
difficulties with the authorities at Luang Prabang, who were
anxious to prevent him travelling towards Vietnam, and it is
unclear exactly where he spent the days before he was struck
down by fever on 19 October. He made his last journal entry
on 29 October 1861, with the stark words: 'Have pity on me,
oh my God'. Twelve days later he died in a camp beside the Nam

Khan River, only a few kilometres from Luang Prabang, and here his servants who had remained with him through this fatal illness buried him.

Mouhot was mourned both in Paris and in London, and interestingly it was to the Royal Geographic Society in the latter city that his family sent his manuscripts and natural history collections. While he is best remembered for the manner in which he brought an awareness of the wonder of the Angkor temples to the Western world, his explorations into northeastern Thailand and the Mekong River valley near Luang Prabang were of great importance. His descriptions of the Mekong were eagerly read by a new generation of Frenchmen eager to find out more about the Mekong, the river he had once described as rushing through high gorges with a sound like the stormy sea. In a very real sense, Henri Mouhot was the first of the modern band of explorers for whom unlocking the secrets of the Mekong was the ultimate goal. By the time his journals were published this goal was being eagerly discussed in Saigon, the capital of the new French colony of Cochinchina.

5

The Mekong Explored:
From Hope to
Disappointment

'Would you not be the man to try and ascend the river for six
or seven hundred leagues to see what occurs in Tibet, in the
interior of China?'
  'Why not?'

*Exchange between Admiral de la Grandière, Governor of Cochinchina,
and Commander Doudart de Lagrée in 1866, recorded in Félix Julien,*
Lettres d'un précurseur, *Paris, 1886*

As Henri Mouhot lay dying near Luang Prabang in 1861,
France had already embarked on its colonial advance into
Vietnam. Spurred on by the combined enthusiasm of the merchants of Bordeaux, the Catholic missionary lobby, and a navy
thirsting for colonial glory, Napoleon III had ordered the invasion
of Vietnam in 1857. The initial attack directed against the port
of Tourane (Danang) on the central coast of Vietnam failed to
do more than leave the expeditionary force exposed to harass-
ment by the enemy and to the depredations of tropical disease.
By 1859 the French command had moved its forces to southern
Vietnam and besieged Saigon, the one major city in the south
of the country and a commercial centre offering much greater
potential rewards than Tourane.

The Western world was well acquainted with Saigon before
the French forces invested the city in 1859. French mercenary
adventurers who had helped the first Nguyen emperor to gain
the Vietnamese throne and control of the entire country at the

73

end of the eighteenth century had provided accounts of the city.
But among the accounts circulating in Europe none provided a
better picture of the city than that written by John White of
Marblehead, Massachusetts, a lieutenant in the United States
Navy. Published in both Boston and London, White's *A Voyage
to Cochin China* drew on a sojourn of three months in Saigon, in
late 1819 and early 1820, and contains a mass of information
about the city, its buildings and inhabitants in the one hundred
and fifty pages he devotes to the subject. Some of his history is
astray, and he notably failed to recognise that the Imperial
Viceroy he encountered in Saigon, Le Van Duyet, was a eunuch,
clearly mistaking the females he encountered in the Viceroy's
palace as his 'wives and concubines'. But, overall, White gives a
vivid and accurate picture of a lively city, one that still sheltered
under a massive citadel which the Emperor Minh Manh later
destroyed in 1835. Despite the admiration White had for Saigon's buildings, this did not transfer to the inhabitants. 'It would
be tedious to the reader,' he wrote, 'and painful to myself, to
recapitulate the constant villany and turpitude which we experienced from these people during our residence in the country.'

Once before Saigon, the French forces again encountered
strong Vietnamese resistance and could do little more than dig
in for a long siege. And, once again, the help from Vietnamese
Christians promised by French missionaries failed to materialise.
Not until reinforcements arrived in late 1860 was Vietnamese
resistance finally overcome in a decisive battle in February 1861
and Saigon seized. The following year a treaty was concluded
with the court at Hue that ratified French control of Saigon and
of three surrounding provinces. The French now ruled the area
of southern Vietnam that they called Cochinchina.

Among the naval officers who came to Vietnam in the ships
carrying the vital reinforcements was a man whose name was to
become inseparably linked with the Mekong River, Francis Garnier.
Still only twenty-one when he reached Vietnam as a member of
Admiral Charner's staff, Garnier had already demonstrated his
physical courage by diving overboard to save a shipmate who had
fallen into the sea from the *Duperré*, as it sailed at night through
the South China Sea. Hand in hand with this courage, which on
occasion shaded into recklessness, went a passionate conviction of
the need to restore French glory, a glory that had, in his eyes, been

sadly undermined by the loss to England of colonies in North America and India in the eighteenth century. Slight of build, and nicknamed 'Mademoiselle Bonaparte' by his fellow naval officer cadets, it is tempting to see some deep-seated need to dispel any presumption of physical weakness in the passionate pursuit of the goals he set himself. Yet, as his short life showed, neither moral or physical courage were among his failings. Indeed, even his decision to enter the French navy as an officer cadet at the age of fifteen was taken against the energetic opposition of his family. Whatever the modern judgment might be of a man who had no hesitation in proclaiming that 'nations without colonies were dead', he remains, at least for me, a man deserving of admiration.

Garnier's initial service in Vietnam lasted less than a year, but by May of 1861 he had already become fascinated by the Mekong River. This was the fascination he later called his *monomanie du Mékong*. Writing to his parents from Saigon, he recorded for the first time his belief that the Mekong could offer the key to the success of France's new colony in southern Vietnam. With more faith than knowledge, he assured his family that 'The Cambodia River [as the Mekong was still frequently described at this time] with its thousand branches which are navigable throughout, with its gigantic course up which one can travel for a hundred leagues from the sea, will carry to the heart of the new colony all the products of the interior'. Like many who were to come after him, Garnier appears to have been brought to this view by the great size of the Mekong as it flowed towards the sea through Cambodia and southern Vietnam. Neither he, nor others, paused to ask why there was no evidence of the trade along the river's course that would seem appropriate to its size. Despite their lack of detailed knowledge about the river's course, it seemed enough to know that somewhere to the north the Mekong flowed through China. With envious recognition that the British had already established a major commercial outpost at Hong Kong, men like Garnier thought that the Mekong could provide the French with their own access to the fabled riches of the Middle Kingdom.

After convalescence in France to recover from a tropical disease contracted in Vietnam, and then a period of unwanted service ashore in France, Garnier seized an opportunity offered to him to return to Vietnam. He was to become an *inspecteur des affaires indigènes*, a native affairs officer, in the embryonic civil

*Francis Garnier,
second-in-command of the
Mekong River Expedition
and a man who admitted to
having a* 'monomanie du
Mékong'. *(From Francis
Garnier,* Voyage
d'exploration en
Indo-Chine, *Paris, 1885)*

administration of what was now the colony of Cochinchina. By
the middle of 1863 he had taken up his post in Cholon, Saigon's
twin city and the centre of the colony's commercial activity, which
was dominated by Chinese merchants. He carried out his duties
with characteristic energy, but his hopes lay elsewhere and he was
aware that, as Cochinchina was not showing any financial return
to the French state, powerful voices in Paris were debating whether
to withdraw from the new colony. As early as June 1863 he was
arguing to his colleagues that it was vital to French interests that
the Mekong should be explored. Then, in January 1864, in
company with his friends and fellow officers Eliacin Luro and
Henri de Bizemont, he put this idea forward in a formal minute
to the colony's governor, Admiral de La Grandière. In the same
month he wrote to a friend in Paris: 'I have joined the colony's
native affairs administration, but with quite another aim than of
remaining there; it is with the goal of undertaking a voyage of
exploration to Tibet . . . I do not know if I will succeed.'
   Throughout 1864, as the metropolitan authorities vacillated
over whether to abandon their colonial possession in southern

Vietnam, Garnier was one of the most active voices in arguing forcefully for the maintenance of the new French position. In doing so he conjured up a vision of the great commercial opportunities that awaited any nation ready to tap the riches of western China by way of the Mekong River. In 1864, writing under the thinly disguised pseudonym of G. Francis, Garnier published an influential pamphlet, *La Cochinchine française en 1864*. It was a document that mixed passionate advocacy with either doubtful or questionable claims about the prospects for the colony. But most strikingly of all, the pamphlet argued for the exploration of the Mekong in terms of the certain riches that would be found as the result of such an enterprise. Britain's position in Hong Kong, Garnier grudgingly admitted, placed that country in a dominant position so far as China's coastal trade was concerned, but the resources of the interior of China were still to be exploited.

He had no doubt that the riches were there and that the Mekong offered a way to them. Quite without positive knowledge of either Yunnan or the Mekong River, Garnier wrote confidently that his countrymen should 'take the measure of the unknown riches enfolded in the valleys and mountains that enclose these rivers'. He went on: 'If one believes the travellers' tales, these valleys contain active and industrious peoples who trade with the Celestial Empire. What is certain is that the Chinese province of Yunnan each year sends many workers to the mines of amber, serpentine, zinc, gold and silver that lie along the upper course of the Mekong.'

At first Admiral de La Grandière had reacted cautiously to the proposal Garnier and his colleagues had sent him, but he too became an enthusiast, so much so that he was later to claim that the whole idea of exploring the Mekong was his own. In mid-1865, while he was on leave in Paris, La Grandière gained the approval of the Minister of the Navy and the Colonies to send an expedition up the Mekong and he returned to Saigon to take charge of its organisation.

Garnier had played a vital role in bringing about this decision to mount an expedition. Now he was determined to be one of the expedition's members. At first La Grandière was

Doudart de Lagrée, the leader of the French Mekong Expedition. (From Francis Garnier, Voyage d'exploration en Indo-Chine, Paris, 1885)

disposed to deny him this wish. The governor found the younger man overly ready to press his views beyond the point of discretion usually expected from a junior officer. In the small, introspective world of Saigon, however, Garnier's passion for the expedition could not be easily denied simply because of personal animus. Moreover, La Grandière was shrewd enough to recognise both Garnier's undoubted abilities and the desirability of seeing this troublesome spirit absent from Cochinchina. When La Grandière chose the personnel for the projected journey in early 1866, Garnier, by now promoted to the rank of lieutenant, was included on the list, not as its leader but as second-in-command.

La Grandière wanted a more senior officer as the leader of the expedition and his choice fell on the French representative in Cambodia, another naval officer, Commander Ernest Doudart de Lagrée. Age, temperament and experience set Lagrée apart from Garnier. In 1866, Lagrée was forty-two, Garnier's senior by sixteen years. He was a graduate of France's most renowned educational institution, the Ecole Polytechnique. After distinguished service in the Crimean campaign, Doudart de Lagrée had sought a posting in Indochina in the hope that the warmer climate would cure a chronically ulcerated throat that prevented him from serving at sea. As his letters show, the cure failed to eventuate; and the Mekong Expedition was led by a man in frequent and sometimes severe pain. This state of affairs never dampened his enthusiasm for the expedition's task, but in contrast to Garnier his enthusiasm was that of a man who was reserved and contemplative by nature.

In addition to Garnier as second-in-command, the personnel consisted of another four principal explorers: two naval doctors, Clovis Thorel and Lucien Joubert; a young sub-lieutenant, Louis Delaporte, who was to be the expedition's artist; and finally and controversially, the youngest member, Louis de Carné, aged twenty-three. Although selected to represent the Ministry of Foreign Affairs, de Carne clearly owed his inclusion to the fact that he was Governor de La Grandière's nephew. From the beginning, both Lagrée and Garnier made little secret of their belief that the young diplomatist had been unwisely chosen for the journey that lay ahead.

Despite the magnitude of the task facing the expedition, there is abundant evidence of inefficient planning, a fact that is all the more strange given the military background of all but one of the principal explorers. At first glance it might seem that the expedition's material needs were adequately catered for. To meet costs along the way, there were gold bars, Mexican dollars and Thai coins. Packed into 150 cases were more than 500 kilograms of hard rations, biscuits and twice-baked bread. There were over 300 kilograms of flour. And since this was a French expedition, the commissary in Saigon provided more than 700 litres of wine and 300 litres of brandy. There were also fifteen cases of trade goods, though only one of scientific instruments. Yet there is little evidence that thought was given to how all these cases were to be transported, or how any surplus was to be returned, as the group's instructions required.

To the already large party of six principal explorers were added three interpreters (one French, one Cambodian and one Lao), four French military men, two Filipino soldiers and seven Vietnamese militiamen. Although it did not seem of great moment as the expedition prepared to leave Saigon, Lagrée's party did not have documents giving them permission to enter

Burma or China. In the case of China, it was assumed that these would soon arrive and could be sent after the explorers. As for Burma, while some effort was made to obtain documents from the Burmese court at Ava, not much importance was placed on the need to gain permission from a government judged too weak to exert serious control over its territory.

Even more striking than these inadequacies of planning was the fact that, even before the expedition began, Doudart de Lagrée was well aware of the major physical barriers to any plans for future navigation which would have to be overcome in the early stages of the expedition's travels. While occupying his lonely position as the French representative at King Norodom's court in Phnom Penh, Lagrée had travelled up the Mekong to the remote settlement of Sambor, a short distance to the north of modern Kratie. There, at the very limits of claimed Cambodian sovereignty, he had viewed the mighty Sambor rapids, which stretch across the breadth of the river and many kilometres upstream. Only a month before the expedition was due to leave Saigon, Lagrée recorded his uncertainties in a note that can still be read in a yellowing document held in the French Colonial Archives in Aix-en-Provence. 'These rapids,' he wrote about what he had seen at Sambor, 'are they really impassable?'

As for the Khone Falls, which he knew of but had not seen, perhaps they were not an 'absolute' barrier and could be overcome either through locks or by dragging vessels to the region above the falls by the use of rollers. Given his knowledge, and Garnier's awareness of van Wuysthoff's account of the Khone Falls, it seems necessary to presume that these intelligent men, who in every sense of the word were 'modern' in their outlook, simply could not accept that they would not be able to overcome the physical barriers that stood in their way. This, after all, was an age that had rapidly adopted new technologies and put them to work to build dams, canals, bridges and railway lines. Not least, they were embarking on their enterprise when work had already begun on the Suez Canal, under the direction of a French engineer.

Certainly the official instructions given to Lagrée by Admiral de La Grandière took little account of the possibility of failure. Cast in terms that reflected the prevailing conviction of France's imperial role, the instructions noted: 'In the general interests of civilisation, and more particularly of our infant colony, we have a duty to eliminate those uncertainties attaching to the unknown course of the Mekong and its commercial prospects, and it is with this thought that the journey you are going to undertake has been decided upon'. As leader, Lagrée was enjoined to explore the Mekong River as quickly and to the furthest extent possible. As he and his companions did this, they were to study the resources of the countries through which they travelled, and to determine 'by what effective means one might join the upper reaches of the Mekong to Cambodia and Cochinchina on a commercial basis'.

The expedition left Saigon aboard two steam-powered gun-boats on 5 June 1866. After pausing to acquire trade goods at Kompong Luong, a settlement a little to the north of Phnom Penh on the Tonle Sap River leading to the Great Lake, the French party travelled on to survey the Angkor ruins. Apart from Lagrée, who had already made one short visit to Angkor, this was a new experience for the rest of the explorers. For just over a week, and in a remarkable display of energy, they busied them-selves exploring the accessible ruins, charting their floor plans and, in the case of Delaporte, recording views of the temples both as they existed and in his imagined reconstructions. Garnier described their activities as a 'consecration' of the expedition's scientific purpose. Despite these high-sounding words, the time spent at Angkor had the air of a holiday. There was even a group photograph taken of the explorers ranged along one of the broad temple entrances. Reproduced later as an engraving, it is a sobering reminder that this was the last period when the ex-pedition was not beset by almost daily problems of health and purpose.

Their sojourn at Angkor over, the explorers returned to Phnom Penh before steaming north up the Mekong to Kratie, on 7 July. This was as far as the gunboats could carry them, and now their bulky stores had to be transferred into canoes for the next stage of their journey. If their time at Angkor and Phnom Penh had been emotionally undemanding, the dreary atmosphere of this isolated settlement under the grey skies of the rainy season affected even the enthusiastic Garnier. Few who have not seen

The French explorers at Angkor in the first month of the expedition: Garnier, Delaporte, Joubert, Thorel, de Carné and Lagrée. (From Francis Garnier, Voyage d'exploration en Indo-Chine, Paris, 1885)

Phnom Penh viewed from the river in 1866. (From Francis Garnier, Voyage d'exploration en Indo-Chine, *Paris, 1885)*

these regions can appreciate the general sombreness that pervades upcountry Cambodia in the rainy season. Only the yellow robe of an occasional Buddhist monk or the flowers on the straggling vines of bougainvillea present touches of colour against the darkness of the trees and the distant hills. By mid-July, when the southwest monsoon has set in with its repeated rain storms, the monotonal landscape is matched by a grey sky to further depress the spirits. And, to add to the gloom of the physical surroundings, the explorers now had to confront the Sambor rapids.

As they faced this next, and clearly difficult, stage in their journey, Garnier had another concern, one he recorded in his private correspondence. He worried that Lagrée might be less than pleased with his role as second-in-command of the expedition. The cause for this worry, if cause there was, lay in Lagrée's reserved manner, not just towards Garnier, but towards the other explorers as well. Not only was he older than all the other explorers; both his aristocratic family background and his elite status as a Polytechnique graduate, an 'X', set him apart from the rest of the party. Yet it is difficult to know what Garnier expected. At this stage of the expedition Garnier was an unknown quantity so far as Lagrée was concerned. And, in any case, Lagrée had made clear from the beginning that he would command the expedition in the same manner as he would a naval vessel.

There were more material reasons for worry once the expedition left Kratie on 13 July. The canoes in which they were now travelling made slow progress against the flow of the river, but by the end of the first day the explorers had reached the Sambor rapids. Although still below its high water mark, the river was already swollen and flowing south through the rapids at more than five knots, and had spread to a width of nearly two kilometres. Initially, Garnier found this a cause for optimism. Since further flooding could be expected as the rainy season continued, the rapids which were now clearly visible would be submerged. Then, he speculated, all that would be required was a vessel with sufficient power to overcome the force of the current. Almost exactly one hundred years later, I travelled over this stretch of the Mekong in a boat that possessed the power Garnier had dreamt of. The river in flood was a majestic sight, not least as I was travelling in the closing hours of daylight with the storm clouds framing the dark, distant hills, and as lightning heralded yet another downpour which would raise the river's height even further. Yet even with a powerful inboard diesel the going was slow, and like the French explorers our boatman had to hug the bank so as not to expose his craft to the full force of the current.

Without such a possibility available to them, the explorers had to accept painfully slow progress as their boatmen poled or pulled their canoes along the eastern bank. By 16 July the party had reached the most difficult section of the rapids. No longer were there any clearly defined banks on either shore, and the boatmen had to strain to make even minimal progress. In his journal Garnier wrote that his dream of the Mekong as a route to the riches of China 'seemed from this moment gravely com-promised'. There was no way of knowing where the main channel of the river lay, and the sudden alternation of depths and shallows promised little assurance that any deep-water channels would persist long enough to make them navigable. It took another three days before the party finally emerged into calm waters below the small settlement of Stung Treng.

The expedition had now left the regions owing fealty to the Cambodian monarch far behind. Stung Treng and the regions around it were administered for the King of Thailand by a Lao governor. After the disappointing experience of the Sambor rapids, Doudart de Lagrée decided to explore the Se Kong River which ran into the Mekong at Stung Treng from the east. At the same time he yielded to Garnier's request to make a further survey of the rapids they had just passed. Since they had travelled up the eastern bank of the Mekong, the possibility remained, Garnier suggested, that a navigable passage might be found on the western side of the river.

Leaving Stung Treng on 24 July, Garnier, a French sailor named Renaud and two Cambodian boatmen set off down the Mekong. They swiftly came to the rapids, and as they heard the roar of the water running through them the boatmen began to turn their canoe away towards the eastern bank. Garnier would have none of this. Drawing his revolver, he threatened to shoot the boatmen if they did not continue down the western side. His was a brave but futile gesture, for although the terrified boatmen did as he commanded, with the canoe being tossed and nearly overturned by the turbulent current, it became clear that the channel along which they raced could not be ascended even by the most powerful steam launch. Garnier and his companions returned to Stung Treng to pass this depressing news to their fellows.

Yet while the records make clear that the explorers were disappointed by the experience of the Sambor rapids, they were not downhearted as they prepared to move further north toward the Khone Falls, an obstacle none of them had seen. Then, as they prepared to set out, Garnier and Joubert fell seriously ill. The nature of the 'fever' that struck them down is uncertain. Although Joubert was well on the way to recovery ten days after the onset of his illness, Garnier's attack was more serious. On the basis of Thorel's description of Garnier's symptoms, it is possible he was suffering from scrub typhus. For eighteen days he was either unconscious or delirious and the other explorers began to despair of his recovering. Finally, Lagrée decided that the expedition must move on and they began to travel north with Garnier lying unconscious in one of the canoes. The same day they started north, Garnier, still delirious, fell into the river. Pulled back into the canoe, this sudden shock was followed by a marked improvement, and on 17 August, with the expedition just below the Khone Falls, he came to his senses. Much of his skin was

The Khone Falls lie just above the modern border between Laos and Cambodia. (From Francis Garnier, Voyage d'exploration en Indo-Chine, *Paris, 1885)*

sloughing away, his hair was falling out, and his left leg was partially paralysed. Not until more than a month after the onset of his illness was he again able to perform some of his normal duties for the expedition.

While Garnier's recovery was a welcome development, the French hopes that the Khone Falls might not be a major obstacle were soon dashed. By this stage of the year the Mekong was not far below its highest level and what they saw was awe inspiring, and depressing. Here was a mass of water tumbling over falls and cataracts spanning some eleven kilometres. Some of the falls were nearly twenty metres high, and the jagged rock faces that separated them posed an equally daunting barrier. Any hopes of navigation between the mouth of the Mekong and this region of southern Laos were at an end. From this point on the expedition's essential task became exploration. With this disappointing conclusion in mind, the party clawed its way around the edge of the falls into the deep, more slowly flowing waters upstream. Pausing briefly at a settlement on Khong Island, they moved further upriver to Bassac (modern Champassak), the chief administrative centre for southern Laos, which they reached on 11 September 1866. Here they were given a warm welcome by local officials, and here the party was to remain for three months.

Less than six months after the expedition left Saigon, Doudart de Lagrée faced frustration as well as disappointment. To the extent that it was possible, he had reconciled himself to the fact that the Mekong did not provide the uninterrupted waterway from Cochinchina into Laos that all had hoped for. But the task of exploration still lay before his party, and there is no doubting the enthusiasm that the explorers felt for this undertaking. There was the excitement of viewing the Angkorian period ruins of Wat Phu not far from their camp, and for Lagrée in company with Joubert and de Carné the interest of travel into the plateau lying to the east of the Mekong; though in this latter case Lagrée's succumbing to a serious fever robbed them of much of their pleasure. There is no doubt the explorers relished the exotic, whether this involved dangerous encounters with tigers, as happened to Delaporte, or observing local festivals.

None was more interesting than the water festival held in Bassac in October that marked the end of the rainy season. Indeed, they became part of the celebrations when, during the festival, the local 'king' held a ceremony in which he swore fealty to the Thai ruler in Bangkok. Lagrée attended with his personnel and, to lend lustre to the occasion, he was escorted by his tiny guard bearing fixed bayonets. This presence, Garnier recorded, added 'not a little to the splendour of the affair'. With nineteenth century reserve, Garnier also noted that the boat races they witnessed were accompanied by raucous shouts from the shore that were 'lascivious'. He did not add more. It seems certain that these chants at Bassac were little different from those I heard being shouted out at the water festival in Phnom Penh nearly one hundred years later.

> It has rained a great deal this year, the river has broken its banks.
> There will be much rice and joy. All the women are pregnant, either by their husbands or their lovers. It doesn't really matter.

Or:

> Oh you women, lift up your sarongs so I can tell who among you pleases me the most.

The festival ended with a floating fireworks display as bamboo frames were set on the water to drift past the watching crowd and with a final night of revelry made more boisterous by the eager consumption of local rice alcohol. It was all very exotic, but it did nothing to solve an increasingly worrying situation for the explorers so far as the lack of passports for China was concerned. By now, whatever reserve Lagrée had shown towards Garnier had vanished. Even before the party left Stung Treng, the expedition's leader had written to La Grandière in Saigon praising Garnier's 'intelligence' and 'ardour'. His second-in-command was a man who 'worked unremittingly' and was 'tireless'. His only reason for concern was that Garnier, through his constant energetic activity, might exhaust himself. Garnier was therefore the obvious man to send back down the river in search of the long-awaited passports; and on 2 November he set off, hoping to travel all the way back to Phnom Penh, where it was assumed the passports must be. The effort was futile, for once in Stung Treng Garnier found that a major rebellion was raging in northeastern Cambodia, making any possibility of travelling down the Mekong to Phnom Penh impossible. There was nothing he could do but return to Bassac.

There Garnier found that another kind of frustration had led to an incident of drunken violence and a chase after local women, and in the fracas the interpreter Séguin had threatened one of the French soldiers with a knife. With both Lagrée and Garnier absent, Delaporte had been in charge and he had clapped one of the escort in irons and placed him under the guard of the local ruler's men.

In all the records of the expedition, both personal and official, the issue of sexual frustration among the explorers and their subordinate European personnel rates only the barest mention. The satisfaction the expedition's principals gained from exploration or, in the case of Delaporte, the pleasure he derived from sketching and recording local music, or playing his violin to the delight of the Lao villagers, did not meet the needs of the French military men in the escort and the civilian interpreter Séguin. These men wanted liquor and they wanted women. These were natural enough desires, and ones neither officers nor rankers denied themselves in Saigon. Writing with a trembling hand in the early 1870s, the French Apostolic Vicar of Saigon vehemently condemned the almost universal practice of French officials keeping concubines. But an expedition, for the officers, was a different thing—a time when physical desires should be sublimated to the

greater good of confronting hardship in the name of France. Such
standards had little attraction for the personnel of the escort.

In Bassac the escort lived a life of enforced idleness, at most
engaged in some routine guard duty. Their lack of contact with
the outside world was total. Just occasionally an indication of
the sexual frustrations endured by the party as a whole emerges
obliquely in Garnier's own record of events. He noted his mildly
embarrassed realisation that the women of Laos had come to
seem gracious and 'even pretty'. Whether this was the result of
his long stay in Cochinchina, or because Lao and European
women shared certain physical characteristics, he could not
decide. In the account of his return from Stung Treng to Bassac
he refers, almost with the vicarious pleasure of a voyeur, to
his belief that a young Cambodian girl who had drunk deeply
from his supply of brandy was afterwards an easy conquest for
a youth of the village. But, he continues after this observation,
'I will be as discreet as the tamarind trees that lent their shadowy
silence to the two lovers'. Louis de Carné's comments on the
love life of elephants provide another, not-so-hidden insight into
the way in which sex was not far from the minds of the explorers.
With the coy prurience that characterises much nineteenth century writing, he described the male elephants as being 'lavishly
gallant. They hide their mysterious amours in the depths of the
woods; but they do not the less, on the march, use their trunks
for most immodest sport.'

Having lost so much travelling time waiting in Bassac,
Lagrée recognised that the expedition had to move on in
order to take advantage of the best season of the year, while
making a new effort to obtain the missing passports. In a letter
sent to Admiral de La Grandière in Saigon to apprise him of
their plans, the tone of the expedition leader's words was close
to desperate as he emphasised the urgency of their need. On
another and more delicate matter, for he was writing about the
governor's nephew, Lagrée expressed his concern that de Carné
seemed unable to accept the necessity to make the detailed
observations for which he was tasked, preferring instead to offer
sweeping judgments for inclusion in the expedition's records. This

evaluation was borne out by the jejune tone of the book that de Carné eventually published when the expedition was over.

The decisions Lagrée now took involved splitting the party into three groups. All members of the expedition would travel up the Mekong to where it joined the Mun River, a little to the north of Bassac, and then up the Mun to Ubon. The explorers believed that this was an important Thai regional centre which, given its proximity to the Mekong, warranted their visiting it. From there the main party would continue north, while Garnier would head back overland to Phnom Penh, taking with him three of the most troublesome members of the escort to be sent back to Saigon.

They set off from Bassac on Christmas Day 1866 in weather that was fresh, even cold, for men accustomed to the heat of Cochinchina. To be on the move again was exhilarating in itself, but once more their progress was dogged by familiar difficulties as soon as they left the Mekong to travel up the Mun. Rapids slowed their progress, so it was not until 7 January that they reached Ubon, a settlement Garnier tersely described 'as too large for a village and yet still not a town'. Here the party split into three. Garnier headed south in search of the urgently needed passports; Lagrée, going overland, led the main body of the expedition north towards Khemerat, a settlement on the Mekong; and Delaporte kept faith with the expedition's instructions by travelling back to the Mekong to continue charting the detail of its course north, after which he was to rendezvous with the main party at Khemerat.

Two months passed before Garnier rejoined the expedition. Lagrée and his group had found the overland journey from Ubon to Khemerat relatively easy, aided as they were by elephants to carry their stores. Delaporte, by contrast, had travelled up the Mekong with great difficulty through another massive set of rapids. Even with eight men paddling his light pirogue he could not best the current and had to resort to seemingly endless portages. Nevertheless, throughout this difficult travel he accurately mapped the twists and turns of the river. Then, once Delaporte was back with the main party, the expedition again found the river allowed easy travel by boat and the explorers moved on to Uthen, where they waited for Garnier.

Garnier had lost no time as he headed south in pursuit of

the passports. In the two months that passed between his leaving Ubon and rejoining the main party at Uthen, a small settlement a little to the north of Tha Khaek, he traversed over 1600 kilometres, much of it on foot under the most trying conditions and through areas never previously seen by a European. Most importantly he found that the passports for China for which they had waited so long were indeed available in Phnom Penh, but not the scientific instruments the explorers had asked for, nor any private mail.

By any standards, Garnier's journey was a remarkable achievement, especially for a man who had so recently been seriously ill. But it was marked by one sad event which Garnier suddenly and emotionally notes in his records. Early in his journey towards Phnom Penh his pet bitch Dragonne had run away. His pet since her birth on the gunboat of the same name, she had fretted ever since leaving Saigon, and now she was deprived of her one canine companion, Delaporte's pet dog Fox. 'This', Garnier later wrote, 'was too much for her. The day after this separation she came as usual to sleep beside me in my boat, showing more affection than normal. When I woke the next morning she was no longer there.' For a time Garnier felt inconsolable. Like other travellers in distant regions, not least the unfortunate Henri Mouhot, Garnier found that his pet dog filled a vital emotional need in his life. For the most part, such emotion was something to be hidden. So when he wrote in a letter of his finally rejoining the main party at Uthen, Garnier simply noted that when he saw the tricolour flying above the expedition's camp his 'heart beat a little faster'.

Buoyed by at last being in possession of the passports for China, the explorers continued up the Mekong, diligently recording linguistic data, searching for minerals and medicinal plants and noting the characteristics of Buddhism. The records made during the expedition were sufficient to fill a folio volume of five hundred pages, quite separate from the lengthy narrative of the expedition recorded in another, equally large volume. And all the while Garnier and Delaporte were preparing maps of the river and the regions surrounding it in great and accurate detail. At the same time, and in conformity with the details of their orders, the expedition kept extraordinarily detailed records of the expenses they were incurring. These allow us to know, for example, that between 13 July and 6 August 1866 the expedition purchased 225 eggs as part of their stores.

Just short of a hundred kilometres beyond Uthen, the French party had a new cause for concern. They were certain the Mekong had its origins in Tibet, and so flowed north to south. Yet suddenly the river was no longer flowing from the north; following its course as it turned sharply, the explorers found themselves travelling west. Then, after a period when they again found themselves travelling in a northerly direction, the Mekong's course turned to the southwest. They could not believe that all their assumptions were wrong, but the pirogues on which they were travelling were now set on a course that was contrary to all their expectations. To add further gloom, the countryside through which they were travelling became tiringly unchanging. Garnier later reflected on his own reaction to the situation. He recognised that novelty was an essential in an explorer's experience. Without it, the actual fact of progress along a route was not enough. 'A day without an emotional experience,' he wrote, 'is a disappointment.'

This admission came at a time when the explorers were increasingly anxious to reach the once important city of Vientiane. They knew it had been sacked in the 1820s, but they thought it just possible that there might be some some trace of the rich market described by van Wuysthoff more than two hundred years earlier. Vientiane, after all, was set in unknown territory, outside the area explored by Mouhot in his travels in Laos. Their hopes were not very high, not least because they had already found how hollow were the claims made about the supposed riches of Laos by two of the most erudite geographers in France, Cortambert and de Rosny. Writing in 1862, these pillars of the Ethnographic Society had suggested that Laos might hide riches beneath its soil that could make it another California. At this stage the explorers hoped for rather less, yet even for their more modest commercial hopes the sight of an almost deserted river that greeted them as they drew nearer to Vientiane was depressing. And when they reached the site of the formerly important city, on 2 April 1867, any remaining expectations of its providing commercial opportunities vanished.

It was immediately clear how thorough had been the destruction wrought by the Thai king in 1828. Yet the vestiges that remained of the city's former greatness impressed the explorers. The royal pagoda, Wat Pha Kaew, still preserved its basic form, with delicately carved wooden panels, fading gold leaf on the pillars supporting the roof and decorative chips of glass that glistened in the sun like a gigantic setting of diamond brilliants. Wat Si Saket was virtually untouched by time or the advancing forest, having been the one temple spared by the Thai invaders, and That Luang, the most famous monument in Vientiane, had only recently been restored when the explorers saw it. They had some sense of this great stupa's importance, but they could scarcely know how deeply it was held in reverence by the population of the Lao principalities. Nor, of course, could they have predicted that That Luang was to become in the twentieth century a potent symbol for Lao identity. So much so that when Laos was caught up in the Vietnam War the communist-led Pathet Lao forces used the monument as one of the decorative motifs on their banknotes, aligning the traditional past alongside such decidedly modern scenes as delicately engraved soldiers shooting down American aircraft over the war-torn Plain of Jars.

Two days after reaching Vientiane, the French party was on the river again. At first the fact that they were now travelling in a region that no European had seen before was a matter for pride, but this unknown section of the river quickly turned a grim face to the expedition. Only a few kilometres above Vientiane the wide plains that had spread on either side of the river for most of the distance between Khong Island and Vientiane were replaced by increasingly forbidding hills. And with the narrowing of the river's width came the familiar barrier of successive rapids. The floor of the gorge enclosing the Mekong was now, in Garnier's words, like some giant mosaic, as different coloured rocks projected unevenly above the dark waters of the river. Once again their progress slowed to a crawl and repeated portages were needed to overcome the rapids. Between 5 and 8 April the expedition advanced less than twenty kilometres. Hiring boatmen prepared to travel any distance proved increasingly difficult, and they now faced a further painful handicap: their supplies of boots and shoes were exhausted, torn apart in repeated treks over the river's rocky banks. From this point onwards most in the party

Delaporte's rendering of the great That Luang stupa in Vientiane, drawn at the time of the Expedition's visit in April 1867. (From Francis Garnier, Voyage d'exploration en Indo-Chine, Paris, 1885)

Throughout the Mekong Expedition, the French explorers faced the need to negotiate seemingly endless rapids. (From Francis Garnier, Voyage d'exploration en Indo-Chine, Paris, 1885)

were reduced to walking barefoot over whatever path lay in their way. In April, alongside the rapids, it was a route filled with bruising and cutting stones. In later months the bare feet of the explorers were to traverse grass and mud that swarmed with voracious leeches.

Still puzzled by the fact that their course along the Mekong was taking them in a southwesterly direction, the explorers reached the riverside settlement of Chiang Khan and received news that seemed to make the physical difficulties they had been encountering pale into insignificance. Chiang Khan's deputy governor greeted them with the information that some forty British officers were on their way down the Mekong to bolster the position of British timber interests active in the north of Thailand. If this report were true, the Frenchmen realised, they would lose the remaining justification for their efforts. They would not be able to claim priority in exploring the Mekong or in laying the groundwork for some future extension of political power over a region which they hoped France might eventually control.

When they left Chiang Khang on 14 April, they still had no certain confirmation that a British party was coming down the river towards them, but they feared the worst. Two days later, and to their great relief, they found that there was no British party travelling on the river. Instead they encountered a small survey mission working for the Thai ruler and headed by a French citizen of Dutch descent named Duyshart. He had indeed been engaged in surveying the Mekong, but with a threatening illness and concern for the deteriorating weather conditions he was abandoning his task. Ominously, he made no secret of his judgment that the twin dangers of political instability in the Mekong's upstream regions and the fearsome fevers prevalent there would bring a tragic end to the explorers' efforts.

While they did not discount Duyshart's warnings, at this stage there was no suggestion of doing other than continuing to explore the river. They knew that Luang Prabang lay ahead, and they hoped to gain accurate political intelligence of the regions beyond that settlement. As they gradually pressed further north, the countryside became less forbidding until, on 28 April, their boatmen told them that they would reach Luang Prabang the next day. Now questions of form became important. Despite their lack of footwear, the Frenchmen drew their best clothes from their valises. Even more remarkably, given the circumstances, the escort could still be dressed like men manning an admiral's barge. They donned white shirts and trousers, sailor's collars and straw hats bearing a ribbon with the word 'Mekong' printed in gold. Only then did they prepare to enter the city where Mouhot had been welcomed six years earlier.

They came to Luang Prabang around a bend in the river and found before them the largest settlement they had seen since they left Phnom Penh more than nine months previously. Built on the eastern bank below the dark slopes of hills and mountains that retreated in successively higher waves, the city offered a sharp contrast with the straggling settlements on the river banks to which the explorers had become accustomed. Instead of the succession of minor riverside villages they now saw a city that was growing in political and commercial importance. Garnier and Delaporte reacted positively to Luang Prabang's charm; ever the outsider in this group, Louis de Carné found it 'mean', but for all in the party it was a place to rest. Despite the brave words of their records, they were all exhausted and unready to contemplate further travel for nearly four weeks. Yet, even as their fatigue diminished, the potential for future political impediments to progress was a matter for grave concern.

6

The Mekong Explored:
From Disappointment to
Tragedy

The adventurous part of our journey is beginning, but we are not
organised to undertake adventures, and it is probable we will pay
for this.

Francis Garnier, writing from Luang Prabang to his friend
Eliacin Luro in Saigon, May 1867

A s the explorers rested in Luang Prabang, Doudart de Lagrée
took stock of their position and their options for the future.
The party had their passports for China, issued by the imperial
authorities in Peking, and they believed these would enable them
to enter China without difficulty. Yet even here there was cause
for worry. The area of southwestern China for which they were
headed had been in the grip of an Islamic rebellion for years,
and the explorers had no way of knowing what they would find
when they eventually reached the borders of the Middle Kingdom. But this was a problem that still lay far ahead. The more
immediate worry related to the territory through which they had
to pass once they left Luang Prabang, for it was a jumble of
petty kingdoms and principalities over which no single monarch
exercised firm control. As their official instructions had noted,
'The ideas we have of these upper regions are too uncertain for
it to be useful to provide you with particular instructions concerning these areas'. So, the wordy document continued, Lagrée
was to take 'inspiration' from his general instructions and 'act
according to circumstances'.

One of the 'circumstances' that the drafters of Lagrée's instructions had not envisaged was the fact that he had begun to be affected by an illness that was ultimately fatal. Separate from a chronic throat ailment and the severe bout of fever he had experienced earlier in the journey, he was suffering from amoebic dysentery, the chronic disease which, if left untreated, attacks the intestines and ultimately the liver. As I know through sharply remembered personal experience, it is a disease that saps an individual's energy. In the nineteenth century no cure existed for the condition. Indeed, none was found until the early 1940s. In his weakened state, Lagrée now sought the opinion of the party as a whole as to what the expedition's next step should be. This decision, and the fact that, initially, Lagrée and Garnier favoured different courses of action, became the basis for later controversy as these two men's respective partisans argued over which of the two deserved credit for the expedition's achievements and for the route the explorers had followed.

Doudart de Lagrée's first inclination was to abandon the goal of exploring the Mekong. Given the uncertain nature of political control in the areas to the north of Luang Prabang, Lagrée considered that the expedition might be wiser to take an alternative route into China, following instead the Nam Ou River, which joined the Mekong just above Luang Prabang and which, he believed, would bring them to within striking distance of China's borders. Garnier vigorously argued the contrary view. As he later recorded, he was 'hypnotised by the river'. His passionate advocacy, which was supported by two other members of the expedition, finally won the day. With their future course of action still undecided, word began to filter into Luang Prabang suggesting that a measure of political calm had returned to the regions lying along the Upper Mekong. Garnier seized on these reports to buttress his case and Lagrée now agreed that the expedition should proceed upriver, though he warned that at the least sign of danger the explorers should be ready to abandon their travel along the Mekong.

With this decision made, the explorers busied themselves reducing their stores and equipment to a bare minimum. They could no longer afford the time required to transport a mass of stores over difficult portages, and they made arrangements to send the surplus material back to Bangkok. Extraordinarily, given the fact that the doctors in the party knew that quinine was a specific against malaria—though they still did not know how the disease was spread—among the stores sent back to Bangkok were forty-eight flasks of quinine. Yet even with the urgency that they now felt was essential to their continuing exploration, there was one task that could not be neglected. With permission from the ruler of Luang Prabang, they constructed a monument over the grave where Henri Mouhot lay buried beside the Nam Khan River. They saw this as a solemn, necessary duty, and were delighted to find that Mouhot was remembered with affection in Luang Prabang. They even found his dog Tine-Tine, though to their regret he bared his teeth at them when they tried to approach him.

Urgency or not, it was impossible for all of the French party's time in Luang Prabang to be consumed with worry about the future. From Garnier's and Delaporte's accounts it is clear that solemnity was scarcely possible as the explorers became an object of the greatest interest for the young women in the local prince's household. Once again, in Garnier's description of this interest there is only a lightly disguised indication of the sublimated sexual drives that he and his companions experienced. They watched and appraised the bare-breasted young women who visited their encampment, among them a niece of the ruler, who was immortalised in a drawing by Delaporte. Whether genuinely concerned or not, the Frenchmen questioned their most frequent female visitor about the propriety of her spending so much time in their presence. But this was not an issue, she assured them: with their long beards they could not be less than eighty years old, long past the age when it would be unsafe or unwise for a young woman to spend time with them.

For much of their time in Luang Prabang the city was *en fête*. With the heavy rains of the wet season close at hand, the population seized the remaining dry nights as an opportunity for dancing and gossip. Even the censorious de Carné seems to have been touched by the mood when he grudgingly wrote, 'The nights are beautiful in the East'—though he immediately qualified this observation by continuing, 'and the East is beautiful only at night'.

The explorers left Luang Prabang on 25 May 1867 to begin what were the most physically and emotionally exhausting stages of their travels. Despite his determination to follow the course of the Mekong, even Garnier had doubts about the possibility of going much further. When he wrote from Luang Prabang to his friend Eliacin Luro in Saigon, he admitted that it was 'very doubtful' if the party would be able to pass unhindered through territories owing allegiance to both Burma and China. His concerns were shown to be well founded when, on 18 June, the expedition passed out of territories linked to the Thai king in Bangkok and entered a region tenuously associated with the Burmese court at Mandalay. From here on, their travel became a matter of daily uncertainty as petty rulers gave and withdrew permission for the expedition to pass through their territory, and as the interference of agents of the Burmese government became a further complication.

Amid the constant political uncertainty that dogged them, the explorers faced an ever-increasing range of difficulties. Beyond the physical problems of having to overcome a continuing succession of rapids, they now found that the silver coins they had brought with them were no longer accepted as payment by the porters and boatmen they needed to hire. It was necessary to melt the coins down into bars in order to use them to meet their costs. And, most debilitating of all, everyone was now increasingly subject to serious illness. The explorers endured fevers that on occasion rendered them delirious, suffered bacillary dysentery on a regular basis, and constantly had to remove voracious leeches from their bodies. At various times Lagrée and Delaporte were unable to walk because of leech-induced wounds that had become infected. By early July the state of health of the expedition was, in Garnier's words, 'deplorable'. In the face of almost constant obstruction from local authorities, Lagrée decided to travel to Keng Tung, the most important of the Shan principalities bordering the Upper Mekong, to seek the assistance of that state's ruler in facilitating the expedition's progress. Taking Thorel with him, he left the other explorers in the small settlement of Mong Yawng on 14 August.

For three weeks the main party waited there, racked by fever for much of the time, and without news of Lagrée. Not until 6 September did they receive news from their leader that allowed them to move on. On 13 September they were all together again and by 29 September, having marched overland to the west of the Mekong, they reached the town they called Keng Hung, which is now known by its Chinese name of Jinghong. In 1867 Keng Hung was still part of the collection of minor states known as the Sip Song Panna (literally '12 000 rice fields', but having the meaning of 'Twelve Principalities'). It was ruled by a man in a vassal relationship with both the Chinese and Burmese courts. At last the Chinese passports they carried with them were of importance, for a Chinese official was accredited to the ruler of Keng Hung and exercised a major influence over him. On 7 October 1867 they crossed the Mekong by ferry for the last time. Apart from Garnier and Delaporte, the other principal explorers would only see the river once more, when they briefly returned to Saigon on their way back to France the following year.

The explorers could take great pride in their achievement in crossing into this southwestern region of China, into Yunnan, the region named poetically as 'the Land Beyond the Clouds'. Moving on to Simao, a short distance from Jinghong, they were briefly able to put aside concerns about the next stage of their travels and momentarily to make light of the illness they had all suffered in varying degrees. They were even able to purchase shoes, for they had still been walking barefoot when they crossed the Mekong for the last time. But now there was another division of opinion about how to proceed. Lagrée doubted the worth of trying to follow the Mekong further west. The expedition had reached China, and in his mind evaluating the commercial possibilities of Yunnan outweighed the scientific and geographic information that might be gained if it were possible to follow the Mekong to its source. At the back of Lagrée's mind was almost certainly the thought that the Red River, which flowed from Yunnan into the sea in northern Vietnam, might provide the navigable access to southwestern China that could no longer be sought along the Mekong. For Garnier, the Mekong remained the goal to be pursued, even though the possibility of its being navigated for commerce no longer seemed a reality.

News of a further advance by the Islamic rebels who still exercised control over much of western Yunnan decided Lagrée. The expedition would abandon the Mekong and travel overland to the provincial capital of Yunnan, Kunming. By doing so the explorers would give precedence to those parts of their instructions that called for the expedition to investigate the commercial possibilities of southwestern China. This was a bitter moment for Garnier, who later claimed that Lagrée's decision was not only taken against his recommendation but also against the views of the other explorers. The best he could achieve was an agreement from his leader that, if they received less worrying news about the activities of the Islamic rebels, then consideration would be given to Garnier's trying to make his way to the Mekong at the point where it lay to the west of the ancient city of Dali.

As the explorers travelled towards Kunming, Lagrée's health was steadily declining, aggravated by the winter conditions that they now encountered. It is a remarkable testimony to his physical resilience and mental determination that he was still able to lead the expedition. When they reached the Red River, he considered following it down to the sea, but yielded to Garnier's arguments that if they continued to Kunming this left open the option of further exploration of the Mekong. Garnier's determination to try and reach the Mekong, and the extent to which it placed him at odds with his leader, were not the only sign that tensions had developed within the party. In a telling comment on the mental costs that their long journey had exacted, the members of the party chose to march in isolation from each other as they headed towards Kunming in November and December 1867. They had all spent too long in each other's company. When Lagrée sought companionship he turned increasingly to Delaporte, not to Garnier, his second-in command.

By the time the explorers left Kunming, on 9 January 1868, Lagrée's condition had worsened markedly, and after five days travel he was no longer able to remain seated on the horses they had with them and had to be carried on an improvised litter. When, on 18 January, the party reached Dongchuan, a minor settlement close to Huize, the district capital of this sparsely settled region, it was apparent that Lagrée was gravely ill. He was suffering from severe dysentery, a fever that was probably malaria, and was again troubled by the chronic problem of his infected throat.

The last meeting of the whole expedition took place around Lagrée's sickbed. Now he sought opinions rather than giving orders. Led by Garnier, the explorers reaffirmed their wish to try and reach the Mekong by way of Dali, and Lagrée gave that wish his approval. He asked Garnier to draft instructions for the party that would travel to Dali. The final paragraph of these instructions seemed to owe as much to Garnier's inspiration as to the thoughts of the by now almost totally incapacitated Lagrée. 'If at any time,' the final paragraph read, 'Monsieur Garnier thinks he might easily reach the Mekong, he should do so alone and as quickly as possible.' As a last instruction from the expedition's leader, Garnier could not have asked for more. On 30 January, Garnier, Thorel, Delaporte and de Carné bid farewell to Lagrée. They were accompanied by five men from the escort. Left with Lagrée were Joubert, a French sailor named Mouëllo, and three Vietnamese militiamen.

G arnier and his companions left a dying man behind as they headed west away from Dongchuan. Yet all the evidence suggests that they did not believe this to be so. For Lagrée to have survived as long as he had, despite the ominous signs of the desperate state of his health, seemed a reason to hope for an ultimate recovery. It was a misplaced hope that proved to be wrong before Garnier's party returned. In temperatures that frequently dropped below freezing, Lagrée's condition continued to deteriorate and his throat ailment worsened. Matching his physical decline was his mental anguish as he told Joubert of his doubts about the wisdom of having allowed Garnier to make his trek to the west and his distress that the expedition had failed to find a navigable route into China.

At the end of February 1868, Joubert faced a terrible dilemma. Temporarily, Lagrée's throat had recovered and he was able to eat solid food again, but he was now in great pain from an abscess that had formed on his liver. In a decision of last recourse, Joubert decided to operate. In barely imaginable conditions, Joubert opened an abscess on Lagrée's liver and drained off half a litre of pus mixed with blood. He did not know that there was another abscess, which remained untouched by this surgical intervention. For a brief period the operation appeared successful, but by 6 March it was clear that the end was not far away. Over and over again during the last days of his life Lagrée told Joubert that when he died his papers were to be destroyed. 'A man's work,' he insisted, 'can only be completed by himself.' Reluctantly, and with inner reservations, Joubert agreed.

The end came on 12 March. Believing that Lagrée's body would lie forever in China, Joubert removed his heart and fashioned a lead casket in which to carry it back to France. Conscious of his medical responsibilities, he performed a post-mortem examination and found the second abscess on Lagrée's liver that had escaped his surgical intervention. Then, with Lagrée's body placed in a heavy Chinese coffin, Joubert supervised its burial in the grounds of a pagoda outside Dongchuan's walls. He could not bring himself to burn his leader's papers, preferring to debate this matter with his comrades. There was now nothing more to do but to wait in the cold, isolated settlement whose only active commerce seemed to be in wooden coffins.

Contending though they were with frequently difficult conditions, Garnier's party made remarkably good time as they headed towards Dali. They knew it to be the last settlement of any size close to the upper reaches of the Mekong, but they had virtually no knowledge of the terrain through which they had to travel. They crossed the Yangtze, and in less than ten days, over paths that rose and fell dramatically, covered more than one hundred and fifty kilometres as the crow flies. They climbed higher than three thousand metres at one stage and then back down to six hundred metres at another. At times they marched through forests of thickly blooming rhododendron bushes and clusters of camellia trees. But there were also stretches of their route that took them through bare, exposed landscapes denuded of trees. And evidence of the rough justice of the Islamic rebels appeared when they passed corpses hanging from crudely constructed gallows and left to twist in the wind. By late February the party had moved into territory firmly controlled by the rebels. If it had not been for documents they had obtained from an important Islamic dignitary during their earlier passage through Kunming they would have not have been able to continue.

Finally, on 1 March, they came to Dali, by now accompanied by a French missionary priest, Father Leguilcher, whose isolated mission station was located a few days travel from Dali. As with Luang Prabang, it is still possible to gain a very immediate sense of the sight that greeted the French group as they approached Dali. For all the changes brought by the passage of nearly a century and a half, Dali still preserves its essential character as a walled city. Its setting is dramatic, with Lake Erhai on its eastern flank and, to the west, the Cangshan mountain range rising sharply behind the city to a height of more than two thousand metres. Shortly before a traveller enters Dali, three tall Tang Dynasty pagodas stand to the right of the road, as dominating today as they were in 1868.

Escorted into Dali by Muslim soldiers, the reception the explorers received was inauspicious. Despite the documents they carried from Kunming, the local authorities refused to believe they were French, insisting instead, for reasons never explained, that they were English. Nevertheless, it appeared that the leader of the Islamic rebellion, who styled himself the Sultan of Dali, was ready to receive them. With this arranged, Garnier began planning his next step. He would leave the other members of the party resting in Dali and make a dash for the Mekong, which he now learnt was four days' march further west.

It was not to be. The next day, Leguilcher was summoned into the Sultan's presence and told that the explorers must leave Dali without delay. If they did not, the Sultan told the priest, their lives would be at risk. Only the day before, he had executed three Malays. The sultan observed: 'If I choose not to take the lives of those who accompany you, it is because of their position as foreigners and respect for the letters of recommendation they carry. But let them hasten to depart.'

There was no choice but to retreat to Dongchuan. As they drew closer to that settlement in the last week of March, they began to receive contradictory accounts of Lagrée's condition, first that he had died, then that he was still alive. Finally, on 2 April, they received certain news in a letter brought by a runner despatched by Joubert. Their leader had died three weeks earlier. This was both the practical and symbolic end to the expedition. Garnier now automatically became the leader and he immediately made clear his readiness to take command. Told of Lagrée's requirement that his papers be burnt, he ordered that this be done. Then, determined that Lagrée's body should be laid to rest

The French explorers in May 1868 at the end of the Mekong Expedition, with the mental and physical costs of the journey clearly visible on their faces: in the back row Joubert and Garnier, in front de Carné, Thorel and Delaporte.
(From Francis Garnier, Voyage d'exploration en Indo-Chine, *Paris, 1885)*

in French soil in Saigon, he ordered the coffin to be exhumed and carried with the party as they continued northwards. Another thirteen days of slow and exhausting travel were necessary before the party reached the Yangtze and the opportunity to continue their travel down to the coast by boat. They were, Garnier noted on 26 April 1868, at the end of their energies and resources, but they had 'not lost their courage'.

When, passing by way of Shanghai, the explorers reached Saigon on 29 June, they had been absent for two years and twenty-four days. Whatever the disappointments they had encountered in their survey of the Mekong, it was the recital of the distances they had covered that impressed those who greeted them in the French colony. And with good cause, for during their travels they had mapped in meticulous detail some six thousand seven hundred kilometres that had never been previously surveyed. The course of the Mekong had been established as far as

Jinghong, and they had visited areas of southwestern China that had not been previously seen by Europeans. All this had been achieved under conditions that a modern traveller finds difficult to imagine.

L agrée's body was laid to rest with funerary pomp in Saigon, with his friend from the time of his posting in Cambodia, Bishop Miche, officiating at the burial service. But this was not the end of travels for his mortal remains. When, in 1983, the local authorities in Saigon, by this stage officially known as Ho Chi Minh City, declared their intention of building over the French colonial-period cemetery in which Lagrée's remains lay, the French government arranged for the coffin to be transported to France and taken, eventually, to Saint-Vincent-de-Mercuze, to be placed in the family mausoleum.

In 1868, the other French explorers returned to France to find that the news of their leader's death and of the expedition's return had passed almost without comment. In Paris before the end of 1868, Garnier was at first disillusioned and then angry. Worse, he was, in addition, the target of a bitter personal denunciation by Louis de Carné as the tensions of the expedition flared into accusation and counter-accusation. What he thought had been success now left a bitter taste in Garnier's mouth.

The French state showed little interest in the expedition's achievements. While Garnier was invited to the imperial court and was received by the Emperor, Napoleon III, there was no suggestion at this stage that he would be rewarded with a decoration. The Geographical Society of Paris, it is true, accorded Lagrée and Garnier a shared medal in 1869, but this could only be seen as recognition by the converted. More disturbing for Garnier were the bitter attacks levelled against him. Admiral de La Grandière, the former Governor of Cochinchina, bitterly resented any suggestion that Garnier had been to the fore in conceiving the expedition project. Whatever honour was to be gained, La Grandière argued, some should be his. If Garnier's account is correct, the admiral hovered between threats and pleas, finally begging to have the instructions he had signed included in the report of the expedition that Garnier was now preparing.

In a mood of growing annoyance and frustration, Garnier

aired his feelings in a series of articles for the influential *Revue Maritime et Coloniale*, beginning in April 1869. In these articles he traced the ironic contrast faced by a man who had returned to France from exploring 'distant countries' only to find a 'profound indifference of opinion towards all that is associated with national grandeur'. It was a general problem, but he would testify to a particular example in relation to the Mekong and the countries through which it flowed.

> A recent voyage of exploration finally made it possible to pull together the scattered facts that we possessed on this region in a certain fashion. This journey, which has brought a lively response in England, which has had its initial findings published in Germany, is scarcely known in France despite the fact that it was led by a Frenchman, Commander Doudart de Lagrée, who unhappily died near the end of his glorious undertaking.

On top of all the other instances of slights and personal antagonism, there seemed only the most limited interest within the government itself about what the explorers had found on their travels. Replying to a circular from the Ministry of the Navy and Colonies, other departments of state showed little enthusiasm to subscribe for the detailed and sumptuously illustrated report that Garnier and his associates were preparing. While the Quai d'Orsay committed itself to five sets of the two volumes of text and two of maps and plates, the Ministry of War subscribed for one set only, and the Ministry of Fine Arts was unprepared to make a decision before publication. The Ministry of Justice stated that it had no funds available. More than a century later, this official report, which was only ever printed in 300 sets, has become a prized bibliographic rarity.

Worst of all for Garnier's peace of mind, the suggestion was bruited about that he was seeking to diminish the importance of his dead leader. This was essentially an unfair charge, but Garnier was to some extent responsible for its being levelled. In the atmosphere of petty backbiting and official parsimony that was prevalent, he set out to publicise the expedition and, unwisely, his own role as leader in the final months. On one public occasion, he failed to mention the duties carried out by de Carné; in a later discussion of the French party's journey, he failed to mention de Carné at all. Then, in addressing the Paris

Geographical Society, he allowed himself to be described as the 'leader' of the Mekong Expedition. This should probably be seen as nothing more than a young man's folly, a case of enthusiasm overcoming good sense. Whatever the explanation, Garnier had ensured that he had brought the tensions and disagreements of the past out into the open.

De Carné led the charge, but he spoke for others—friends and colleagues of Lagrée—who resented Garnier's thirst for glory. His claims notwithstanding, it seems doubtful that he spoke for the other members of the expedition. De Carné's accusatory letter was published in the Paris newspapers. Lieutenant Garnier, he asserted, was misleading the public and seeking to create the impression that he had led the Mekong Expedition for nearly twelve months rather than merely for the final three. His letter ended in a bitter fashion: 'I summarise, Monsieur, by protesting against the omission of my name from the document I have indicated, against the newspaper articles you have written from time to time to draw attention to yourself to the detriment of your travelling companions, and finally against the claims you have made concerning the command of the expedition.'

In the final analysis, de Carné's attack did not have widespread importance, partly because only a limited few were interested in the controversy. When he penned his attack, de Carné had little more than a year to live. He had returned home gravely ill with dysentery. For a brief period there was a remission, but he was dead at the age of twenty-seven, before the end of the Franco–Prussian War, the event that dominated the thoughts of French society during 1870 and 1871. He was deeply and bitterly mourned by his father, the Count de Carné, who arranged the posthumous publication of his son's account of the Mekong Expedition in both French and English editions. The book, *Travels on the Mekong*, lacks the clarity of Garnier's text and is deeply flawed by de Carné's tendency to sneer at so much that he encountered. His difficult personality was marked by an unwavering conviction of the rightness of all his judgments and a readiness to write of peoples and societies of which he did not approve in the sharpest terms. This is a point that emerges strikingly in some of his unpublished notes which his father included in a preface to de Carné's book. 'The Chinese', de Carné had written two years before his death, 'are not only old, they are decrepit.' China, he continued, was 'Lazarus in the grave': it 'already stinks'; and the country was separated by an abyss from even 'the most corrupted Christian nation'.

As de Carné's life slowly slipped away, Garnier was completing his account of the expedition. A bare two months before the outbreak of the Franco–Prussian War, he was honoured by the Royal Geographic Society of London with the award of the Patron's Medal. No greater accolade could be bestowed than that given by Sir Roderick Murchison, president of the Society. He spoke as the foremost authority on exploration of his day: the man whose judgment was appealed to when questions of priority were in dispute; the arbiter who had declared that John Speke had indeed discovered the source of the Nile. When Murchison assessed the achievement of the Mekong Expedition, he called it 'the happiest and most complete of the nineteenth century'. 'Happiness' for a man such as Murchison was, of course, no simple hedonistic value. What he spoke of was the happiness of duty done and task achieved. A year later, and as a further testimony to the extent to which some names are remembered and some forgotten, Garnier shared a special award at a geographical congress in Antwerp. The man who shared his award was David Livingstone, Livingstone of Africa, a name that has survived in the annals of exploration while Garnier's, Lagrée's and their comrades' have been largely forgotten.

Why should this have been so? Why did the explorers of the rivers of Africa, above all the Nile, and to a lesser extent the Amazon in South America, succeed in capturing the Western imagination in a way that never was the case for the Mekong? And why was the Mekong never immortalised in Western art in the way that Giovanni Bernini immortalised the Ganges in his famous Fountain of the Four Rivers in Rome's Piazza Navona? The answers, so far as Africa and India are concerned, lie, I think, in the fact that the Mekong and the Indochinese region through which it flowed came into Western knowledge at a late date. Much of Africa was still the 'Dark Continent' when Burton, Speke and Livingstone undertook their explorations, but Egypt and the Nile were firmly established in the minds of Europeans as one of the great sources of Western culture. It was 'natural' for nineteenth century Europe to wonder what lay beyond the known land of Egypt, for Christendom had memories of the Queen of Sheba as well as Cleopatra. And there were also the legends associated with Prestor John and the fascination that the Christian Church in Abyssinia held for generations of clerical scholars.

The place of India and the Ganges in the Western mind was more ambiguous, but nevertheless more firmly established than was ever the case for Indochina and the Mekong. Alexander of Macedon had reached India and contemplated travelling down the Ganges before his troops refused to travel any further to the East. Knowledge of India and of the major river that watered its eastern territories remained in the background for over a thousand years, but was rekindled with the Portuguese advance into the subcontinent in the sixteenth century. From the time that Vasco da Gama reached the Indian coast in 1498, the West was simultaneously fascinated and repelled by the civilisation its representatives encountered. It is, of course, a matter of record that fascination combined with the opportunity to profit from India's wealth readily overcame the sense of revulsion that Westerners felt in the face of what they saw as the barbarities of Indian custom and religion.

The fascination exerted over the Western imagination by the Amazon River was linked to a different set of interests. A preoccupation with this great river was an integral part of the Iberian advance into South America which, so unlike the experience of the Iberians in sixteenth century Cambodia, led to the establishment of colonies of settlement inextricably linked with Christian evangelisation. Such colonies were never established in the countries of Indochina, not even in the twentieth century, when colonial society to an overwhelming extent was characterised by small European communities living as a thin veneer on top of the majority indigenous society.

As the later account of the Mekong's history will show, the river did exercise its own fascination over generations of Frenchmen. But this was a fascination that was essentially practical and material rather than cultural. Only Garnier among the explorers of the nineteenth century seems to have moved close, in any consistent fashion, to seeing the Mekong in terms that went beyond the utilitarian. Individual travellers might marvel at its grandeur, but for those in Europe who were fascinated by exploration the preoccupation was with regions that had a different, longer place in Western minds.

In the bitter period following the Franco–Prussian War, Garnier's restless spirit sought a new outlet for his energies. Now happily married and the father of a young daughter, his eyes turned once again to China and to Yunnan. As was the case in 1864, when he wrote of the riches that were bound to be found in China and brought down the Mekong, Garnier's enthusiasm took precedence over certainty of knowledge as he described to a friend his plans to return to Asia. No one could realise the wonder of it all:

> . . . it is not at all depressing; Laos is marvellous. But even more so is Yunnan with its great mineral resources; with the high blast furnaces, the hissing machines, the forges, the rolling mills that Europe could install there in abundance, what might it not become? But what of Tibet? And what of the western provinces of China, those provinces which are, up till now, the source of silk transported in an uncertain fashion, with expensive intermediaries who, from stop to stop, from hand to hand, raise the price ten times before the goods arrive at warehouses on the coast . . . ?

His hopes for further exploration now combined with the prospect of commercial gain through tapping into China's trade in silk and tea, Garnier obtained leave from the navy and embarked for the East in October 1872. He had completed his work on the official report of the Mekong Expedition, and now he yearned for new adventures. It was, in the most literal sense, a fatal decision. For after solitary travel in China between May and July 1873, he returned to Shanghai to find a letter from the Governor of Cochinchina, Admiral Dupré, asking him to return urgently to Saigon to discuss 'matters of importance'.

Perhaps it is appropriate that the final chapter in Garnier's life combined recklessness and raw courage with a readiness to disregard the formal channels of command linking France's colony of Cochinchina and the authorities in Paris. And it may be thought fitting, too, that his involvement in what became a disastrous foray into Tonkin, the northern region of Vietnam, had a direct link with his membership of the Mekong Expedition. When he reached Saigon, he found that the 'matters of importance' Dupré wished to discuss with him were linked to the beleaguered presence in the northern Vietnamese city of Hanoi of Jean Dupuis. A French arms dealer who had transported weapons up the Red River to Kunming, Dupuis had met Garnier and the other explorers in Hankow during the final stages of their journey towards the sea in 1868. Despite Dupuis' later denial, it seems almost certain that it was then he learnt from the explorers of the possibility that the Red River could offer a route into China. And he had found that it did indeed do so. But now he was in Hanoi, where the Vietnamese mandarins who administered the region were refusing to let him travel up the Red River, on this occasion to sell a cargo of salt in Yunnan.

At this point the historical record becomes blurred. The best evidence is that Dupré asked Garnier to travel with a small force to Hanoi to assist Dupuis and, if possible, to use the opportunity to establish a new colonial possession in northern Vietnam. Even allowing for Garnier's inveterate enthusiasm, it is difficult to conclude anything else in the light of his letters to his wife, Claire, and brother Léon. Writing to the latter just before he set off for Hanoi, in October 1873, his mood was clear: 'As for instructions, carte blanche! The Admiral is relying on me! Forward then for our beloved France!'

A little more than two months later Garnier was dead. For a brief period he seemed to have carried all before him as, once he had relieved Dupuis, he gained control of Hanoi and other strongpoints in the Red River Delta. But when the Vietnamese counterattacked, aided by Chinese Black Flag bandits, on 21 December, Garnier's reckless spirit proved his downfall. After driving back an enemy attack he led his small force outside the citadel walls behind which they had been sheltering. His aim was to achieve a decisive victory. Instead, he became isolated, fell into an ambush, and was stabbed to death. As a final indignity, the enemy severed his head from his body and carried it away.

By the time Garnier's body, his severed head now reunited with the torso, was finally returned to Saigon, after a French withdrawal from Hanoi had been negotiated, there was a new governor in place, the austere Baron Victor Duperré. He made clear that he was unprepared to treat Garnier as a dead hero. He refused a request from Garnier's widow for lead from the Saigon shipyard to be used as an outer coffin. Next, to emphasise that Garnier was disgraced, Duperré issued orders that there should be no general mourning as the coffin was drawn to the cemetery. Only those who could justify their presence on the basis of personal friendship had the governor's permission to join the funeral cortège. When Garnier's body made its last journey, fewer than half a dozen mourners walked behind the hearse. A decade was to pass before public honours began to be paid to Garnier's memory: streets named after him in Paris and the provinces, a vessel given his name in the navy, and finally the statue erected at the southern end of the avenue de l'Observatoire. As was the case with Doudart de Lagrée, Garnier's remains were finally removed from their resting place in Saigon in 1983 and lodged in the base of this statue.

Garnier's death did not end the controversy that had emerged over the leadership of the expedition. Indeed, less than a year after Garnier fell beneath the lances of the Black Flag bandits outside Hanoi, Lagrée's closest friend and fellow naval officer, Captain Bonnamy de Villemereuil, published a pamphlet taking up the issue. He insisted that Lagrée, or 'la Grée' as he chose to write the name, 'by a simple exposure of the facts . . . must be considered the true explorer of the Me-Kong and of Indochina'. In short: 'The time has come to remove any confusion of the name and to say when speaking of the exploration from 1866 to 1868: *the expedition of de la Grée in Indochina.*'

Viewed from afar, the dispute seems pointless. Garnier generously acknowledged the role of Lagrée in his published works, even if he was given to self-promotion in some of what he wrote. But with the controversy joined, Garnier's brother Léon felt the need to defend him, while de Villemereuil and Félix Julien, another of Lagrée's friends, kept harking back to the essential fact: Lagrée led the expedition for most of its duration. Remarkably, the controversy had not died when I first started reading the expedition's manuscript records in Paris in September 1965.

Learning that Monsieur Georges Taboulet, a former colonial

official in Indochina, was an authority on the Mekong Expedition, I called to see him at his apartment. We met in a study filled with books and memorabilia connected with the expedition, including a plaster bust of Garnier that stood on Taboulet's desk. As I sat in the fusty, overheated atmosphere, Taboulet denounced those who failed to recognise that, while Garnier may not have been the leader of the expedition until the final months, it was incontestable that he was the driving spirit throughout its long and difficult journey. I think that, to a large extent, this judgment is correct, certainly from the time the French party left Luang Prabang. The irony is that, whatever their disagreements over the route to follow, it is clear that throughout the expedition Lagrée and Garnier treated each other with respect. The post-facto arguments of their partisans have been a poor monument to their memory.

As for the other principal explorers, with the exception of Louis Delaporte they rapidly faded from public gaze. De Carné had died in 1871, the same year that Lucien Joubert left the navy to take up a provincial medical practice. He died in 1893. His fellow naval doctor, Clovis Thorel, also left the navy in 1871 and lived on in Paris until 1911. Maintaining a close relationship with Louis Delaporte, Thorel introduced the younger man to his future wife in 1876. By this date, Delaporte had become closely associated with the growing interest among French scholars in the art and culture of Angkorian Cambodia. In 1873, Garnier had hoped to have Delaporte join him in his Tonkin adventure, but before this could take place Delaporte was ordered to begin a survey of the temple ruins at Angkor. Afflicted by a tropical illness, he soon had to return to France. Based in Paris, he devoted himself to the collection and exhibition of material brought back from the Cambodian ruins, first while still in the navy, and after 1880 in various civil appointments. In 1881, he made a final visit to Angkor, but after four months was again forced by illness to return to France. From then on, until his death in 1925 at the age of eighty-three, he devoted his life to research on the art and archeology of Cambodia, assembling the nucleus of the superb sculpture collection that may now be seen in the Musée Guimet in Paris.

Today, Garnier, Lagrée and the others are little remembered outside France, and little enough there. As Frenchmen, their achievements and their failures have remained, essentially, the preserve of French writers addressing a French audience. When the region they so painfully traversed became part of a wider international interest, it did so in terms of the Vietnam War, a period many would rather forget. Yet the aim of the Mekong Expedition encompassed far more than its French membership suggests. The French explorers were seeking a way into China, a goal harking back to Marco Polo and stretching into the present, when the Western world still struggles to find the right way to deal with the giant nation that so fascinated those early explorers.

7

Gunboats and 'Conquered Hearts': Exploration and Imperial Rivalry along the Mekong

Two Frenchmen . . . Mouhot and de Lagrée, died during their travels in these regions; following in their footsteps, seeking to emulate these friends of Laos and to make myself useful to my own country as well as to yours, I evoked their protective spirits as you asked me to, calling on them to help us and guide me constantly.

Auguste Pavie, addressing his Lao companions at the start of his
first mission to Laos, in January 1887.

The French government's lack of interest in the Mekong Expedition, which was such a source of anguished annoyance for Francis Garnier after he returned to France in 1868, was for the most part not matched by the Frenchmen serving in Cochinchina. For these men the expedition had promised not only the expansion of geographic knowledge and the opening up of commercial opportunities but, ultimately, the prospect of a future French advance into previously unknown territories. The most notable exception to these generally held views was that of Admiral Duperré. Yet even in his case the mean-spirited denial of full funeral honours to Garnier, in 1874, probably had as much to do with concerns about naval officers acting in accordance with clearly stated instructions as with any views he might have held about the desirability of expanding France's colonial possessions.

As France recovered from the humiliation of defeat in the

Franco–Prussian War, Garnier had not been a lone voice in calling for a larger colonial presence in Asia. Occupying only part of Vietnam was for many an unsatisfactory compromise. Then there was the 'protectorate' over Cambodia. This arrangement denied Siamese influence over the weak kingdom, but also the risk of British expansion, for the Bangkok court was, in many French minds, thought to be a British surrogate. But the protectorate over Cambodia did little to boost French commerce, and the key to commercial success was still judged to be linked to China. Yet, as things stood, the Mekong apparently did not provide the practical route into Yunnan seen as essential to that success.

Slowly but surely a range of views on what should be done to advance French interests began to coalesce. There should be further exploration of the Mekong and re-examination of the possibility of in some way overcoming the difficulties that lay in the way of using it for navigation. Concurrently, it was judged essential that this exploration should now extend to lands lying to the east of the river's left bank. This was necessary because the court in Bangkok claimed a degree of suzerainty over these isolated regions and, once again, that could mean the British might take advantage of their good relations with Siam to hinder French interests in the future. Finally, and most importantly in terms of these broad aims, France should move to impose its authority over Vietnam. Doing so would once and for all eliminate an unsatisfactory partial control of a country whose ruler seemed determined to undermine France's position in Cochinchina, who had once again embarked on the persecution of native Christians, and who was blocking efforts by the French to open up commerce with China by way of the Red River.

Already, while the explorers had been slowly making their way up the Mekong in 1867, the colonial government in Saigon had seized control of further Vietnamese territory. Disregarding the protests of the court at Hue, the French had marched into the western provinces of Cochinchina that had remained under Vietnamese sovereignty after a peace treaty was concluded in 1862. Now, in the aftermath of Garnier's failed attempt to establish a new French position in Tonkin, restless minds in both Saigon and Paris could not accept the status quo. Of growing concern in French eyes was the readiness of the Vietnamese emperor, Tu Duc, to move closer to the Chinese government at a time when marauding bands of Chinese soldiers—part bandits and part government auxiliaries—were active in northern Vietnam and in regions to the east of the Mekong River. To be defied by Tu Duc was bad enough, but making the situation more worrying was the concern that Britain was poised to do what the Mekong Expedition had failed to achieve, to find a trade route into Yunnan, in their case by way of northern Burma.

It was not quite the 'Great Game' of the Indian Northwest Frontier, but the same readiness of the British and the Russians to assign the worst possible motives to their rivals characterised the manoeuvring and assessments of the French and British as they eyed each other in Southeast Asia. For both—the British already controlling much of Burma, and the French in Cochinchina—the prospect of developing a commercial route into China was a key consideration. And for both, though achievement of the goal was slow and tortuous, it eventually became accepted that Siam (Thailand) best served their purposes by remaining a buffer state. The critical issues were those associated with regions lying on the periphery of Burma, Siam and Vietnam, for these were political entities that did not fit well into either of the contending European powers' views of what states should be.

Lagrée and Garnier had found this out to their painful cost in the course of the Mekong Expedition. A small state along the upper reaches of the Mekong might be ruled by a 'king' or 'prince' but owe some form of allegiance to one, two or even three more powerful rulers. The country we call Laos today was a classic case in point. When the explorers travelled along the Mekong in the mid-1860s, they called the region they passed through above the Khone Falls 'Laos'. This term included areas to the west of the Mekong that now form part of modern Thailand, and which were then semi-independent of their more powerful suzerain in Bangkok. When they reached Luang Prabang, the explorers found a state that accepted the status of being a vassal to no less than three suzerains, the rulers of Bangkok, Peking and Mandalay. And, finally, at Jinghong they found a court that was in dual vassalage to Mandalay and Peking.

At the same time, they were aware that the Vietnamese court at Hue claimed to have rights over areas along the Mekong's eastern bank as well as in upland regions of what is today northwestern Vietnam. These regions, such as that now made famous by the Battle of Dien Bien Phu, were not inhabited by ethnic Vietnamese but rather by groups of Tai-speaking people. For the French, the Vietnamese claims were of particular interest, for they knew that Vietnam, like China, had different views of territorial boundaries from those held by Indian-influenced kingdoms such as Thailand and Cambodia. The latter might think of borders as something porous and shifting. But for the Vietnamese, in theory at least, borders were fixed on the ground. Whatever the actual degree of control the Vietnamese court actually exercised, it would not admit the right of any other state to share sovereignty over lands it claimed lay within its boundaries. Already, those Frenchmen in favour of a further colonial advance could see the value of France being able to adopt succession rights to those claimed by the Vietnamese court. And such a claim to succession rights would gain them lands to the east of the Mekong.

These were all matters that needed further investigation, and one of the first to undertake a survey of upland regions to the east of the Mekong was Dr François Jules Harmand. A medical doctor by training who had been posted to Saigon, there was much that was unattractive about this energetic worker on France's behalf. He comes into historical view as a member of the party that accompanied Garnier in the seizure of Hanoi in 1873. At the beginning of the enterprise, Harmand was full of praise for its leader but, when Garnier was killed and the French force had to withdraw from Tonkin, Harmand changed his tune. They had failed, Harmand wrote to his mother, because Garnier 'had sacrificed everything to his ambition'. Fired with a desire to see French control over the whole of Vietnam, and deeply anglophobic, Harmand in 1877 was authorised by the colonial authorities in Saigon to carry out an exploration of regions of Laos lying to the east of the Mekong.

He had already shown his capacity for travelling under difficult conditions in the course of exploring regions of modern Cambodia to the west of the Khone Falls in 1876. In doing so he recorded his dismissive views of the local population, views that were not to change throughout his life wherever he went in Indochina. Cambodians, he observed, were an 'indolent' race, who were 'content to drop a few seeds into very fertile soil and wait until the Chinese arrive to purchase their harvest and transport it to Phnom Penh'. The Chinese inhabitants of Cambodia were, if long-term residents, likely to share many of the attributes and superstitions of Cambodians, 'while still being superior to them'. But, if they were new arrivals, this group was 'extremely insolent and feared'. As for the Vietnamese, they had a 'singular mixture of qualities and vices'.

Harmand's experiences in Laos in 1877 did nothing to improve his views of the various ethnic groups living there. With rare exceptions he characterised those he encountered, whether Lao, upland hill peoples, or Vietnamese, as 'obstinate', 'discourteous' or, in the case of senior officials, given to the 'pretence' of European manners. Speaking no Lao, and only a little Vietnamese, Harmand had constant problems in gaining information throughout his travels. With a temper that seems constantly to have been on a hair trigger, he shouted and raged at those whom he thought were obstructing him, resorting on occasion to physical violence, as when he slapped the face of a local dignitary he judged less than helpful. Refused the gift of food on another occasion, he responded by shooting randomly at the domestic animals in the farmyard of the man involved.

Harmand felt no sense of shame about his actions. Indeed, they were all recorded in the account of his travels that was originally published in the influential Paris magazine *Le Tour du Monde*, the same journal in which both Mouhot's and Garnier's account of their travels first appeared. If his views seem extreme to a modern reader, it is certain they did not appear so to most of his contemporaries. Moreover, those same contemporaries could not fail to be impressed by Harmand's stoic acceptance of the hardships he encountered and survived in the course of his travels. Like the members of the Mekong Expedition, he suffered frequently from fevers and dysentery and endured fierce heat and torrential rain. He, too, was forced to accept that at the end of the day his legs would be host to voracious leeches. And like them he walked for part of his travels barefoot, in his case in order to save shoes that were rapidly wearing out. 'My education as a traveller is definitely not yet complete,' he wrote in July 1877. 'I still need to learn how to walk barefoot on thorns and rocks.'

In terms of his contribution to geographic knowledge and, for him more importantly, the possibility of developing a commercial route from the Mekong eastward to the coast of Vietnam, Harmand's exploration was a mixed success. His account of travelling in the Bolaven Plateau was an important contribution to knowledge. But his traverse of the country lying between the Mekong at Lakhon and Quang Tri, on the Vietnamese coast, gave little support to the Vietnamese court's claims that these were regions in which it exercised influence. To the contrary, it was clear that the petty states he passed through were linked in a tentative way to the ruler of the principality of Ubon, which in turn was a vassal of Bangkok. Slowly it was becoming clear that if France was to gain control of the Mekong and the regions around it this would have to be done at the expense of the Thai court in Bangkok.

Harmand's exploration of Laos was followed five years later by a mission placed in the hands of another, but very different, medical doctor, Paul-Marie Néïs. Having proved his credentials by an earlier exploration among the hill peoples living in the mountains of Central Vietnam in 1880, Néïs was commissioned by the French authorities in Saigon to survey areas to the north and west of the Mekong in 1882. Leaving Saigon in December 1882, he followed the well-known route up the Mekong that Lagrée's party had pioneered, and joined his doubts to the widespread view that it would never be possible to overcome the barrier to navigation of the Khone Falls. This realistic judgment contrasts sharply with the enthusiastic assessment he made of the agricultural potential of the regions around Bassac. In the future, Néïs later told an audience in Bordeaux, this was an area that could become Saigon's 'granary'. Despite spending some nineteen months on his mission, including eight long months in Luang Prabang, Néïs's travels yielded no major geographic discoveries, though he was an earnest if less than skilled cartographer, and he did note the existence of previously uncharted rivers that ran eastward to the Vietnamese coast rather than west to the Mekong.

The real interest of the record Néïs kept of his travels, and its significance for the French administration, lay in the account he gave of the continuing unrest in regions increasingly under potential and actual threat from Chinese bandits. Narrowly escaping from one of these invading groups, his experience could only give further ammunition to those who were arguing for the necessity of France's playing a role that would combine imperial advance with the imposition of peace and order. Achieving some form of French control over the Lao regions would prevent Britain from extending its influence beyond Burma. And ensuring that peace and order prevailed was, of course, essential for the development of prosperous commerce as well as for the much-vaunted pursuit of France's *mission civilisatrice*.

In contrast to Harmand, Néïs was sympathetic to the local populations he encountered and actively concerned for the well-being of his escort. He even spared from corporal punishment one of the Vietnamese militiamen among them who tried to poison his much-loved Pointer dog and who stole some of Néïs's funds to support an opium habit, though his magnanimity did not extend to his sparing the miscreant a spell in Luang Prabang's unsavoury gaol. It is tempting to attribute these generally benevolent attitudes to his being a Breton, an identity he shared with Auguste Pavie. With Bretons a group often seen in France as outsiders, a people still conscious of their separate Celtic heritage, it is perhaps not too fanciful to make this judgment. Whatever the explanation, it was characteristic of Néïs that he should have invited the ruler of Luang Prabang and his officials to celebrate Bastille Day with him during his sojourn in Luang Prabang. Equally characteristic of his personality was his concern to visit Mouhot's grave near Luang Prabang and, having found that the monument built over it by the members of the Mekong Expedition had decayed, to raise a cross over the grave site. Like his predecessors, Néïs knew the costs exacted by extended travel in often inhospitable regions, the endless battle with leeches, the need to walk barefoot and, above all, the inescapable fact of repeated bouts of 'fever'. And like the Mekong explorers before him, Néïs knew that he could combat malaria with quinine, though he was still unaware of what caused its onset.

Extended bouts of 'fever' combined with the torrential rain of the wet season appear to explain Néïs's long stay in Luang Prabang. During much of this time he could scarcely move from his bed, a fact that did not prevent him from continuing to record what went on about him as well as the progress of his own illness. Writing to Dr Harmand, who was now the French Consul in

Bangkok, Néïs's lengthy medical description of his condition, which can still be read in the French archives, begins with the disclaimer that he could make no excuse for the 'orthography' and the 'French' of his account since it has 'been written either during or between attacks of fever'.

Néïs's travels and his reports of the disorder that now reigned in sections of northern Laos represented yet another building block for the advocates of an overall French expansion in the Indochinese region as a whole, as they sought to construct a policy platform from which that advance could take place. Meanwhile, there would have to be a final reckoning with the Vietnamese court to end a situation that the French, both in Saigon and Paris, found increasingly intolerable.

Between 1881 and 1887 France steadily, and in many cases bloodily, moved to assert its control over the whole of Vietnam. The details are not important for later events involving the Mekong, though it is notable that among the harsh measures taken to ensure Vietnamese compliance with French wishes some of the harshest were advocated by that arch-colonialist, Dr Harmand. Although Vietnamese resistance was never fully extinguished, French domination of Tonkin (northern Vietnam) and Annam (central Vietnam), by the late 1880s, combined with its established position in Cochinchina, meant that one vital piece in the colonial jigsaw that was to become French Indochina was firmly set in place. The same was true, by this stage, of Cambodia, or at least of the territory of Cambodia over which France had instituted its 'protection' in the 1860s—two western provinces, including that in which the Angkor ruins were located, still remained under Siamese control, only returning to Cambodian sovereignty in 1907. Yet France's position in Cambodia was only assured after three uncertain years between 1884 and 1887, after French gunboat diplomacy on the Mekong led to a major rebellion against French control.

Ever since the conclusion of the treaty granting France a 'protectorate' over Cambodia in 1863, French officials in Phnom Penh, and their superiors in both Saigon and Paris, had looked on King Norodom with an ambivalent eye. Many were offended by what Le Myre de Vilers, the Governor of Cochinchina, described as Norodom's readiness 'to join the refinements of European comfort to the luxury of Asia'. Yet it had been the French who, in an effort to ensure that Norodom did not resist their authority, had ensured that he was able to afford the comfort and luxuries with which he surrounded himself. It had been the French who had given him the Empress Eugénie's prefabricated palace, after it had been used for the opening of the Suez Canal, so that it could be erected in the grounds of the Phnom Penh palace compound on the banks of the Mekong. And it had been the French who chose to be amused, rather than censorious, when Norodom asked for details of how executions were carried out by firing squad, and then immediately used his newfound knowledge to execute errant members of his female establishment.

Despite Norodom's undoubted fallibilities, his indulgence in alcohol and addiction to opium, his readiness to tolerate the presence in his court of members of Indochina's demimonde, and his financial prodigality, there were some who recognised that he was a man of consequence: a man revered by his people. One of those who saw this most clearly was Auguste Pavie, the man who played such an important role in exploring Laos and bringing the principalities based along the Mekong under French control. While still serving in Cambodia, in 1881, Pavie described the passage of the king and his court through the countryside:

> To meet in one's travels the Asian monarch and the Cambodian court returning from an excursion in oriental style, with disorder adding to its curious character, is really good fortune.
>
> Two hundred elephants, rolling the ancient seats, gilded or black, which they support, carry the king and the princes under roofs of scarlet bamboo screening and pass like a parade, filled with women of the harem and with dancers half naked beneath their scarves. They disappear with the horsemen, the carriages, and those on foot, in a cloud of dust, leaving the impression of an unforgettable enchanted picture.

Pavie's sympathetic description of the king and court was given sharper focus by another official, Etienne Aymonier, who also was numbered among those French officials that combined administration and scholarship with exploration. Writing at the end of the nineteenth century, Aymonier insisted that:

The attachment of the Cambodians to their hereditary chiefs is as profound as it is sincere. The nation has long been accustomed to the idea of not separating its own existence from that of the royal house. The monarch is the living incarnation, the august and supreme personification of nationality.

Just how true these words were was demonstrated some years before they were written. By the early 1880s French officialdom's patience with Norodom was wearing thin. French troops had had to put down a rebellion led by one of Norodom's half-brothers, Si Vatha, who then retreated to the jungle fastnesses beside the Mekong near the Sambor rapids. In actions that echoed King Satha's attempt to gain support from Manila in the sixteenth century, the king himself had tried unsuccessfully to enter into a secret treaty with the Spanish government. And, against strict French direction, Norodom had allotted the rights to the kingdom's opium farm to one of his court cronies, without consulting his 'protectors'. This last act he sought to excuse as the result of his having been drunk at the time. Two factors finally brought a French decision to act against him in 1884. There was renewed concern that the British were seeking to increase their influence in Siam, a prospect that prompted French officials to tighten their grip over Cambodia. At the same time, the newly appointed Governor of Cochinchina, Charles Thomson, decided to increase French control over the kingdom and that an end had to be put to Norodom's financial profligacy. To achieve this goal Thomson told the king that, henceforth, France would be responsible for collecting the kingdom's customs duties.

Norodom was outraged. If he agreed to the French demands, Norodom wrote, 'It will be thought that the king has lost all authority over his subjects'. With Thomson adamant and Norodom refusing to yield, there was a brief period of deadlock. Determined to overcome the king's obdurate refusal to bend to French will, Thomson set in train arrangements that would force Norodom to agree to cede the right to collect customs duties or, as a final step, remove the king from the throne. He already had a willing substitute in another of Norodom's half-brothers, Sisowath, a classically Herodian figure who had made clear his readiness to do whatever the French asked of him years before. Now Thomson summoned military reinforcements to Phnom

Penh to back his démarches. These reinforcements included three gunboats brought up the Mekong from Saigon and then anchored directly in front of Norodom's palace.

The stage was now set for one of the best known *tableaux* in nineteenth century Cambodian history. On 17 June 1884, Thomson strode into the king's private chambers within the palace in a brusque display of lèse-majesté, waking Norodom with the noise of his entry. He then read aloud the terms of new administrative arrangements for the kingdom which gave France much greater power over Cambodia's affairs than it had previously exercised. Hearing these terms, Norodom's interpreter, Col de Monteiro, a Cambodian of Iberian ancestry who had once also acted as an interpreter for Doudart de Lagrée, is said to have cried: 'Sire, this is not a convention, it is an abdication'. Thomson's aides hurried de Monteiro from the room, leaving a furious Thomson confronting a worried Norodom.

At this point, if one of the accounts of this dramatic encounter can be trusted, Thomson pointed to the gunboats moored within sight of the palace. If Norodom refused to sign the new convention, Thomson told him, he would be confined aboard one of the gunboats. 'What will you do with me aboard the *Alouette*?' the king is supposed to have asked. 'That is my secret,' was Thomson's reported reply.

Literally outgunned, knowing that his half-brother Sisowath was a French pawn, and recognising that Thomson would indeed force him from the throne if he failed to sign the new convention, Norodom buckled under. The gunboats returned down the Mekong and the kingdom seemed, for the moment, at peace. It was an illusion, and within less than a year a full-scale rebellion against French control was in force. Given the fact that gunboats on the Mekong were vital to Thomson's having gained Norodom's acquiescence, there is historic irony in the fact that a French army post sited on the Mekong just below the Sambor rapids was the first target for a rebel attack when the rebellion began. More than two years were required before the French, making major concessions to Norodom, were once more able to claim that their 'protection' of Cambodia was untroubled.

Not surprisingly, this notable example of gunboat diplomacy is almost totally forgotten in contemporary Cambodia, where the tragedies of recent decades have eroded an historical tradition that, in any case, placed as much emphasis on supernatural intervention as on chronology and the detail of human motivation. Indeed, even before the breakdown of Cambodian society that began with the country's descent into war in 1970 and was followed by the horror of the Pol Pot years, the events of 1884 had been transformed into something much closer to legend than to history. When I talked to Pirou de Monteiro, the great-great-grandson of Col de Monteiro, in 1966, he told me a tale of his ancestor being brutally treated by the French and held in prison for years. In fact, as the records make absolutely clear, none of this happened. Col de Monteiro escaped punishment by the French and, as the nineteenth century drew to a close, ended his long official life siding with them against Norodom, serving finally as a minister in the kingdom's tame cabinet.

The last great nineteenth century mission of exploration linked to the Mekong was carried out by Auguste Pavie. It was he who, with a dedicated band of assistants, filled in the remaining blanks on the map of the regions lying to the north and east of the great river. Yet important though his exploration was in geographic terms, Pavie's most notable contribution was political in character. His actions set the stage for the drama that ended with France gaining control of the territories bordering the Mekong that today make up the country we know as Laos.

Pavie had an unlikely background for the task he undertook and the results he achieved. In considerable contrast to his predecessors, such as Lagrée, Garnier or Harmand, Pavie was decidedly not a member of the officer class. Born into a modest family in the Breton town of Dinan in 1847, Pavie joined the army in 1864 and was sent as a member of the marine infantry to Cochinchina in 1869. After service back in France during the Franco–Prussian War, Pavie, having reached the rank of sergeant-major, returned to Cochinchina in 1871 and joined the colonial administration's post and telegraph service. Almost immediately, he was sent to take charge of the telegraph office in the Cambodian port settlement of Kampot.

By any standard, this was a lonely posting however scenic its surroundings, which can still be appreciated today. Nestling beneath the steeply rising Elephant Mountains and sited beside a wide river, Kampot in the nineteenth century was several days journey from Phnom Penh. Pavie was one of a very few Europeans living in the small, isolated settlement, but it was an atmosphere in which he thrived. The soldier become telegraphist began to transform himself into a profound student of Cambodian society. Without formal training, he mastered the Cambodian language and steadily developed a deep understanding of the country's culture. He also began to demonstrate his remarkable physical hardiness. He walked, barefoot by choice and always wearing a characteristic wide-brimmed hat, over wide areas of Cambodia, charting his travels and recording all that he found of interest. His physical capability did not seem to match his appearance. Writing of him in the 1880s, a French officer observed: 'At first glance his appearance was against him. Thin, with a sickly appearance, below average height, he said of himself that he had the air of being a weak individual.' But the same commentator went on to note that 'beneath this appearance of physical weakness, there was a wealth of intelligence put to work with an energy and a strength of will without equal . . .'

After nearly a decade of service in Kampot, Pavie was recognised as a man whose knowledge of Cambodia warranted more important duties than those of a telegraphist in a small port settlement. Most importantly, his talents were recognised by the first civilian governor of Cochinchina, Le Myre de Vilers, a man closely linked to the colonial lobby in Paris who acted as Pavie's patron for many years. After Pavie successfully oversaw the construction of a telegraph line between Phnom Penh and Saigon in 1879, he was then commissioned to carry out the much larger task of linking Phnom Penh and Bangkok telegraphically. Closely involved in the planning and construction of this second line, Pavie so impressed his superiors that in 1886 he was transferred from his previous duties into the French diplomatic service. This new appointment certainly reflected an admiration for Pavie's undoubted abilities, but it had a broader significance.

Pavie's new appointment came at a time when the two imperial protagonists, France and Britain, were moving towards a final resolution of their respective claims in and around the Indochinese region. This was an age of unrestrained, though not always unanimous, imperial ambition. In France, politicians such as Prime Minister Jules Ferry spoke in terms that echoed Francis Garnier's proposition that 'nations without colonies were dead'. Failure to pursue a forward policy, Ferry argued, would see 'Germany in Cochinchina, England in Tonkin, in other words, the bankruptcy of our rights and our hopes'. Advocates of British expansion were no less determined to advance their goals. The journalist, and later British proconsul, James George Scott, characterised the Third Anglo–Burmese War fought in 1885 as a justified pre-emptive strike against French expansion. And, he argued, while his country had no designs upon the Lao states along the Mekong, a railway linking Moulmein, in Burma, with Chiangmai, and Chiangmai with Bangkok, would serve British interests and keep France from exerting its baleful influence over Siam. Increasingly, all of the interested parties recognised there was the need to decide, once and for all, who had authority in the petty states that lay along the course of the Mekong. While Siam was still reluctant to agree to a French demand that a commission be appointed to determine the boundaries of these states, it did accept a French demand that they should appoint a diplomatic officer in Luang Prabang. In Paris it was decided that no one could fill this position better than Auguste Pavie. In 1886 he was named French Vice-Consul in Luang Prabang.

When Pavie left Bangkok to take up his appointment, the political situation in much of the area over which Luang Prabang claimed authority was close to anarchy. The ruler of Luang Prabang, Oun Kham, was a frightened old man, and with some cause. Promises of Siamese protection had proved largely ineffective and territory to the north and east of the Mekong was in the hands of roving Chinese bands who claimed to be under the authority of the government in Peking but who seemed to the Lao to be bandits. For Pavie, this situation was no deterrent, and in his highly personal account of this period of his life in Laos he was rhapsodic in the description he provided of his view of the Mekong, when he reached it from Siam. Then, like so many before and after, he recorded his charmed reaction to his first sight of Luang Prabang in February 1886. He set down his feelings in staccato phrases:

Conquered and charmed, an impression remains with me: dry fishermen's nets strung up along scaffolding; boats pulled half out of the water along the strand; rafts crossing noisily over the Nam Khan's rapids into the Mekong; white and gold pagodas roofed with coloured, varnished tiles; tall houses built in wood and low huts constructed with palm leaves, their roofs covered with thin strips of bamboo; lightly dressed men and women climbing up and down the muddy and steeply rising banks between small gardens and providing an appropriate splash of brilliant colour; as a final note, and not too far distant, high mountains, dark green in colour, with tufts of cloud rising from the the Nam Khan and dispersing about them.

It all seemed idyllic, but this judgment soon proved to be an illusion. In late April, Pavie received news that a mixed group of Chinese and Tai irregulars—bandits in French eyes—were marching on Luang Prabang. They were led by a Tai-speaking warrior known both as Cam Oum and as Deo Van Tri, the latter the name given to him by the Vietnamese. Hurriedly returning from a mission aimed at finding another route from the Mekong into northern Vietnam, Pavie found Luang Prabang virtually undefended. The force of Siamese soldiers that had previously been stationed there had left for Bangkok. For the moment all he could do was to consult with Luang Prabang's ruler and await developments.

In early June 1887, the mixed Chinese and Tai group entered Luang Prabang, preceded by trumpeters and brandishing black, yellow and red flags. For a few days there was an uneasy standoff. Then, on 10 June, the invaders attacked, sacking the town and seeking to capture Luang Prabang's ruler. Alerted to the beginning of the attack, Pavie, who was stationed on the right bank of the Mekong opposite the town, sent his Cambodian auxiliaries to help the ruler and his household. Braving the shots of the attackers, these men succeeded in saving the ruler and some members of his household and brought them to the other side of the river. Once there, with much of Luang Prabang on fire, Pavie placed Oun Kham in his boat and, as part of a convoy of vessels, small and large, headed downstream. It would have been a dramatic scene with the flames of the burning town reflected in the Mekong and sharply visible against the dark hills rising from the river. Pavie and his party eventually reached Pak Lai after a precipitous passage of the rapids that lay in their way, a passage that would never normally be attempted in darkness. The Frenchman revelled in the event, admitting that 'despite myself, I could not regret being part of this brouhaha'.

Whether he realised it or not at the time, this 'brouhaha' was a vital step in France's acquisition of control over the whole of the Mekong. Oun Kham, Luang Prabang's ruler, was full of gratitude to Pavie and now sought to gain French protection for his principality. This, in Pavie's eyes, was one of the events, perhaps the most important, that led to his choosing as a subtitle for his own account of his long years of service in Laos the words 'the conquest of hearts'. From 1888 onwards, Pavie was at the centre of French manoeuvring to gain control of the whole of the Mekong valley from its border with Cambodia to the territories claimed by China close to Jinghong, the point at which Lagrée's explorers left the river in 1867. He continued his almost ceaseless travel, including taking part in an assessment of possible ways to overcome the Khone Falls as a barrier to navigation of the Mekong in 1890, an episode to be treated in the next chapter. He was French Consul in Bangkok in 1893, when French naval vessels blockaded the entrance to the Menam River and forced the Siamese government to agree to French control over territory to the east of the Mekong. There was still work to be done before, in the first decade of the twentieth century, France established its definitive control over all of the territories that made up French Indochina. But even before that time, 'our river', as Paris politicians and colonial publicists routinely called the Mekong, was firmly in French hands.

The gunboat diplomacy of 1893 did not end Pavie's pioneering exploration work. Working with an enthusiastic team of assistants, including yet another remarkable doctor–explorer, Lefèvre, who left a vivid record of his experiences in upland Laos, Pavie and his associates traversed the territory to the north and east of the Mekong. They eventually covered some 30 000 kilometres in the course of two major surveys, preparing detailed maps of the regions they passed through. When Pavie finally retired in 1904, he could justifiably claim to have been one of the most important explorers of his generation. He spent the rest of his life still closely engaged in colonial affairs and published the results of his travels in ten magnificent volumes, finally dying in 1925 aged seventy-eight.

How should we judge Auguste Pavie? Like Garnier before him, he was a man of his time. His belief that his successes reflected a conquest of the hearts of those who came under French control may seem self-deluding now. Pavie certainly did not see matters in these terms. Moreover, there is no doubting the genuineness of the gratitude of Luang Prabang's ruler, nor of many other members of the Lao elite at a time when Western concepts of nationalism simply did not exist among them. He was, of course, a colonialist, with all of the negative baggage that is associated with that word nowadays. Perhaps one can make no other final judgment than to note that he was a man of great energy and intelligence who was devoted to the advance of French interests, and a great explorer in his country's name. Rightly or wrongly, the fact that so much of the Mekong now lay within French hands owed much to the work of August Pavie.

There are other names that deserve brief mention in the catalogue of French explorers linked to the Mekong in the closing years of the nineteenth century. Among them is that of Prince Henry of Orleans, the pretender to the extinct French throne, who travelled along the Mekong's course in Yunnan in 1895 before turning west to investigate the headwaters of the Irrawaddy. And there was Dutreuil de Rhins. Born in 1842, he led an adventurous life that took him to Vietnam in the 1870s, and in the company of Pierre de Brazza to the Congo in the 1880s. In company with another Frenchman, Joseph-Fernand Grenard, Dutreuil de Rhins left Paris in 1892 with the aim of travelling through Central Asia to Tibet in order to fulfil a vaguely described scientific mission. By April of 1895 their party had reached the eastern Tibetan plateau and, Grenard was later to claim, located the source of the Mekong. Everything suggests that they were indeed close to that source, but with the ground covered with snow and with watercourses still frozen there was no way the explorers could fix the source's location with any certainty. Not long after, tragedy of the kind so familiar in the annals of the Mekong's exploration struck the small French party. Following a confrontation between the Frenchmen and local

Khamba inhabitants, Dutreuil de Rhins was shot and killed. Grenard survived to claim the discovery of the Mekong's source, but the paucity of detail in his description of what he and his companion had found meant that the question of where the source of the Mekong actually lay remained unresolved.

8

Navigating the Mekong: Challenge, Illusion and Defeat

> The navigability of the Mekong . . . there is a task worthy of raising the passions of our century with its love for great undertakings . . .
>
> *Admiral Paul Reveillère, writing in 1887*

Among the French officials linked to efforts to navigate the Mekong, few if any were more eager to achieve this goal than Paul Reveillère. Cut from the same nationalist cloth as Francis Garnier, this naval officer had been one of those who argued forcefully that France should retain its hold over the colony of Cochinchina when, in the early 1860s, it seemed possible that the government in Paris might abandon this newly acquired possession. Later, in the 1880s, when he was at the head of the French naval contingent based in Saigon, he doggedly sought to prove that the Mekong could, indeed, become an important commercial artery linking southern Vietnam with the Lao states to the north of the Khone Falls. In his passionate belief that such a development was possible he, like many before and after him, placed hope before reality. This was an attitude that led to feats of courage and endurance as well as controversies of comic absurdity. But, in the end, disappointment was heaped on disappointment. In a phrase embraced by many French authors to describe such a situation, the final judgment about the possibility of using the Mekong for commercial navigation was that it was 'The End of Illusions'.

Reaching this judgment took many decades, and the tale of how it was finally reached must be sketched in broad strokes. As early as the first weeks of the Mekong Expedition's slow course up the Mekong, when its members encountered the Sambor rapids, Garnier had recorded in his journal that he feared the whole enterprise aimed at finding a commercial route into China was 'compromised'. Yet curiously, though perhaps understandably given his emotional investment in advocating the Mekong as a route into China, Garnier was not ready to accept that the existence of the Khone Falls and the presence of repeated sets of rapids represented a fundamental barrier to the uninterrupted use of the Mekong for navigation. Both in his more personal account of the expedition, and in its official publication, he acknowledged that 'without gigantic construction work' it would be impossible to navigate through the Khone Falls. This was a view that his leader, Doudart de Lagrée, had communicated to the Governor of Cochinchina before the end of 1866. And it was also the view of Louis de Carné. When his account of the expedition was published in both French and English editions in 1872, his judgment was emphatic. 'These cataracts,' he wrote, 'offer an insurmountable obstacle to steam navigation.'

Yet, when the official account of the expedition was released in 1873, Garnier was positive that the barrier of the falls could be overcome one way or another. Perhaps, he wrote, it would be possible to construct a road or a railway around the falls. Or again, and here he seems to have moved to the borders of fantasy, it might be possible to build a canal linking the Cambodian Great Lake with one of the tributaries that ran into the Mekong on the river's right bank above the Khone Falls. In any event, he asserted, 'The river will remain the most convenient way to transport native merchandise downstream between Bassac and Phnom Penh'. He had in mind, he wrote, timber and what he described as 'marble'. In the final analysis, he never made clear just how this would be done. If nothing else, his reference to the possibility of exploiting timber resources in southern Laos strikes a resonant chord today.

Despite the experience of the Mekong Expedition, and perhaps explaining Garnier's later readiness to look for some way—any way—to rescue his dream of the Mekong's navigability, speculation about the possibility of finding a way to overcome the

Khone Falls as a barrier and to chart the best way through the rapids above and below the falls never really ceased. For a period in the 1870s the Red River in northern Vietnam was seen as a possible alternative way into China, but this route never captured the enthusiasm generated by the Mekong. In 1869, only a year after the Mekong Expedition had ended, a naval lieutenant, Mourin d'Arfeuille, and an army captain, Pierre Rheinhart, set out from Saigon to make a further detailed reconnaissance of the Mekong, both below and above the Khone Falls. Their account, which can be read in the colonial archives preserved in Aix-en-Provence, was accompanied by meticulously prepared charts. But it gave little encouragement to those who felt that Lagrée and his companions might have overlooked a passage around the falls that could be used for steam navigation. The best these two men were able to offer was the assurance of a Chinese merchant in Stung Treng that at times of low water it was possible to manoeuvre a light craft up the falls.

Travelling further north, d'Arfeuille and Rheinhart made an equally dispiriting assessment of the Khemarat rapids. These were the rapids that Delaporte had found so difficult to overcome in 1867. Two years on, these later explorers reinforced his views of the difficulties of passing through the rapids in either direction. To travel downstream, they reported, particularly during the period of high water, it would be necessary to use a solidly built raft. To do otherwise, and to use a light craft, would risk being sucked down in the many whirlpools that the rapids created.

By the early 1880s, as France slowly put the humiliation of its defeat by Prussia behind it, the voices of the enthusiasts for colonial expansion were growing stronger, and among them were advocates of a renewed effort to establish steam navigation on the Mekong above Phnom Penh. The ultimate goal was the same as that which had been pursued by Garnier—the hope of finding a way to access the fabled riches of China. The political imperative was the presumed need to pre-empt a British advance from their bases in Burma towards the Mekong and so into southwestern China. The first new steps along the navigational path so greatly desired by the Mekong explorers were taken in August 1884. Then, a naval despatch boat commanded by Lieutenant Campion showed that it was possible to take a small steam-powered vessel through the the Sambor rapids. A year later the then Captain Reveillère pushed the limits of steam navigation further up the river. As Luc Lacroze, a French writer who has devoted an entire book to the subject of efforts to navigate the Mekong, points out, Reveillère, a man without any sense of false modesty, laid claim to being the person who conceived it possible to use steam-powered vessels to navigate at least as far as the Khone Falls. Reveillère's reasoning was simple. The Mekong might not be navigable throughout the year, but it was certainly possible during periods of high water. Lagrée and his fellow explorers, Reveillère argued, simply had not had enough time to make a proper assessment of what could, and could not, be done.

Over the next three years, Reveillère, either in person or directing the efforts of officers under his command, showed that it was indeed possible to travel by steam-powered vessels as far as the Khone Falls when the Mekong's water levels were high. Difficulties had to be overcome. To facilitate passage of the Sambor rapids and areas further north, it was necessary to carry out blasting operations to remove rocks from preferred channels. And even at high water it was found that there were problems with flooded forests lying just below the surface of the river. Submerged trees lurked as a constant threat to a vessel's keel, propeller or rudder. But the Khone Falls were reached in 1887, and Gallic gallantry was shown by naming the bay where the first steam vessels to reach the falls dropped anchor 'Margueritte', after the wife of the most senior French official in Cambodia who had accompanied the party making this voyage. By now, the possibility of navigating the Mekong had attracted commercial interest. When these first vessels reached the falls one of those on board was a Monsieur Blanchet, a representative of the Compagnie des Messageries Fluviales de Cochinchine, the French company holding the government concession for commercial navigation in Cochinchina and Cambodia.

The fact of a successful transit by steam vessels as far as the Khone Falls signalled a new round of claims that a way could be found to navigate through or around them. Or, if navigation itself was not possible, then a very short rail link, of no more than two kilometres, would suffice to trans-ship goods from below to above the falls. This was certainly the view of Lieutenant Frésigny, who captained one of the two vessels that reached the falls. Moreover, with hope springing eternal, Frésigny was still not prepared to abandon the possibility that somewhere to the east of the waters where his vessel lay in the Baie Margueritte, there might just be a passage through which craft could steam. Although it was clear that no vessel could overcome the obstacles posed by the known complex of falls and cascades that stretched over many kilometeres, the possibility that there might be an as yet unexplored navigable passage remained in Frésigny's and others' minds.

The same hopeful enthusiasm infected the views of Camille Gauthier, a businessman and vocal admirer of Lagrée and Garnier. As efforts were under way to determine the practicablity of navigating the Mekong below the Khone Falls, Gauthier conceived the idea of travelling down the Mekong from Luang Prabang to Phnom Penh. This, he argued, would reveal the opportunities for developing the (still untested) natural resources of Laos, a development he very much hoped to profit from himself. Setting off from Luang Prabang in December 1887, Gauthier travelled by raft along the length of the river, reaching Phnom Penh at the end of January 1888. His was an adventurous journey, as his raft was tossed and buffeted by rapid after rapid, particularly between Luang Prabang and Vientiane, and then through the Khemerat rapids. And, at the end of his journey, Gauthier had to admit there were long sections of the river that simply did not lend themselves to steam navigation. As for the Khone Falls, and despite hearsay reports that local craft were able to ascend and descend through one dangerous passage, Gauthier reluctantly concluded that linking the river above and below the falls would depend on either building a canal around them or constructing a railway to effect trans-shipment.

Gauthier's hopes for commercial advantage faded quickly too, for when he sought a financial subvention from the French government he was rebuffed with the advice that support was already promised to the Compagnie des Messageries Fluviales. Yet, if nothing else, his conclusion that the Khone Falls were, indeed, an impossible barrier to navigation was one of the last nails in the coffin to which this idea was consigned. As interested opinion gradually came to accept that trans-shipment was the only way goods could be carried from one side of the falls to the other, one last bizarre episode temporarily called Gauthier's judgment into question. At its heart was a doctor practising in Saigon who also hoped to profit from agricultural exploitation of a large island in the Mekong not far below the Khone Falls. This was one Dr Mougeot.

In early 1890 Mougeot announced that he, in company with a Monsieur Pelletier, had found a passage through the Khone Falls that could be navigated by sizeable vessels. His announcement created a sensation in Saigon, but questions were soon being asked about the claim. Why, most importantly, had this passage not been discovered before? The explanation Mougeot offered was twofold. First, it was because the Siamese authorities, who still controlled this section of the Mekong, did not wish the French to know about the passage and had intimidated the local inhabitants into not revealing its existence. And, second, the passage that Mougeot now proudly named after himself and his companion Pelletier might previously have been obscured by the low hanging foliage of trees at the entrance to the passage. And, in any event, he was of the opinion that the current of the river was now less violent than when the Mekong Expedition travelled up the river in the 1860s. This supposed diminution in the force of the river's current was what made use of the 'Passe Mougeot–Pelletier' possible.

It was not long before Doudart de Lagrée's champion, Captain Bonnamy de Villemereuil, once more entered the lists on his late friend's behalf. In the 1870s and 1880s, Villemereuil had been ready to contest any suggestion that Francis Garnier deserved credit that was due to the leader of the Mekong Expedition. Now, from retirement in the Bordeaux region, Villemereuil was determined not to allow Mougeot to claim credit that he believed still remained due to the man who had died so tragically in China twenty-three years before. Citing the words of both Lagrée and Garnier to bolster his case—but, as Luc Lacroze points out, in one case adding and in the other case removing words that did not bolster his case—Villemereuil deplored Mougeot's claim to have found a new way through the Khone Falls that the explorers had overlooked in 1866 and 1867. What Mougeot and Pelletier were calling a new discovery was a passage that had been identified over twenty-five years earlier. If it was to have a name, the passage should be the 'Passe Doudart de Lagrée'.

Adding to the interest provoked by Mougeot's claim to have found the passage that had so long eluded those who sought to navigate the Mekong was the conclusion reached by Auguste Pavie when he travelled down the river from Luang Prabang to Saigon in 1890. Reaching the Khone Falls in early August, Pavie recorded his own descent in a canoe at the same time as the descent of three sizeable Chinese-owned vessels measuring twenty-five metres in length and drawing a draught of one and a half metres. With the removal of trees along the banks of the passage he had travelled through and blasting of rocks in the river bed, it would be possible, he suggested, for a steam vessel to navigate through the falls at high water.

In the midst of these claims and counter-claims about the navigability of the Khone Falls and the priority to be accorded the discovery of a passage that could be used by a steam vessel, the first actual attempt to steam from south to north through the falls took place. On 5 October 1890 Ensign Guissez pointed the bow of his small gunboat, the *Argus*, to the north and started to ascend the passage that Dr Mougeot wanted to claim as his own. By this time of the year the water level was already beginning to fall. The *Argus*, drawing 1.3 metres, could go no further than a short distance up the passage, which at times narrowed to five or six metres and was less than a metre in depth. After dousing the fires in the vessel's engines and emptying its boiler, Guissez and his crew attempted to make further progress by trying to pull it forward with ropes. But even this was to no avail as the boat's keel continued to snag on the bottom of the passage. The best that could be done was to careen the *Argus* and spend the dry season charting the passage that was supposed to lead to the calm waters above the falls, while clearing away, as far as possible, rocks that lay along the course they still hoped to travel.

The following September, and then again in August 1892, Guissez once more tried to take the *Argus* up the passage of water he had entered in 1890, each time failing to move forward more than a few hundred metres. Indeed, viewing this area of the falls today, it seems amazing that he was able to achieve even this much through a narrow and treacherous channel against a fierce current. Finally, it was too much even for Lieutenant Guissez, as he now was, and after his final unsuccessful effort he declared himself convinced that he could not possibly achieve the goal of piloting his vessel to the northern side of the Khone Falls.

This was all too much for Dr Mougeot. Previously he had eulogised Guissez's attempts to take the *Argus* through the passage. Now he ridiculed the lieutenant's conclusion that the passage could not be traversed, claiming that if only Guissez had tried harder success would have been possible. In a final attempt to prove his point Mougeot now purchased a vessel himself, *La Marthe*, which was a little over fourteen metres in length and drew less than a metre. Leaving Saigon in September 1893 he began his own assault on the falls. If Mougeot's own account can be believed, once the vessel entered 'his' passage in early October all was going well and there were only five hundred metres of difficult water to traverse when the helmsman allowed *La Marthe*'s stern to strike a submerged tree. The port propeller was damaged and failed. With only one propeller to contest the current, *La Marthe* could not move forward and Mougeot's effort to show that it was possible to navigate from below to above the Khone Falls was at an end. He returned to Saigon levelling dark accusations against the helmsman (who deserted shortly after the failed attempt) and making clear his feelings that the Compagnie des Messageries Fluviales was the cause of his troubles. His argument was that the existing navigation company feared that Mougeot would defeat it in competition for a contract to carry out commercial navigation on the upper Mekong.

In fact, the failure of the *Argus* to surmount the Khone Falls had already brought about a new approach by the French authorities even before Mougeot launched his unsuccessful attack on the falls. The tensions between France and Siam that were to lead to the gunboat diplomacy of July 1893, when France blockaded the Menam or Chao Phraya River below Bangkok, were affecting French foreign and colonial policy well before that date. Determined to assert control over the Mekong Valley in areas still claimed by the Siamese government, the French decided to place French gunboats on the river above the Khone Falls. In order to do this, it was now realised, the only practical course of action was to construct vessels that could be carried over the islands that lay along the line of the Khone Falls and then to relaunch these in the calm waters north of the falls. Contracts were let in France for the construction of two gunboats with shallow draught. When completed, these were shipped in parts to Saigon and assembled, not without controversy, in the Saigon naval arsenal after the shipyards of the Compagnie de Messageries Fluviales submitted an absurdly overpriced tender for this work. Named *La Grandière* and *Le Vay le Massie*, the vessels were finally launched in August 1894 and placed under the command of Lieutenant Georges Simon.

By mid-September, and with both gunboats at the foot of the Khone Falls, Lieutenant Simon faced the problem of transporting his charges across the islands that separated the calm waters to the north and south. Before undertaking this task he took a decision to substitute another vessel for *La Grandière*, which was already in need of major repairs despite its short time in service. His choice fell on a small vessel belonging to the Cochinchinese administration, the *Ham Luong*, which could be demounted into two parts. While waiting for the arrival of the two gunboats, iron railway lines had been laid from Margueritte Bay to the northern end of Khon Island, a distance of about three kilometres, and the next task was to position the vessels on a carriage built to run along the rails. As *Le Massie* was being manoeuvred onto this carriage, a tree floating down the river struck and derailed it. By the time the carriage had been repaired, the water level in the bay had fallen so sharply that Simon had to abandon any hope of placing his vessels on the rail lines that had already been laid down.

Undaunted, he set his force of Vietnamese coolies to work building another line from a more easterly point on Khon Island towards the north. This task, which took more than a month, could only be partially completed, for the new route was nearly five kilometres in length, while the rails available only stretched for three. When the trans-shipment of the two vessels finally began on 15 October the first three kilometres were covered relatively quickly, with Vietnamese manpower hauling and pushing the boats forward. But then it was necessary for teams of men to continue the vessels' advance by picking up sections of rail from behind the carriage bearing the boat and relaying them,

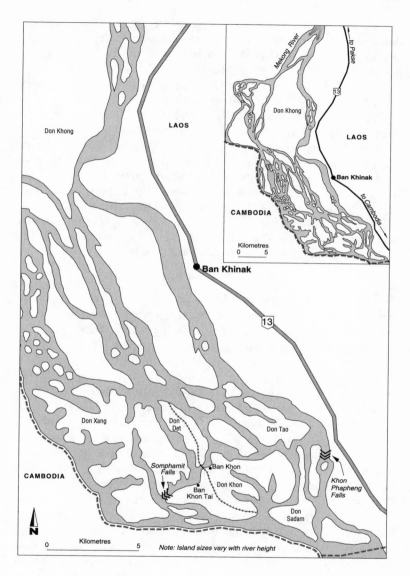

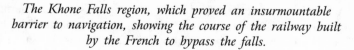

The Khone Falls region, which proved an insurmountable barrier to navigation, showing the course of the railway built by the French to bypass the falls.

a few dozen metres at a time, over and over again. This physically demanding work took place amid the frequent downpours of the late rainy season so that the workers were more often than not labouring in mud and drenched to the skin.

At last, on 1 November 1893, a French vessel was afloat above the Khone Falls. The workforce of Vietnamese coolies, many of whom had tried unsuccessfully to run away during these operations, and the small number of Europeans led by Simon were exhausted and debilitated by tropical disease. Further transshipments of vessels across Khon Island would have to wait for another year. But exhausted or not, Simon immediately assumed his command of the two vessels that had been transported, with the grand title of 'Chef de la mission hydrographique du Haut-Mékong'. A new chapter in attempts to navigate the Mekong had begun. Now the aim was to determine how to deal with the rapids lying further north of the Khone Falls.

B etween 1894 and 1903 French naval officers engaged in intensive surveys of the Mekong where its course runs through modern-day Laos. Their initial preoccupation was with the Khemerat rapids. Subsequently, they extended their efforts to the course of the river above the modern Lao capital of Vientiane, through to Luang Prabang and finally to a section of the Mekong a little above the tri-border region where the boundaries of Burma, Laos and Thailand meet today. There is no denying the energy of those involved and the skill and dedication shown as apparently impassable obstacles were overcome by boats and crews tried to their limit. But apart from a brief role undertaken by one of the French gunboats, showing the French flag in a dispute over the control of a minor Lao state, Muong Sing, in 1895, the essential result of the reconnaissance of the river was to affirm the near-impossibility of the Mekong's ever being used for sustained and uninterrupted navigation by cargo vessels of any size. The hopeful words contained in many official French reports notwithstanding, it was to be a sceptical English observer, one H. Warington Smyth, who captured the situation best when he commented on Lieutenant Simon's achievement in taking the vessels as far as the major rapids system at Tang Ho.

Lying about fifty kilometres above the modern tri-border area, in a region where the Mekong runs between Burma and Laos, Tang Ho was the point at which Lagrée and his companions abandoned any effort to continue their travels on the river itself and chose instead to walk beside it. The rapids at Tang Ho, Garnier wrote in June 1867, were 'insurmountable'. This, finally, was Simon's own conclusion, a fact somewhat at odds with the enthusiasm his having reached Tang Ho generated among those who still dreamed of the Mekong as a commercial and strategic route. As Warington Smyth commented:

> Statements about the navigability of the river have been so constantly reiterated by persons who wished it to be navigable that when they [the French] obtained command of it in 1893 there is no doubt that most Frenchmen believed they had obtained a navigable waterway into Yunnan. Not only is this not the case, but it does not even form a high road for their own Laos acquisitions . . .
>
> Lieutenant Simon has, in my humble opinion, done a magnificent job in a plucky and sailorlike manner. One would like to have seen and helped him at it . . .
>
> And one would like to know what the two years' voyage necessary to get the *Grandière* and the *Massie* to Tang Aw [Tang Ho] cost, and what they will do there and how they will get down again.
>
> Something has been said about 'inspiring terror'; one feels inclined to hope the *Nats* [local spirits] and the cormorants are duly impressed, but inspiring terror in the Laos could have been done much more cheaply.

These comments appear in Warington Smyth's lengthy published account of his five years of service as Director of Mines in Siam. Tinged as they are with more than a little of the supercilious outlook of a Cambridge graduate for whom France and the French could only be regarded as inferior, they held a fundamental truth. For, once at Tang Ho, Simon could not return down the Mekong until the following high water season. Warington Smyth was not the first or last British observer to dismiss the possibility of the Mekong's being used for navigation into China. This had been the firmly expressed view of the noted Scottish explorer–journalist, Archibald Colquhoun, who crossed the Mekong in western Yunnan province in the early 1880s, at the same point at which Marco Polo is supposed to have done so. And George Morrison—'Chinese Morrison', the famous Australian doctor turned journalist—barely mentioned the Mekong when he crossed at the same point as Colquhoun in 1894. He certainly did not entertain any thoughts of the river's commercial possibilities.

Yet for all his sense of British superiority, which even extended to his trying to teach the rowing methods of his Cambridge college to the Lao crew who paddled his canoe, Warington Smyth too was not immune to the fascination of the Mekong. He mocked the French and their obsession with the river, but he confessed his own strong feelings for it.

> Few can regard the Me Kwang without feeling its peculiar
> fascination. That narrow streak, connecting the far countries with
> the distant ocean, what scenes it knows, what stories it could tell
> . . . From its cradle as the Gergu River in the Tibetan highlands
> to its end in the stormy China Sea it never sees a populous city
> or a noble building . . . No wonder one sat and watched it by
> the hour listening to its tale.

For the French, the story that was told involved the disbandment of the hydrographic survey flotilla in 1903 and, over many years, the making of efforts to improve the length of time it took to travel by the Mekong from Saigon to Vientiane and Luang Prabang. The most notable step forward involved the construction of a permanent rail link between the water below and that above the Khone Falls, with docking facilities and steam-powered cranes at either end of the line. Begun in 1897, the railway line initially followed the temporary track laid down under Simon's directions. If one description of travel on the line joining the river below and above the falls is any guide, the transit in these early years was a rough and ready affair. Describing her visit to the countries of French Indochina in 1909, and publishing in the *Tour du Monde* magazine, Marthe Bassenne gives us a picture of passengers, freight and local travellers all jammed together on open rail wagons in an atmosphere of 'chaos' as the small locomotive struggled along the track. Once at the northern end of the line, travellers transferred into a craft of thirty-two metres, the largest size able to navigate through the constricted channels before reaching open water. It was not until 1920 that a bridge was built between Khon and Det Islands, extending the line

The bridge built by the French to carry the railway between Khon and Det Islands above the Khone Falls still stands today, now only used by ox carts and two wheel vehicles.

further north to a more satisfactory embarkation point above the falls. With its tiny locomotive running on narrow gauge rails, this effort to overcome the problem posed by the existence of the Khone Falls finally came to an end in 1940, amid the dramatic changes that followed Japan's entry into Indochina in the year before the outbreak of the Pacific War.

Over the years, efforts continued intermittently, and very much at the mercy of fluctuating budget provisions, to ameliorate travel on the river itself. Rocks were cleared from the riverbed, navigable passages clearly marked and a channel was dredged along the left bank of the Mekong to overcome the problem posed by the Sambor rapids. But all this work took place against the twin disappointments faced by those who had been advocates of the Mekong's commercial role. Any lingering doubt that the Mekong could be used to tap the riches of China had vanished forever when Lieutenant Simon could take *La Grandière* no further than the Tang Ho rapids. The gunboat had subsequently continued to navigate the Mekong at times of high water, but in

1910 and while said to be carrying treasured Lao art objects for display in Paris, it sank in the Mekong downstream from Luang Prabang. Its cargo has never been recovered.

As for the presumed riches of Laos, these never eventuated during the period of French colonial control. There were opportunities for minor agricultural development on the Boloven Plateau in southern Laos and some possibilities for the exploitation of timber. But this latter commodity, despite Garnier's earlier enthusiasm, was difficult to extract, and the repeated rapids along the Mekong's course plus the major barrier of the Khone Falls made thoughts of floating timber downriver to the ports in Phnom Penh and Saigon dubious at best. It is true that there were occasional efforts to use the river in this way, and these included one heroic effort by a Norwegian commercial adventurer, Peter Hauff.

Unknown by historians until an account of his life was published by his granddaughter in 1997, Hauff was in many ways typical of the Europeans who sought private gain in Indochina at the turn of the century. The son of a sea captain, Hauff began his career in Indochina in 1894 at the age of twenty-one working in a Saigon agency house. Fathering children by both a Lao and a Vietnamese woman during the fifteen years he spent in the region, his diaries reveal him as a man of great energy who was fascinated by the exotic world in which he lived, approaching it with a sympathy frequently lacking among the French officials of the time. In 1902, in a remarkable if essentially meaningless achievement, he succeeded in manhandling a sixteen-metre boat through the Khone Falls from south to north. This involved a notable show of spirit and the capacity to organise and inspire his local crew. It did not alter the conclusion that the falls could not be navigated by boats on any regular, commercial basis. A little later, Hauff undertook a commission to ship a collection of logs from Luang Prabang to a river port in the Mekong Delta. This too was a remarkable effort, involving no fewer than twelve hundred logs assembled in a series of rafts. The fact that the logs finally reached the Mekong Delta was indeed a triumph of determination in the face of endless obstacles. It did not, however, herald any continuing use of the Mekong for the despatch of timber out of Laos. In fact, for most of those who were associated with Laos while it formed part of French Indochina, this lightly populated kingdom was seen as a tropical lotus land for those ready to turn their backs on the more 'serious' aspects of colonial endeavour.

What is more, and in the face of all the difficulties that had to be overcome in navigating the Mekong, the gradual development of a road system running to the east of the river's left bank undermined whatever claims could be advanced for the desirability of trying to improve navigation. Diehard supporters of the Mekong as a means of travelling and shipping freight between Saigon and locations in Laos, including, unsurprisingly, the Compagnie des Messageries Fluviales, could not prevent a steadily developing tendency for the colonial authorities to favour the use of land transport over use of the Mekong. This became the more marked as efforts were directed towards linking Laos with ports on the Vietnamese coast, leading to the completion in 1930 of an all-weather road between Quang Tri in central Vietnam and Savannakhet in southern Laos. Eventually, Saigon was linked with Laos by way of Colonial Route 13, which went to Tay Ninh in southern Vietnam before passing through Kratie and Stung Treng in Cambodia to continue on around the Khone Falls.

Even in the more leisurely days of French colonial rule, the time taken to travel from Saigon to Vientiane and Luang Prabang on the Mekong seemed excessive to most observers. It was one thing, in the 1930s, to spend a comfortable thirty-two hours on the *Jules Rueff*, the most modern offering of the Compagnie des Messageries Fluviales, travelling from Saigon to Phnom Penh, and quite another to continue the journey further north. Despite the existence of the railway at the Khone Falls and the various improvements that had been made to the river route, it still took a passenger thirty-seven days to travel from Saigon to Luang Prabang in 1935. The trip required no less than seven or eight changes of vessel, with the size in each case determined by the time of the year, and thus the level of the river. Freight services took much longer. When British Naval Intelligence produced a handbook on the Indochinese region in the early years of the Second World War, the information it gave on the Mekong as a navigable route was succinct and to the point . . . at the end of the 1930s it took longer to travel by river from

Saigon to Luang Prabang than to travel by boat from Saigon to Marseille.

What remains today as a memory of the decades of attempts to use the Mekong as a route for navigation? There is little enough that would be recognised by members of the Mekong Expedition which set off from Saigon in 1866. The only recognisable building still standing from that time is the French Customs House on the waterfront. In a wonderful piece of historical irony, it now houses a museum dedicated to Ho Chi Minh. In Phnom Penh, only the *phnom* remains from the time when Lagrée and his companions paused before their long and painful journey to the north. Kratie and Stung Treng are still the names of the settlements the explorers passed as they drew closer to the Khone Falls. Still isolated and at the outer reaches of the Cambodian state, the architecture of shophouses strung along the river dates from a much more recent time. It would still be familiar to those who travelled the river in the 1930s. But, when one comes to the falls, the descriptions left behind by Delaporte—writing for Garnier who was recovering from illness— and de Carné are as accurate today as they were in late 1866.

Delaporte wrote of the thunderous sound of the water pouring over the falls and of the effect of so much water foaming over the rocks being like that of a 'furious sea'. De Carné was no less impressed. 'Here,' he wrote of the Khone Falls, 'the water is broken up as it dashes into a gulf, raising a sparkling pillar of moist dust on which there rests a rainbow.' The falls are just as impressive today, still untamed and still providing an impassable barrier to any form of navigation, short of the lightest of craft manoeuvred through them at low water. Each time I have seen the falls, I have been left with an overwhelming sense of the unstoppable power of the river as it surges on its southwards course.

In sharp contrast, the remnants of the railway built by the Frenchmen who came after the Mekong explorers are a testimony to the fragility of colonial hopes. It is still possible to follow much of the course of the line that was laid from the south to the north of Khon Island and across the bridge that has remained to link Khon and Det Islands. What one traces are the remnants of the permanent way, with some of the ballast still lying where it was placed more than ninety years ago. But the rails are not there, for they have been pulled up to be used as rough bridges across watercourses or as fencing around houses. The concrete loading docks are still there, though without any trace of the cranes that once stood on them. Most evocative of all the signs of the defeated past are the small locomotive and its tender which sit, forever immobilised, rusting away amid the deep green of lush tropical foliage.

Travelling north it is easy to sense the frustration that generations of Frenchmen felt as the Mekong alternates between wide, deep reaches of water before suddenly narrowing to become a mass of white water rushing through rock-strewn rapids. At intervals, the markers that were installed to aid navigation still poke above the water, with splotches of faded green and red paint showing where a boat may or may not pass. For the rest, the ruins at Wat Phu, Wat Si Saket and That Luang in Vientiane and, remarkably, the old quarter of Luang Prabang survive to be viewed today, little changed from how they were seen by generations of French travellers.

The river is still used for travel, but not at all as was expected by those who laboured so long and with such difficulty in the past. Ocean-going vessels reach as far as Phnom Penh, and passenger ferries ply the Mekong up to Kratie. Once above the Khone Falls, sizeable boats are able to navigate the river at high water over stretches of its course. But once the level of the water drops, these vessels must be moored till the next rainy season. In 1990, amid enormous fanfare, the Chinese government despatched large tug-drawn cargo barges down the Mekong in what was claimed to be the beginning of a regular service between Simao Port, just north of Jinghong, and Vientiane. After a few trips at the time of high water, the service lapsed. There simply was not sufficient cargo to justify such a service, which could only operate for a brief period each year. Equally, the planned hovercraft service that was to operate from Chiang Khong on the Thai side of the river into China has not proved viable. High costs and a lack of tourists have meant that this dream, too, has had to be abandoned. In place of these grand and expensive forms of travel, the most efficient means of navigating the Mekong that has emerged in recent times is the use of the light skiffs powered by large engines. These are the so-called 'long tail boats', familiar to anyone who has seen them operating on the Chao Phraya River in Bangkok. They travel at high speed along the river in a rush of spray and with ear-shattering noise.

The Mekong will never cease to be a means of travel, but it seems likely that this use will further decline as work continues to upgrade the roads, which increasingly provide a preferred alternative for the transport of goods and passengers. Poor road conditions and insecurity have meant that this alternative has been slow in reaching its full capability, but this is a case in which progress, however slow, is relentless. The dreams of men such as Garnier, Reveillère and Simon, the commercial hopes of the directors of the Compagnie des Messageries Fluviales, the belief that a railway was the answer to the barrier of the Khone Falls—all these have proven misplaced. When I visited Khon Island in 1998, I met the man who had driven the last train over that railway. Now in his nineties, but looking much younger, he spoke with pride of his job as an engine driver and of how the French had given him a medal for his services. He reinforced my long-held belief that there is something special about the commitment to their tasks among those who work on a railway, any railway. I did not find his pride misplaced. Rather, I saw in him a symbol of all those hopes that had gone before and which were, as he surely soon would be, simply a memory.

9

Fear and Fascination: The Colonial Years along the Mekong

The gods have disappeared, and ironic Death has left only slaves.

George Groslier, A l'Ombre d'Angkor, *Paris, 1916, writing of the contrast between twentieth century Cambodia and the civilisation of the Angkorian period*

Such a beautiful world, so strongly seductive that one simply cannot leave it without sadness.

Pierre Billotey, L'Indochine en Zigzags, *Paris, 1929, writing of his travels through Indochina in 1928*

The grudging recognition, at the beginning of the twentieth century, that the Mekong could not become the major commercial artery hoped for by so many Frenchmen coincided with the end of what they and their metropolitan admirers frequently called 'The Heroic Age' of colonialism in Indochina. This was a self-serving term adopted by French enthusiasts for their country's colonial role. The exploration of the Mekong and the later attempts to prove it could be navigated had a prominent place in the chronicles describing this period. But the term also encompassed a range of other developments, from the bloody invasions of northern and central Vietnam, in the 1880s, to the suppression of rebellion in Cambodia in the same decade, and the adventurous exploits of August Pavie in Laos in the 1890s. Central to the use of the term was the view that with the passing of the heroic age *Notre Indochine* had become a settled group of

French possessions. What now existed, the publicists proclaimed, was a territorial ensemble in which the prospects for economic success were real, made greater by the rapid expansion of rubber estates in the 1920s, and the necessary firmness of colonial rule was balanced by the worth of France's civilising mission.

From the early twentieth century onward, the Mekong was increasingly viewed as an integral part of this wider, exotic Indochinese world, rather than simply as an object of fascination in itself. It was 'our river' in 'our Indochina'. Yet while the river had been revealed to be of limited commercial importance, and none at all so far as trade with China was concerned, it was still seen as having both a practical and an important symbolic role. Saigon, Phnom Penh, Vientiane and Luang Prabang, as well as a host of minor settlements, owed their existence to the Mekong, or to its delta. Practically, few who travelled between Saigon and Phnom Penh chose to do other than make this journey by the Mekong. And, by the twentieth century, the richness of the Mekong Delta as a prime source of rice was already clear. Symbolically, too, the river was seen as a physical feature that matched the political reality of French rule in southern Vietnam, Cambodia and Laos.

So, for those who visited the countries of French Indochina and wrote of their experiences, the river was always worthy of mention and usually described in admiring terms, such as 'sovereign' or 'majestic'. But increasingly the subjects that interested a visitor were those associated with an apparently stable French presence in Vietnam, in Laos and in Cambodia. For all but a few critical commentators, of whom the prominent French literary and political figure André Malraux was one, Saigon, a city at the edge of the Mekong Delta if not actually on the river's banks, was seen as the city which, more than any other in Indochina, was admirable in the extent to which it gave its French residents the sense of still being in their homeland while living in a tropical world. The public buildings were consciously constructed to reinforce this comforting atmosphere, from the Opera House to the City Hall, and from the prefabricated Catholic Cathedral to the Palais de Justice, the latter looking as if it had been transplanted from southern France.

To sit and drink one's *apéritif* on the terrace of the Continental Palace Hotel in Saigon was to replicate the reassuring comfort of

With French rule solidly established in Cochinchina, the
colonial administration sought to replicate aspects of France, as
with the Hôtel de Ville in Saigon, here seen in 1998 with a
statue of Ho Chi Minh in the foreground.

the cafes and bars along the Champs Elysées in Paris or the Cours
Mirabeau in Aix-en-Provence. But even in this most French of
Indochinese cities the exotic was always present. It was both
desired and inescapable. Above all it was represented by the
indigenous population, which so greatly outnumbered the colonialists. The Vietnamese had their own powerful culture, their
Buddhist temples and their calendrical festivals, all very different
from everything that was French in character. They were cast in
the role of servants in this colonial theatre of life, but they were
servants who, disturbingly, on occasion forgot the parts they were
supposed to play.

A different form of exoticism formed part of the French
colonial experience in Phnom Penh and in the river towns of
Cambodia and of Laos, most particularly Luang Prabang. In
Phnom Penh and Luang Prabang, the presence of Buddhist
monarchies set the tone for much of French colonial life. To an
extraordinary extent, French officials became 'mayors of the
palace' to the rulers of Cambodia and Laos, preoccupied with

dynastic rivalries in the royal families of these small kingdoms and calculating the extent to which it was possible for France to advance its interests through these revered institutions. And not only France's interests, for there is more than a hint of private corruption about the manner in which the succession to the Cambodian throne was decided in 1927, following the death of King Sisowath. While the records in the archives do not make the issue absolutely clear, the balance of evidence strongly suggests that the senior French official of the day, *Résident Supérieur* François Baudoin, threw his support behind one of Sisowath's sons, Monivong, in return for a substantial bribe paid to him by Monivong while Sisowath was still alive.

Frenchmen, official and otherwise, delighted in being present, sometimes as participants and sometimes as spectators, when royal ceremonies and local festivals took place. French officials became an integral part of the ceremonies to wish the Cambodian ruler good fortune at the start of the Cambodian New Year, mingling in their white uniforms with the richly coloured traditional dress of the Cambodian courtiers. In Luang Prabang, also at the time of New Year celebrations, they stood beside the king and his court as the royal elephants were paraded to listen to a sermon preached in their interest by a Buddhist monk. And in both Phnom Penh and Luang Prabang, the French joined the local population in watching the boat races on the Mekong at the time of the water festival marking the end of the rainy season. In doing so, they matched, knowingly or otherwise, the experience of Lagrée and his fellow explorers decades before, when the members of the Mekong Expedition watched the annual water festival at Bassac in 1866.

Few writers offered a more sympathetic view of this apparently politically settled, exotic Indochina than the once popular, and now long forgotten, French novelist Pierre Billotey. His account of travelling through the countries of Indochina in 1928 is a revealing combination of French pride and wonder at the unfamiliar world he encountered. Arriving in Saigon, his first reaction was to feel that he was back in France, so strikingly did the rue Catinat with its boutiques remind him of an elegant shopping street in his homeland. But, almost immediately, he reacted to the differences; to the presence of Indians from Pondicherry, of Chinese and, curiously mentioned last, of Vietnamese. The trees that lined the street running down to the Saigon River were different, as were the flowers, the bamboos and the bougainvilleas that he saw around him.

From Saigon onwards, as Billotey travelled through Vietnam, Laos and Cambodia, the exotic and a sense of colonial tranquillity dominated the impressions he recorded. He did briefly acknowledge that the contemporary calm he witnessed had not always come easily, in that he took note of the exploits of a famous Vietnamese opponent of French colonial control who had been active forty years earlier. This was the feared guerrilla leader De Tham, whose resistance to the French exacted a high cost in lives, both French and Vietnamese. And, in contrast to the enjoyment Billotey took in so many other sights, he admitted that once away from the Mekong he found the flat Cambodian countryside uninspiring. But reflecting on battles fought in the past and the fact that not all was uniformly wonderful only served to heighten his general sense of satisfaction with what he saw.

Like so many before and after him, he was charmed by Luang Prabang. Travelling down the Mekong, he came upon it in the late afternoon. His description of the town is not a paraphrase of Pavie's, but it is marked by the same enthusiastic feeling.

> And, towards the end of the afternoon, a charming plain
> suddenly spread out in front of me, a plain of beautiful
> colours—beige and green and gold—the plain of Luang Prabang
> surrounded by uneven but harmoniously formed hills, such as
> those in the paintings of Hubert, Robert and Poussin.
> A wide avenue of coconut trees, another bordered by hibiscus
> in flower, and wooden houses in a mix of trees, palms and
> bushes; I reach Luang Prabang . . . A little later, from a high
> gallery at the French Commissariat, I contemplate the sovereign
> Mekong, this wide, spreading river in its violet coloured valley.

When Billotey came to Luang Prabang it had a population of about eight thousand. Since Vientiane was the administrative capital of the Lao territories controlled by France, there were only a small number of French citizens living in Luang Prabang. Indeed, throughout the colonial years there were never more than a thousand Frenchmen living in the whole of Laos. Their relations

with the Lao were more than easy, he insists; they were affectionate, though not so affectionate as to prevent the wives of
married French officials insisting that Lao women should not go
bare-breasted as they walked about their streets. He enthused
about Luang Prabang's pagodas and the presence of the royal
elephants. Above all, Billotey's account of his visit dwelt on the
warmth of feeling shown by the French toward the Lao king,
Sisavang Vong, who had mounted the throne of Luang Prabang
in 1904. This was a warmth, he insisted, that was reciprocated
by the ruler, who had studied in France.

There was another side to the relationship between the French
and the inhabitants of Luang Prabang that was already established when Billotey visited the Lao royal capital, but it was not
one about which he wrote. By the interwar years, Luang Prabang
had become a byword for colonial hedonism, a place where the
rules of public behaviour that applied in Saigon and Phnom Penh
were cheerfully broken. Here there was no need for liaisons
between unmarried Frenchmen and Lao women to be conducted
discreetly, and if a man's taste ran to maintaining his own small
harem this was seen as a personal matter. Opium could be smoked
quite openly without the pretence that accompanied such indulgence in Saigon or Phnom Penh. For many French officials, every
device was used to ensure that a posting in this agreeable tropical
haven was extended indefinitely. As the English author Norman
Lewis put it, writing of Luang Prabang in 1950 but describing a
world that had existed for decades, 'Laos-ised Frenchmen are like
the results of successful lobotomy operations—untroubled and
mildly libidinous'.

When Billotey continued his journey it was on the Mekong,
by raft through the series of rapids that lay between Luang
Prabang and Vientiane. There was little that charmed him in the
latter settlement, where there was still abundant evidence of the
Siamese sack one hundred years before and where Vietnamese,
rather than Lao, seemed to be the dominant group of inhabitants.
Soon he was on his way to Phnom Penh, travelling in a succession
of small steam-powered vessels of the Compagnie de Messageries
Fluviales to the Khone Falls. Here he bypassed the falls on the
railway linking vessels to the north and south of this major
obstacle to navigation. And so on he went to Phnom Penh and
to more pleasure taken in the royal palace, the 'Silver Pagoda'

with its floor paved entirely with silver tiles, the royal dancers and another group of royal elephants. Then, after Phnom Penh, there was Angkor, with Angkor Wat the final temple visited, a building which Billotey ranks as one of the four greatest master-pieces ever constructed by man.

As a travel book of the period, Billotey's *L'Indochine en Zigzags* is no worse, and a good deal better, than many of its kind. It is not really surprising that the author gives little serious attention to the interests of the indigenous inhabitants of the regions he visited. As a Frenchman of his time, he describes them, if at all, in the clichéd terms that were current even among the most sympathetic of French observers. He quotes George Groslier, a dedicated student of Cambodian culture, whom we first met extolling the wonders of Wat Phu. Speaking to Billotey, Groslier described the Cambodians as 'excellent people, but immensely tired . . . doubtless less adroit than the Vietnamese, but more artistic and incomparably superior in moral terms'. The views Groslier expressed were widely held. For him and for others the fall of the Angkorian empire had meant the death of a civilisation. It had left a Cambodian population who were moral but who had the mentality of slaves. Indeed, this claim that Cambodians possessed *la mentalité d'esclave* was still to be heard, uttered quite unashamedly by French men and women, when I first went to Phnom Penh in 1959.

The book's most striking deficiencies lie in the way in which, as a picture of colonial life along the Mekong, it shows virtually no awareness of the largely unacknowledged fears that lurked in the minds of the French community, fears that surfaced in the face of the least sign of challenge to French authority. For in any account of colonial life in Saigon, in Phnom Penh and in Vientiane and Luang Prabang, as well as in the other minor settlements that lay along the Mekong, the presence of fear, as well as fascination, can never be ignored.

Despite the pleasure to be found in the fascinatingly exotic world in which they lived, the French residents of Indo-china had to accept the worrying truth that there were elements of this world they could never understand, or trust. Even in Laos, seen as the most submissive of colonial possessions, there were a number of instances of resistance to French rule in the first three decades of the twentieth century. These were forcefully suppressed, and French officials comforted themselves with the thought that those involved were drawn from minority ethnic groups rather than the 'loyal' lowland Lao of the Mekong River valley.

In the case of Cambodia, the so-called '1916 Affair' was less violent than the brief challenges to French authority that had occurred in Laos. But in some ways it was much more puzzling to the French; an example of an event which they neither predicted nor, when it was over, really understood. Starting at the end of 1915, but growing quickly in size the following year, crowds of Cambodian peasants flocked to Phnom Penh to protest to the king about the burden of taxes and corvées levied in the name of the Cambodian government but, in fact, imposed by the French. At times the number of Cambodians massed outside the palace beside the Mekong numbered as many as ten thousand, and estimates of the total number who came to present their grievances to the king ran as high as one hundred thousand. While there were a small number of violent incidents associated with this large-scale movement of protesters in the provinces, including an uncertain number of deaths, the affair was bloodless in Phnom Penh itself. And, after hearing the king's assurances that he would seek to ameliorate their situation, the protesters dispersed and returned to their homes. Throughout the whole episode, as French reports of the period make clear, the protesters simply ignored French officials as if they had no relevance to their interests. As 'calm was restored', to use a favourite French administrative phrase, King Sisowath travelled up and down the Mekong to act as a soothing presence in areas near Kompong Cham and Prey Veng, which had been prominent regions of protest.

Despite the largely violence-free character of these demonstrations, the colonial authorities were deeply disturbed. They were acutely conscious that the protesters had turned to the king to seek redress, emphasising the extent to which the Cambodian monarch was still regarded as the source of authority for the local population despite the control the French exercised over him. At the same time, they were frustrated by the fact they could not discover any central figure or group responsible for organising the protests, which appeared to have emerged spontaneously. This was the more worrying since these events occurred at a time when there was a constant awareness in Indochina that metropolitan France was locked in a deadly struggle against Germany. Any challenge to authority was seen as having the potential to hinder the French war effort. This fact led one official in Phnom Penh to argue vigorously, if inconvincingly, that German agents operating out of Bangkok were undoubtedly behind the demonstrations. At the same time, the 1916 Affair was also viewed by the French in Cambodia against the background of unsettling events in Cochinchina.

Anti-French demonstrations in Cochinchina in 1916 sharpened the fears of the colonial administration that the Vietnamese population was ready to take advantage of France's embattled state as the war in Europe dragged on without an end to the conflict in sight. When, in February 1916, a band of Vietnamese secret society members attacked the Saigon Central Prison in an attempt to free one of their leaders, French fears of their colonial subjects' 'disloyalty' seemed all too justified. Since the attack took place at a time when France was at war, the colonial authorities tried the Vietnamese involved before a military council of war. Fifty-one were found guilty and sentenced to death by firing squad. In an act designed to cow any further challenges to their control, the French carried out the executions, six at a time, with the leaders of the attacking group forced to watch while their followers were shot before they, too, were executed.

The prospect of further Vietnamese uprisings and the memory of this example of Vietnamese 'treachery' during the war haunted the minds of Frenchmen, both official and unofficial, for years to come. Such fear was the justification for the extraordinary slaughter that took place even before the war ended when there was an attack on the French and Vietnamese prison personnel on the island of Puolo Condore (modern Con Son), off the coast of Cochinchina, in April 1918. One Frenchman and two Vietnamese employees of the administration were killed. In suppressing this challenge, the French, in return, killed seventy-five Vietnamese prisoners.

One index of the deep and pervasive nature of this fear among the colonists that they might lose control over those whom they ruled may be found in the reports carried in the Saigon

newspapers of the execution of Vietnamese who had been convicted of crimes against French men and women. In *L'Opinion*,
the *Courrier Saigonnais* and *L'Impartial*, information was provided
in excruciating detail. The account of an execution was usually
preceded by a recapitulation of the crime for which the sentence
was being exacted. Then followed an account of the mounting
of the guillotine: the collection of the condemned man from his
cell, with a description of the final *toilette* as the executioner
shaved his neck; whether or not he drank the brandy customarily
offered; and finally the scene at the scaffold, not forgetting the
stench of blood when the blade had fallen.

There is no reflection of this pervasive sense of fear in
Billotey's account of his travels, and even for those French men
and women who were residents rather than visitors in the
countries of Indochina there was a curious feeling of ambiguity
about their relations with the local populations of Cambodia,
Laos and Vietnam. For while the presence of fear meant that
'trouble makers' if apprehended were treated very harshly, the
French found a measure of reassurance in the presence of men—
and they were almost always men—who were not just content
to enjoy the benefits that flowed from cooperation with the
colonial power but were ready to go further and to speak in
favour of *collaboration*.

In Cambodia and Laos, with rare exceptions, the small elites
linked to the royal families were mostly passive supporters of
French rule. Even the very earliest stirrings of nationalism in
Cambodia in the 1930s were directed more at the French readiness to staff the lower ranks of their administration with
Vietnamese rather than Cambodians, not at the French themselves. It was different in Cochinchina, the oldest of the French
possessions in Indochina. There, a small but influential group of
Vietnamese were prominent in the 1920s in calling for active
political cooperation between Vietnamese and French residents
of the colony, apparently genuinely believing that such cooperation was possible. Associated with the Constitutionalist
Party and led by a talented descendant of an old mandarin family,
Bui Quang Chieu, these men are now seen as little more than a
footnote in Vietnamese history—from the point of view of
Vietnamese communist historians, the footnote must be cast in
pejorative terms since the Constitutionalists were ready to work

with the imperial oppressor. In a number of cases drawing their wealth from landholdings in the Mekong Delta, they presented themselves as worthy of playing a part in the direction of the colony in a manifesto published in the Saigon newspaper *l'Opinion* in 1926, declaring:

> Doctors, engineers, industrialists, businessmen, farmers, former civil servants, we present ourselves to the electoral college with the knowledge that we are not pursuing any personal advantage since each of us occupies in society a material and moral position which is able to assure us of a decent and independent existence.

But even such reasonable men could not fully earn the trust of the colonial residents. They might not be revolutionaries, but theirs were not the only voices emerging from the ranks of the educated, and relatively prosperous, members of the colony's Vietnamese bourgeoisie. Why should the Constitutionalists be seen as true friends of France when, only a year before, another Saigon newspaper, *L'Echo Annamite*, had carried a polemic against French rule cast in venereal terms. Arguing that there had been greater 'progress' in Japanese-administered Korea and Formosa (Taiwan), a writer using the pseudonym De Tu (Disciple) offered his vision of progress in Cochinchina:

> Consider the matter closely. Before the conquest there were virtually no brothels in the territory of the Annamese [Vietnamese] empire. Since then they had sprung up like mushrooms in all the European urban centres.
> These are facts which speak, and eloquently so.
> Mathematically, in this matter, civilisation equals syphilisation.
> Long live the speculum!

Satire this undoubtedly was, but in a colonial ambience criticism of any kind was seen as an offensive reflection of an unreadiness on the part of the colonised people to know their place. And, fundamentally, that was a place that might involve liberty and even fraternity, but certainly not equality.

Little of this sense of underlying concern was communicated from Indochina to metropolitan France in the 1920s. It was certainly not a matter that weighed on the mind of the young

André Malraux when, in 1923, he embarked on his 'Indochina Adventure'. This was one of the more bizarre episodes of the interwar period, yet it was one with links back to the visit of the Mekong Expedition to Angkor in 1866, and to Louis Delaporte's later long involvement with the Angkor ruins. Turning twenty-three just days after arriving in Saigon, Malraux had already made his mark in the hothouse literary world of Paris before he conceived his plan to steal statuary from an Angkorian period temple.

His decision to travel to Cambodia was, in itself, a reflection of the exotic appeal that Indochina exercised over his countrymen. Louis Delaporte's untiring work in publicising the architectural and artistic glories of the Angkor temples had stirred French interest, among both scholars and a more general public. A visit to see the temples became the goal of almost all who visited Cambodia, whether as an official or as a tourist. It was an opportunity to see the past accomplishments of a people who now, in a phrase popular with a number of French writers, 'had fallen from their antique glory'. Travelling up the Mekong to Phnom Penh, and then by the Tonle Sap River to the Great Lake and the small provincial town of Siemreap, the number of visitors to the famed ruins steadily increased from the beginning of the twentieth century.

Among those who wrote their admiring accounts of Angkor, few if any were more influential in French literary circles in the early decades of the twentieth century than the naval officer and enormously popular author, Louis Marie Julien Viaud, who wrote under the name of Pierre Loti. He published his *Un Pèlerin d'Angkor* (An Angkor Pilgrim) in 1911, describing a visit he had made ten years earlier. As with his other books, Loti's descriptions are presented in richly luxuriant prose tinged with romantic melancholy that frequently borders on the extravagant. This is particularly so in this book, dedicated as it was to the memory of his brother who had died years before in the East. Loti was ambivalent about his experience of travelling on the Mekong to Phnom Penh. The Mekong, he allowed, was a 'majestic' river, but its banks were 'monotonous'. But he could only marvel at the Great Lake, at its size and at the sight he saw as dawn broke over it, turning the clouds on the horizon into a momentarily solid background of 'mountain masses'.

It is when he reaches the temples themselves that Loti is in his true element. Describing his visit to the great walled city of Angkor Thom, he says:

> The forest, always the forest, and always its shadow, its sovereign oppression. One feels it to be hostile, murderous, brooding with fever and death; in the end one wants to escape it, for it imprisons, it tests you . . . And then when even the few birds that are singing stop, you wonder what has caused this sudden silence . . .

The cause of these unsettling feelings was a sudden heavy storm which, when it finally ended, left Loti in a state of 'infinite sadness'.

Yet, amid this picture of the dark forest's threatening atmosphere, of torrential rain storms, and of later images of snakes slithering beneath his sleeping platform, Loti succeeds in summoning up a picture of the ruined temples which is richly evocative. There is no confirmation that Malraux had read Loti's account of Angkor, and the best evidence is that he was introduced to Cambodian art by a German dealer and scholar, Alfred Salmony. But it would be surprising if he did not know, or had not heard, of Loti's account. Pierre Billotey certainly had, for he contrasts the cleared land around the temples he saw during his visit with the forest Loti describes. Clearly, Malraux knew enough of Angkor to be aware of the work of French scholars who were reclaiming the temples from the jungle and establishing a chronology of their construction. Most importantly he had read the account provided by the archeologist Henri Parmentier of a small jewel of a temple, Banteay Srei, that lay some sixteen kilometres north of the main temple complex and which had only been discovered by a French survey team in 1914. This was the temple from which Malraux, who read Parmentier's account in Paris and who, in 1923, was in severe financial straits, decided he would steal some statuary. Once successful, he believed, he could sell his loot at vast profit in New York.

Notwithstanding the rich irony of the future Minister of Culture in General Charles de Gaulle's government having engaged in an act of cultural vandalism in Cambodia, the incident is frequently dismissed as unimportant or qualified as youthful folly by Malraux's admirers, particularly those in France. Strikingly, it was left to an American writer, Walter Langlois, to publish the first exhaustive account of the episode many years after the event. Yet, in seeking to steal statuary from the exquisite Angkorian period temple of Banteay Srei, André Malraux was not acting on a sudden impulse. Along with his wife Clara and a childhood friend, Louis Chevasson, both of whom accompanied him to Cambodia, he was well aware of the illegality of what he was going to do—not least because he had been told of the ban placed on the removal of materials from the Angkor temples when he visited Hanoi prior to setting off from Saigon for Cambodia. There, he had discussed the Angkor ruins with members of the revered French cultural institution, the Ecole Française d'Extrême-Orient.

Malraux later presented a highly romanticised account of his journey into the forests surrounding the Banteay Srei temple in his novel *La Voie royale* (The Royal Way), first published in 1930. The reality, as Clara Malraux made clear in her own account published many years later, was more prosaic. The party came prepared with ox carts on which to transport their spoils and Cambodian workmen to assist them. Cutting one of the supremely beautiful *apsaras* from the temple's central building using stone saws, Malraux and Chevasson had this and some smaller pieces placed in the packing cases they had brought with them on the carts. Falsely labelled as 'chemical products', these cases were then transported to a vessel on the Great Lake and consigned to Saigon. It seemed, briefly, that Malraux and his companions had succeeded in their plan.

But they had not for, unknown to them at the time, their every movement had been followed once they reached Siemreap. Shortly after the vessel in which they were travelling with their spoils reached Phnom Penh they were arrested and taken into custody. While charges against Clara Malraux were dropped, her husband and his friend were finally brought to trial in July 1924 and found guilty. Malraux was sentenced to three years imprisonment, while Chevasson's sentence was eighteen months. With their counsel appealing against the verdict, claiming that Banteay Srei was not covered by the prohibition on the removal of cultural items from Indochina, Malraux and Chevasson moved from Phnom Penh to Saigon to await the results of a further trial.

By the time the trial and sentencing took place, interest in the case had grown among Malraux's literary friends in Paris. All manner of arguments were marshalled to undermine the verdict against Malraux and Chevasson. They were, it was said, to be admired rather than criticised for their enterprise. Malraux's burgeoning reputation in Paris was sufficient to rally a host of literary and artistic figures to circulate a petition on his behalf. Unexpectedly, I found evidence of how seriously this support from the cultural elite was taken when I was working in the Cambodian archives in 1966. Looking for material relating to an earlier period, I came by chance on the letter book for 1924 that contained copies of correspondence relating to Malraux's first trial. Glued in the letter book were carbon copies of messages exchanged between Phnom Penh, Indochina's administrative headquarters in Hanoi, and Paris. These were typewritten, but scrawled across a message at the time of the trial was a hand-written warning. 'Take care,' it said, 'this has become a political affair.'

Political or not, Malraux and Chevasson were again found guilty in the appeal court hearing in Saigon. But their sentences were reduced and the question of whether the temple they had robbed did, indeed, fall within the ban on the removal of cultural items was left unresolved. As a result, they never entered prison. The support they received from their fashionable friends in Paris and the underlying concern that white French citizens should not suffer penalties that would certainly have been imposed without hesitation on France's colonial subjects saved Malraux and his accomplice from suffering little more than inconvenience. In reading of the period, there is a sense that the theft came to be regarded as, at worst, a diversion from more serious issues. The looted statuary was returned to Banteay Srei and may be seen in place today. Inaccessible for many years, while war and insecurity afflicted Cambodia, the temple remains largely undamaged, contrary to the account given by one of Malraux's biographers and admirers, Axel Madsen, who writes of Banteay Srei having been destroyed by Khmer Rouge and North Vietnamese troops in 1970.

When Malraux returned to Saigon in 1925 it was in a quite different role from that of temple robber. Now he embarked on a brief but energetic period as a journalistic critic of the colonial regime. He became a key figure in the publication of the newspapers *L'Indochine* and its successor *L'Indochine enchaînée*. Just how much effect Malraux's excoriating articles on the failings of

French colonialism actually had is a matter for debate. Certainly he was at the forefront of those who pointed to the inequities of life in Cochinchina, and his reports of a trial held in Phnom Penh following the murder of a French official, Bardez, made clear the shortcomings of the justice system in Cambodia when the authority of the colonial power was called into question. Interestingly, though he did not pursue the matter at great length, one of his trenchant editorials focused on the exploitation of land in the Camau region of the Mekong Delta. While he could not have been aware of all the facts involved, in writing of the social problems associated with the delta region Malraux was discussing an area that was to become a key support base for Vietnamese communism in later years.

The agricultural potential of the Mekong Delta was clear even before the French established their colony in Cochinchina. In the early colonial years, the hope was that French *concessionnaires* could take advantage of the rich soil of the delta and the presence of cheap labour to establish rewarding agricultural enterprises, particularly in the cultivation of rice. This was not what happened. As the area of land was constantly expanded through massive drainage programs, those who benefitted were not for the most part Frenchmen but a growing class of land-rich Vietnamese who linked their fortunes to the colonial government. By the 1920s this group controlled over 80 per cent of land in the delta either in their own name or on behalf of a small number of absentee French landlords. They exploited their tenant sharefarmers mercilessly, lending funds at usurious rates and demanding upwards of 40 per cent of each crop in payment for the use of land.

By 1930 the growing inequities between landowners and tenant farmers and day labourers were contributing to a steady growth of rural discontent, which was reflected in major demonstrations in the delta in 1930 and 1931. This situation was exacerbated by the Great Depression when many landlords were bankrupted. But instead of this leading to a more equitable distribution of landowning, the French administration preferred to consolidate ownership in the hands of those large landholders who survived the economic downturn.

Some of the rural poor living their disadvantaged lives in the delta turned to religions with strong millenarian overtones in the hope of finding spiritual solace for their earthly suffering. The syncretic Cao Dai religion, with a leadership structure of a 'pope' and 'cardinals', both male and female, and saints as diverse as Shakespeare and Victor Hugo, was founded in Tay Ninh, a little north of the delta in 1926. It soon gained a strong foothold in the delta in the 1930s and remains strong there to the present day. The Hoa Hao sect, which is probably best seen as an offshoot of Buddhism with its stress on the rejection of materialism, was founded in 1939. For others, particularly after the foundation of the Indochinese Communist Party, the forerunner of the Vietnamese Communist Party, in 1930, the appeal of revolutionary political doctrine was strong. The contrasts between prosperity and poverty were too strong for it to be otherwise. In his detailed study of the Mekong Delta's society and politics the French historian Pierre Brocheux quotes a couplet from a popular song that sums up the feelings of those who had not benefitted from the economic development of the region. As they worked under the burning sun, rice transplanters who were day labourers sang:

> The rich wear sapphire jewels and dress in cashmere shirts.
> We, the poor, bear the harnesses of horses and the yokes
> of buffaloes.

Harnessed and yoked as they were, these peasants were a ready reservoir of recruits for the communist cadres who worked in the delta during the 1930s and preached that release from oppression could be gained through revolution.

No such revolutionary element emerged in Cambodia and Laos in the period leading up to the Second World War, though in both there were initial but limited stirrings of nationalism in the 1930s. But throughout French Indochina, events in Vietnam in 1930 and 1931 reinforced the concerns the French colonialists had long felt but seldom articulated about their long-term hold over their colonial possessions. In those years there was first a mutiny by Vietnamese troops against their French officers, in the northern garrison town of Yen Bai. French retribution here was swift, with some fifty mutineers quickly sentenced to death and guillotined and villages suspected of complicity bombed. But soon there was a much greater challenge to the colonial authorities. In 1930 and 1931 there were major uprisings against French rule in the north-central Vietnamese provinces of Nghe An and Ha Tinh. Taking place against a background of local famine in some of the poorest areas of the country, debate continues over whether these protests and accompanying violence were promoted by the fledgling Vietnamese communist movement or simply exploited by its members. Whatever was the case, for a period the French administration lost control of the countryside. To reassert control the administration resorted to aerial bombardment of protesters and unleashed the Foreign Legion to bring the Vietnamese peasants to heel. Reports at the time made clear that the Legion acted with great brutality. So it was not surprising, but still striking, to find, when examining the Colonial Archives in Paris, that there were records to show that the order had been given that nine out of ten Vietnamese taken prisoner by the Legion's units should be killed. That orders along these lines had been given had long been presumed; now the evidence I found, in the form of a carbon copy on flimsy paper, left the issue beyond dispute.

No further rising of comparable size took place in the years up to the outbreak of the Pacific War, though communist-led uprisings in the Mekong Delta in 1940 were serious enough to bring brutal French repression, with the Foreign Legion once more unleashed to restore order. The memory of challenges to the French never went away. Official pronouncements about the state of calm that existed throughout Indochina were made against the background knowledge that this was a calm that could suddenly be shattered. The effects of the Great Depression still lingered as the 1930s drew to a close. Yet, in the eyes of almost all observers, the Mekong still flowed through a French Indochina in which colonial rule was presumed to be secure, even if more open to disturbance than once was thought possible. The error of this assessment was soon to be revealed.

Concentrating on French colonialism and the countries that made up French Indochina has meant neglecting the Mekong where its course runs through China. In the far south of China's Yunnan province another form of colonialism was slowly beginning to take effect from the early years of the twentieth century. When the members of the Mekong Expedition passed through Jinghong in 1867 this settlement was part of the Sip Song Panna, the collection of twelve small states ruled by Tai-speaking 'princes' who owed multiple allegiances to stronger suzerains. In Chinese eyes these were troublesome territories whose rulers frequently did not know their proper place in the Chinese scheme of things. 'A handful of wriggling worms' was how one nineteenth century Chinese official described them. In the case of Jinghong, which was the name of the state as well as of its capital, the most powerful of its suzerains was the Chinese emperor. In the diplomatic manoeuvring that took place at the end of the nineteenth century, Jinghong was awarded neither to France nor to Britain. Instead, it was accepted as lying within the bounds of the Chinese empire despite the very limited presence of ethnic Chinese within the state.

Initially, the incorporation of Jinghong in China had little effect on its majority non-Chinese population, the Dai people, linguistic cousins of the Lao and Thai. In the period of instability that followed the Chinese Revolution of 1912, this region of Yunnan was far removed from the major events of the time. By the 1920s, there was a slow seepage of Han Chinese into Jinghong and the establishment of a limited government presence there. An American missionary who passed through Jinghong in 1919 noted that there were 'only the officials, the soldiers and a few merchants' in a fort the government had constructed. For the rest, the area retained its identity as a northerly version of the Lao world that was now controlled by France.

Further west and north, the Mekong existed as a barrier to be crossed, just as it had been in Marco Polo's time. With a forbidding topography of steep gorges rising directly from the edge of the river or malaria-ridden valleys running away from it, this was not an area that offered opportunities for settlement and agricultural exploitation. This was a situation that remained unchanged until decades after the Chinese communists gained power in 1949. During the Second World War, the Mekong was crossed and recrossed by the enormous convoys of vehicles that traversed the Burma Road, but in these upper reaches the river remained, as it had for centuries, a barrier to be traversed with the minimum of delay. Indeed, until the 1980s, the story of the Mekong is, again, largely the story of events along its course through the countries of Indochina.

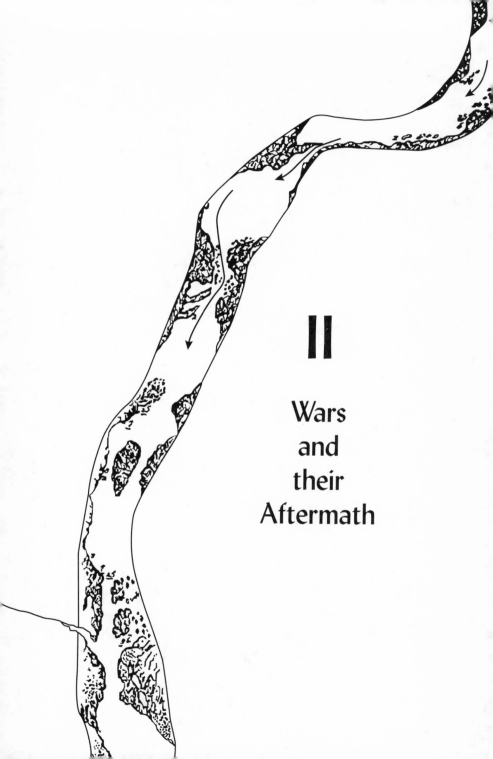

II

Wars
and
their
Aftermath

10

War, Failed Peace and
Plans for the Mekong

Born in equivocation, this conflict developed after 1946 like a
cancer, slowly gnawing away at the convalescent French body
politic, first affecting the army and its officers, then the nation's
finances, and finally the whole foreign policy of our country.

> *Philippe Devillers,* Histoire du Viêt-Nam de 1940 à 1952, *Paris,*
> *1952, characterising the First Indochina War*

In order to promote increased cooperation in the area and to
deny the general area of the Mekong River Basin to Communist
influence or domination, assist as feasible in the development of
the Mekong River Basin as a nucleus for regional cooperation
and mutual aid.

> *United States National Security Council report recommendation,*
> *September 1956*

During the Second World War a pro-Vichy regime, headed by
Admiral Decoux as Governor-General, continued to exercise
administrative control over the countries of French Indochina. It
did so at the pleasure of the Japanese, who permitted this exercise
of apparent French sovereignty in exchange for what Tokyo saw
as a vital concession to its interests: the unfettered opportunity
to move troops unhindered through the countries of Indochina
and to use their territory for the stationing of its aircraft. The
Japanese aircraft that sank the British battleships *Prince of Wales*
and *Repulse* in December 1941, leaving Malaya and Singapore
without naval protection, took off from airfields in Cambodia.

Then, as the tide of battle began to swing decisively against them, the Japanese in March 1945 no longer saw any benefit in allowing the French to exercise even the constrained power they had retained to this point. In a swift and effective coup de force they overturned the Decoux regime and embarked on a belated effort to promote 'independent' states in Laos, Cambodia and Vietnam, while maintaining effective control over all three countries.

This was a climactic moment, for it was recognised, most particularly in Vietnam, as a sign that French colonialism's days were numbered. From this point on, and with the Vietnamese communists led by a remarkable set of talented individuals of whom Ho Chi Minh was only one, the stage was slowly being set for three decades of bitter hostilities, the years of the First and Second Indochina Wars. First the French and then the Americans sought to stem the tide of communist revolution but, as hindsight has made crystal cl ̄ their efforts failed and the countries along the Mekong tha. ̄e made up Indochina all finally came under communist control in 1975.

Like so many young Australians attending high school or university, my awareness of the war that was taking place in the countries of French Indochina between 1946 and 1954 was limited in the extreme. The conflict in Korea, in which Australian troops were engaged, had a reality for me that simply was not matched by the events taking place in Vietnam, Laos and Cambodia. There was an exception, it must be said, in the case of the accounts that appeared of the Battle of Dien Bien Phu. Yet even that epic battle made less impact on my mind than the newspaper coverage of the Battle of Kapyong, in April 1951, when the 3rd Battalion of the Royal Australian Regiment was awarded the United States Presidential Citation for the part it played in halting the Chinese advance down the Korean Peninsula. History plays strange tricks, so that while the major wars in the countries of Indochina stand out in any discussion of post-1945 Southeast Asia, the other 'alarums and excursions' of the first decade after the end of the Second World War are frequently forgotten. For many, if not most, Australians at the time, the Malayan Emergency and political volatility in Indonesia were more demanding of attention than the beleaguered struggles of the French to retain control over their colonial territories in Indochina.

So, when I went to live in Cambodia in 1959, it was a surprise to find myself surrounded by people for whom the First Indochina War was a vivid memory. More than that, I slowly came to realise that the peace which appeared to prevail in Vietnam, Cambodia and Laos was of the most fragile and vulnerable kind. Throughout the countries that had formed French Indochina and which, after 1954, were all independent, political tensions both great and small threatened to plunge the whole of the Indochinese region back into conflict. In 1959, the lands along the Mekong were only briefly absolved from the turbulence that had so often been part of their history, and even this absolution was not complete, particularly in the Mekong Delta.

Even this fact was hard to recognise at first. Like Pierre Billotey, thirty years before, my first contact with Indochina was with Saigon. And like him I was struck by the combination of French chic and Asian exoticism that hung about the street that he encountered as the rue Catinat, but which by 1959 had become Tu Do or Freedom Street. From the square by the venerable Continental Palace Hotel and the former opera house, this tree-shrouded street ran down to the Saigon River. Walking past its cafes and curio shops, a first-time visitor's impression was of a city which was surrendering its French colonial past slowly and grudgingly. The hotel in which I stayed, the Majestic, was French in style and furnishing, down to the surprise inclusion, for an Australian in 1959, of a bidet in the bathroom. It stood across the road from the venerable headquarters of Denis Frères, Indochina's equivalent of Hong Kong's great trading house Jardine Mathieson. Yet there was one feature of Saigon's street life that was charmingly, and quite definitively, Vietnamese. This was the distinctive national dress of the women. Seeming universally slender and narrow-hipped, they floated by in their *ao-dai* (pronounced ow-zai), a long tunic split to the waist and worn over silk or satin trousers. Whether one sought a metaphor that evoked flowers or butterflies to describe the impression they left as they passed, these women were grace itself.

The misleading impression of pervasive calm left by a brief stop in Saigon was reinforced by the sights that greeted me in Phnom Penh. Here was a city that many thought was the most attractive in the whole of Southeast Asia. It was no longer the collection of wooden buildings and garbage-strewn streets with open sewers that Lagrée, Garnier and their companions encountered in 1866. As the French consolidated their control over Cambodia, they had laid out the centre of Phnom Penh in a grid pattern, the streets lined with trees in a nostalgic effort to recall the cities of their homeland—an echo of Provence. Some of these streets were named to honour past Cambodian kings and officials, but many others were tributes to men who had played a part in consolidating France's hold over the country, including the grand boulevard running southwards from the Phnom honouring Doudart de Lagrée. (It is difficult to know what members of the Cambodian royal family thought of the fact that a major thoroughfare running through the European Quarter commemorated Charles Thomson. This was the man who in 1884 had forced King Norodom to accede to his wishes under the threat of French gunboats moored in front of the royal palace.) The palace compound and the Phnom, topped by a pagoda and a tall stupa, were the city's most distinctive features. Yet nothing was truly old here. Built in a style that owed much to the Grand Palace in Bangkok, the Royal Palace in Phnom Penh with its roofs of shining multi-coloured tiles was a late nineteenth and early twentieth century creation, designed and paid for by the French. Even the pagoda and the stupa crowning the summit of the Phnom were modern replacements for older constructions.

Phnom Penh was a city where royal ceremonies were still a vibrant part of life. The grandest of all took place in the throne hall of the palace on occasions such as the celebration of the Cambodian New Year, an event that occurred in April, one of the hottest periods of the year. While the members of the Cambodian court looked relaxed in their white cotton tunics and richly coloured silk *sampots*, sarongs drawn up between their legs so that the wearers looked as if they were clothed in seventeenth century pantaloons, the attendant diplomatic corps sweated in a variety of unsuitable dress. In my own case it was my ambassador's heavy-weight tails, which I had borrowed for the day. Yet even standing for two hours in 40 degree heat could not dull the exoticism of this ceremony. It was replete with the sounds of the court brahmins blowing on their conch shells, the boom of gongs to indicate when homage was to be paid, and the sight of a palace servant crawling across the floor to hand the king his spectacles and his speech of welcome.

This was a world that could easily be satirised, as had been done cleverly by a former British defence attaché who had served in Phnom Penh—Andrew Graham, in his novel *A Foreign Affair*. But it was no less exotic because of this, and no less important to the majority of Cambodians. Not to all, for ceremonies such as this were deeply offensive to the then unknown Pol Pot. Even more offensive to him, it is safe to presume, were the *soirées dansantes*, the dancing evenings, presided over by Prince Sihanouk, Cambodia's former king and, at this time, its unchallenged political leader. These were events at which Sihanouk led a band of princes, warbled French pop songs and watched as his guests sipped vintage champagne. In 1959, Pol Pot was still using his birth name of Saloth Sar and working as a teacher in Phnom Penh. He had already made his views of royalty clear in an obscure Khmer-language student journal published in Paris six years earlier. 'Monarchy,' he had written, 'is an unjust doctrine, a malodorous running sore that just people must eliminate.' It was a view from which he never departed.

Leaving aside an expatriate presence of less than ten thousand, Phnom Penh's population of some 500 000 persons was divided, in ethnic terms, into three more or less equally sized groups— Cambodians, Chinese and Vietnamese. They appeared to live in harmony, with government in the hands of the Cambodians, major commerce in the hands of the Chinese, and petty trade handled by the Vietnamese. The divergent interests that existed between and within these groups were not immediately apparent. Much more obvious to a newcomer was the pervasive presence of the still large resident French community.

French men and women frequented the city's cafes and bars in greater numbers than any other group of expatriates. Theirs was the largest group of foreigners to be seen at the Cercle Sportif and Société Nautique, in the old La Taverne restaurant opening on to the post office square, and in the Bar Jean by the river or the seedy Zig Zag run by a lugubrious ex-legionnaire. It was members of the French community who stood out as 'characters'. There was Dr Grauwin, the famed 'Doctor of Dien Bien Phu', who was determined to live out his life away from France and who was the first port of call for expatriate males suffering from sexually transmitted diseases. And there was Pierre Mathivet de la Ville de Mirmont, the debonair aristocrat who was deputy head of the French diplomatic mission. A man of great charm and surpassing elegance, Mathivet rotated his 'first' and 'second' wives, as he called them, through Phnom Penh, and kept a gibbon in his house.

As an apparent sign that little had changed in the relationship between Cambodia and France, when state ceremonies took place the French ambassador was accorded a special position, ahead of and separate from the rest of the diplomatic corps. This was an honour that infuriated many members of the official American community, for they knew that it was their dollars that were essential to the Cambodian state's survival, at least in the fashion to which many elite Cambodians had become accustomed. And here was the nub of the situation. Throughout the countries that had once formed Indochina, however much France clung to its past links and as Frenchmen pretended that it was possible to live a life that was unchanged from colonial times, the dominant external power in the region was the United States. Its presence, through its diplomats and its military training teams, was steadily changing the political equations that had been brought into being in 1954. In that year France had admitted defeat in the First Indochina War, and Cambodia, Laos and Vietnam, the last divided between communist and non-communist control, faced the future as independent states. The illusion of calm that I saw in Saigon and Phnom Penh masked the legacy of eight bitter years of war and the reality of a deteriorating security in the countryside, particularly in South Vietnam.

The story of the First Indochina War has been told and retold many times. It was a war which saw the Vietnamese communist forces grow from a collection of poorly equipped guerrilla bands to an army that could overcome the cream of French troops in a setpiece battle at Dien Bien Phu. France's defeat in this battle was the climax of the war, though not a signal for the immediate end of hostilities. But the strategic skill of the Vietnamese commander, General Vo Nguyen Giap, the fundamental errors of the French High Command and the courage displayed on both sides of the battle have tended to distract attention from the equally important developments that took place far to the south of Dien Bien Phu, in the Mekong Delta.

There, where social and economic deprivation among the peasant population had made the region a fertile recruiting ground for the communist cause, a different kind of warfare took place.

It was a war that was no less bitter because it lacked the main-force engagements that took place in the north of Vietnam. There were no 'meat grinder' battles amid the canals and paddy fields of the delta. Instead there was a ruthless contest for control between French-led forces that operated from fixed, fortified bases and the communists who were able to blend into the population in a classic illustration of Mao Zedong's dictum of the guerrilla's need to act as a fish in the population sea. And if this choice was not open to them, they could retreat to areas such as the U Minh Forest, a vast region of swamps and forest cover in the west of the delta that was almost impenetrable for the French. Cruelty and torture were used by both sides. Apologists for the communists have maintained that the guerrillas' use of terror was 'selective', in contrast to the readiness of some French units to exact vengeance on whole villages. At the very least, an attempt to draw up a balance sheet that evaluates which side was more, or less, 'humane' faces enormous difficulties.

The war in the delta was one in which fear reigned at night as small government units that could claim 'control' over territory in the daytime retreated to their vulnerable posts at nightfall. The description that Graham Greene provides in *The Quiet American* of Fowler's misadventure when his car breaks down between Tay Ninh and Saigon is set in an area a little to the north of the Mekong Delta, but it can readily be taken as an accurate depiction of the fear and insecurity that were an essential part of the war in the region where the great river makes its final passage to the sea. By 1953, with the war now routinely described in France as *la sale guerre*, the dirty war, for its costs in casualties and the way in which it was being fought, the communists had established a dominant presence in the western part of the Mekong Delta. This judgment does not rely on the claims made by the communists at the time but rather on the official war map prepared on the orders of the Commander-in-Chief of the French Forces in Indochina, General Henri Navarre.

Saigon during the First Indochina War lost much of its image as a city of French chic mixed with Asian exoticism. Instead it became a city of extremes, of fine food served in restaurants that were screened from the street by wire mesh erected to act as a barrier against the grenades thrown by communist guerrillas mounted on motorbikes; of French women still dressed in the latest fashions, as local dressmakers ran up copies of the Paris collections; and of a vast network of casinos, opium dens and brothels. The most famous of the institutions catering to a range of vices was the Grande Monde, a vast 'dancing' establishment that was run by a vicious quasi-military group of Vietnamese gangsters, the Binh Xuyen. Led by Bay Vien, a man of cruel temperament whose only show of compassion appeared to be directed towards the pet tiger and python that he kept in his home, these criminals drew immense profits from gambling and prostitution. And underlying the moral decadence of the city was the fact that the Binh Xuyen operated with the approval of the French administration.

Further up the Mekong, in Cambodia and Laos, the impact of the First Indochina War on the settlements along the river was limited, at least in terms of direct military clashes. Phnom Penh, Vientiane and Luang Prabang were all affected by the war, but they were never subjected to the pattern of urban guerrilla violence that plagued Saigon. In Laos, there was one notable engagement that took place on and by the river even before full-scale hostilities between the French and the Vietnamese communist forces broke out in December 1946. This was a battle that took place at Tha Khaek, a small riverside town in southern Laos, in March 1946.

In the confused circumstances that followed the end of the Pacific War, the return of the French to Laos was opposed by an embryonic Lao nationalist movement, the Lao Issara (Free Lao). This was a group that had many political faces, some radical, some clearly conservative, and many with political opinions in between. Among the radicals was the man who came to be known as 'the Red Prince', Prince Souphanouvong, a physically powerful man with a bluff but engaging manner. One of three sons of the second most important royal family in traditional Laos, Souphanouvong's education in France, where he qualified as an engineer at the elite Ecole des Ponts et Chaussées, left him with two personal legacies that might, at first, seem likely to have been mutually exclusive. On the one hand, not least as the result of working on the waterfront during his university vacations, he had imbibed a stimulating draught of leftist ideas. These ideas, which were later reinforced by the experience of fighting both the French and the Americans and by marriage to a Vietnamese woman with communist beliefs, stayed with him all his life. On the other hand, and never interfering with his left-wing views, his time in France had convinced him that there were capitalist pleasures that need not be forgone. His taste for good wines and cigars was equally a matter of lifelong conviction.

When the Pacific War ended, Souphanouvong was in Hanoi, cementing ties with the Vietnamese communists, ties that would last throughout his life. Returning to Laos, with an escort of Vietnamese communist soldiers, by this stage known as the Vietminh, Souphanouvong became an important figure in a Lao Issara provisional government that pledged to gain independence from the French. By January 1946, the French had made clear their determination to resume control over Laos. When, in March, they embarked on a series of military actions to reassert their hold over the whole of Laos, Souphanouvong was in Tha Kaek at the head of a mixed force of Lao and Vietnamese. Unlike his colleagues elsewhere, he chose to fight against the much stronger forces at the colonial power's disposal. It was a courageous but foolhardy decision. The French forces attacked Tha Kaek with artillery and air strikes, forcing Souphanouvong and his mixed Lao and Vietminh forces to abandon the town and to seek refuge across the Mekong on the right bank, in Thai territory. Souphanouvong was among the more than a thousand Lao and Vietnamese casualties in this brief but costly engagement. As he crossed the Mekong towards Thailand, a French aircraft strafed the boat in which he was making his escape, wounding him seriously. He recovered to make his way eventually to Hanoi, and later back to Thailand to become a member of a Lao Issara government-in-exile.

For the remainder of the First Indochina War, hostilities in Laos were mostly waged away from the Mekong, in the highlands to the east and north of the river. There were some minor engagements not far from its banks, and a small flotilla of French gunboats operated on the Mekong to interdict supplies being sent down the river from Laos into Cambodia to aid the small pro-communist movement in that country, but for the most part the Mekong did not play a vital part in the First Indochina War away from its delta. Only in the last full year of the war was there anything like a departure from this pattern. In early 1953, General Vo Nguyen Giap, the Vietnamese communist military commander, demonstrated his forces' increasing capabilities by making a major thrust into northern Laos directed towards the royal capital of Luang Prabang. As his troops advanced towards Luang Prabang, there were sharply contrasting reactions from the population of this city and that of the administrative capital, Vientiane, much further south along the Mekong. In the latter, panic reigned for a period with many inhabitants deserting the city, either to flee further south or to cross the river into Thailand. But in Luang Prabang, in considerable contrast, there was an atmosphere of untroubled calm as the Lao king made clear that he had no intention of leaving his palace beside the river, and as a Buddhist monk credited with second sight assured the city's population that all would be well. And it was, for when they were within two days march of the royal capital the Vietminh forces stopped and retreated for reasons that have never been clearly established.

Later in the same year, and in developments closely linked to the famous Battle of Dien Bien Phu, General Giap again directed his troops to make a major attack into Laos. As the French expeditionary force assembled at Dien Bien Phu with the twin aims of preventing a Vietminh advance towards Luang Prabang and drawing their opponents into a major battle, Giap once again sent his forces deep into Laos in December 1953. One Vietminh force started down the Nam Ou River from the far north of the country. If they had continued down this major tributary of the Mekong, they would have reached Luang Prabang, but after drawing off the now increasingly stretched French the Vietminh again withdrew to the north. The more important Vietminh strike was mounted much further south on the river at Tha Khaek, the site of Prince Souphanouvong's brave but futile resistance to the French in 1946. After briefly capturing and holding Tha Khaek, and then striking at a French base even further south, the Vietminh again withdrew as Giap completed his preparations for the epic siege of Dien Bien Phu.

The fall of Dien Bien Phu in May 1954 ensured an end to

the First Indochina War and, after tortuous negotiations in Geneva, an agreement for an armistice between the French and Vietminh forces was signed on 20 July 1954. The wide-ranging Geneva Agreements of the following day covered broader political matters. Their content, and the intent of those who negotiated them, are still matters of controversy. In particular, the United States which by 1953 had assumed a major role in financing the French war effort in Indochina, has been a target of criticism for its readiness to underwrite a new, anti-communist regime in southern Vietnam. So far as the future of the Mekong was concerned, the river's course below the Chinese border now ran through one country, Laos, in which the pro-Vietnamese communist Pathet Lao movement controlled two provinces; through another, Cambodia, where King Sihanouk had succeeded in preventing the small local communist movement from gaining any international recognition; and through a new southern Vietnamese state, the American-backed Republic of Vietnam. In China, the Mekong ran through a country which, for the United States and its allies, was an ideological enemy. When, with the end of the war in 1954, discussion began about ways to capitalise on the Mekong's economic potential, there was simply no thought given to including China in development plans for the river.

A s the 1950s drew to a close, there was steadily growing evidence that the arrangements negotiated under the Geneva Agreements were falling apart. Nowhere was this more clear than in the Mekong Delta where the communist Vietminh presence had been so strong during the war years from 1946 to 1954. By 1955 the United States had made abundantly clear that it regarded the Republic of Vietnam (South Vietnam) as the region in which a line had to be drawn against the futher advance of communism in Southeast Asia, and to do this the Americans needed a Vietnamese leader on whom they thought they could rely. The man they backed to lead an anti-communist government based in Saigon was Ngo Dinh Diem. While unquestionably a nationalist, he was a remote figure who had spent much of the war in exile from Vietnam and who combined his devotion to a bleakly austere form of the Catholic faith with the unyielding certainties of an ancestral Confucian background.

Never a popular figure, Diem did not lack either the courage or the determination to act against his enemies. From 1956 onwards, and particularly from 1958, he pursued policies to counteract the continuing hold that he knew the communists exercised in the Mekong Delta. There was little that was subtle about his approach to the problems he faced. Relying on military and civil officials who were disproportionately Catholic in religion, and who were often from central and northern Vietnam rather than from the south itself, Diem embarked on a program of wholesale arrests of those suspected of being communists. At the same time, his government reinstated the rights of landlords who, in many cases, had not had any contact with their lands, or the peasants who farmed them, for up to a decade. These peasants now found they had to pay high rents to men they often had never seen. This situation contrasted with the arrangements that the communists had skilfully instituted during the time they had exercised control over areas of the delta, when rent charges were suspended.

By 1959, as resentment of Diem's methods grew and the communist guerrillas increased their activity in the delta, Diem's government proclaimed a new law which gave special military courts the right to sentence to death within three days those convicted or suspected of attacks against the state. In a sinister new twist, these courts travelled through the delta with a portable guillotine for use against those convicted. Today the guillotine is on show in Saigon (Ho Chi Minh City) in the War Crimes Exhibition, a museum devoted principally to the actions of American troops during the Second Indochina War and housed, with an evident sense of Vietnamese irony, in the former United States Information Service building.

The war that was being fought in the paddy fields of South Vietnam had moved up several notches in intensity by 1963, bringing an increased American military presence in the form of advisers to the South Vietnamese army. The communist forces, now almost universally referred to as the Vietcong (the Saigon government's term for the communists), were steadily gaining strength. Although we now know that the efforts of these guerrillas in South Vietnam were directed by Hanoi, most of the men and women active in the communist cause were southerners and they were about to show their capabilities in a major engagement. In the first week of the new year, on 3 January 1963, a battle took place in the Mekong Delta that saw the beginning of a new and deadly phase in the undeclared war between the communist and non-communist forces in Vietnam. Forgotten by many, more than thirty years later, it was an event that foreshadowed South Vietnam's and America's ultimate defeat at the hands of the communists. It was the Battle of Ap Bac.

Learning that there was a concentration of Vietcong troops near the delta village of Ap Bac, some sixty kilometres southwest of Saigon, the commander of South Vietnam's Fourth Army Corps ordered troops of the Seventh Division to attack the communists. The government troops, estimated to outnumber their opponents by a factor of ten, were assisted by an American helicopter unit. Neither of these facts prevented the engagement from being a debacle, marked by gross failures of leadership and command on the South Vietnamese side. Of fifteen American helicopters involved, four were put out of action and three Americans were killed. Losses on the South Vietnamese side were much heavier, more than sixty killed and a hundred wounded. The true number of communist casualties was never determined. When the Vietcong troops withdrew under cover of darkness they left behind only three bodies.

News of the battle at Ap Bac hit Saigon like a storm. Spending a month in the South Vietnamese capital at the time, I heard the question asked by Vietnamese and foreigners alike: How could this have happened? But it seemed this was a question that was not even being asked at the highest levels of the American Embassy and its military mission in Saigon. In fact, when the American Commander-in-Chief for the Pacific, Admiral Harry D. Felt, arrived in Saigon just after the battle at Ap Bac he lauded it as a South Vietnamese victory. There were some in the American military who recognised what had happened and what it could portend for the future, among them John Paul Vann, the flawed and controversial subject of Neil Sheehan's biography, *A Bright Shining Lie*. For the rest, most senior Vietnamese and American officials seemed unable to accept the implications of the battle. As we now know, and well before the final communist victory of 1975, the Mekong Delta could never again be claimed as an area under the certain control of the American-backed government in Saigon.

The Battle of Ap Bac was still in the future when a start was made in efforts to tap the Mekong's economic potential. The conclusion of the First Indochina War, and the unresolved political issues remaining after a temporary peace was ushered in by the Geneva Agreements, provided the background to the establishment of the Committee for the Coordination of Investigations of the Lower Mekong Basin (the Mekong Committee) in 1957. This was the first organisation to develop a comprehensive scheme for the economic exploitation of the river once it flowed out of China's Yunnan province. To a large extent, the Mekong Committee was a child of the Cold War as it was played out in Southeast Asia. Well before the commitment of American troops as advisers to the Diem government in South Vietnam, policy makers in Washington had begun formulating plans to prevent the spread of communism in post-Geneva Southeast Asia that involved the Mekong River. The aim, as set down in one of the earliest documents dealing with the river and prepared by the National Security Council in 1956, was to 'deny the general area of the Mekong River Basin to Communist influence or domination'. How this was to be done was initially only addressed in very broad terms, for there was little detailed up-to-date technical information available about the river and its tributaries.

In developing its policies, Washington was able to consult a report completed in early 1956 by a team from the United States Bureau of Reclamation. This report, which suggested a range of sites suitable for hydro-electric exploitation, reflected an initial United States view that the Mekong could be developed along the lines of the Tennessee Valley Authority (TVA), the vast engineering works begun in the American South during the Great Depression of the 1930s. Washington was also aware of discussions that were taking place in the Economic Commission for Asia and the Far East (ECAFE), a United Nations specialised agency, and was anxious to prevent this body taking the running in something that the Americans increasingly saw in strategic as much as in economic and developmental terms. Despite initial United States opposition, an ECAFE-sponsored survey of the Mekong in 1956, which did not include American participants, produced a report in 1957 that was to remain important for plans drawn up for the Mekong over the next few years. Reflecting a consensus present in both developed and underdeveloped countries of the world at the time, the ECAFE team's report was based on the premise that a major part of what was required to exploit the Mekong's resources was the construction of large dams on the river's course.

The largest of these dams, the ECAFE report suggested, could be located a short distance upstream from Vientiane at Pa Mong. Moving downstream, additional potential dam sites were identified at the Khemerat rapids, the Khone Falls and the Sambor rapids, all locations familiar as barriers encountered by travellers on the Mekong over many centuries. It was also suggested that a dam might be built to regulate the flow of water in and out of Cambodia's Great Lake. Although the ECAFE report made clear that a great deal of work would need to be done before it would be possible to describe the impact of dams in these locations, it did recognise that their construction would have wide-ranging effects. In the case of the dam site proposed at the Khemerat rapids, for instance, the report acknowledged that damming the Mekong here would result in the flooding of Savannakhet, then as now the largest town in southern Laos. The Pa Mong dam, it was acknowledged, would if constructed lead to the relocation of some 250 000 people who lived in areas that would come under water.

Formally established in 1957, the Mekong Committee's membership consisted of four of the five riparian countries along the lower course of the river, namely Cambodia, Laos, Thailand and South Vietnam. At this time all four countries had budgets that were heavily dependent on American economic aid. The fifth riparian state, Burma, showed no interest in joining the committee, and in this Cold War era no consideration was given to China's membership. The People's Republic of China, it must be remembered, was not even a member of the United Nations at this time. The determination of the United States to be heavily involved in shaping developments was now reflected in the work that was undertaken in late 1957 by a retired senior officer from the US Army Corps of Engineers, Lieutenant-General Raymond A. Wheeler. The recommendations made to the Mekong Committee by General Wheeler were to shape its course of action until the Second Indochina War put an end to any prospect of completing the major projects associated with the Mekong itself. Emphasising the importance of American interests, despite the involvement of other external aid donors such as France, Japan and Australia, an American became the administrative head of the Mekong Committee and the largest contribution to the committee's costs came from the United States.

Wheeler's report placed great emphasis on the collection of technical data as a prelude to the actual construction of any dams on the Mekong, but in terms of where these dams might be located it was in agreement with the 1956 ECAFE report in identifying Pa Mong, in Laos, and Sambor, in Cambodia, as locations worthy of detailed study. A dam at Pa Mong, proponents argued, had great economic promise and would be the largest ever built in the world. It would provide a range of benefits—alleviating flooding in Laos and Thailand, providing irrigation for northeastern Thailand, generating cheap electricity, and improving navigation both upstream and downstream. A dam at Sambor, similarly if less dramatically, would improve navigation, generate electricity and provide irrigation. These were benefits that would be available to Cambodia, Laos and Vietnam.

Strikingly, the reports written during this period discussing the Mekong's future were cast in overwhelmingly positive terms. Difficulties and negative costs were not ignored, but they took second place to the benefits that were seen as clearly outweighing them. This was a time when big dams were seen as good in themselves on all sides of the global ideological divide. It was the era of the decision to build the Aswan High Dam in Egypt and the Kaptai Dam in the Chittagong Hill Tracts of Bangladesh. In the minds of the policy makers of the period, the possibility that developing the Mekong's economic potential would act as a counter to communism as well as bringing benefits to populations in countries in desperate need of development offered a potent mix of altruism and presumed good strategic sense. Moreover, it would be less than fair to suggest that all who became involved in the work of the Mekong Committee thought only in

Cold War terms. Observing the work of the Australian engineers who began survey work in Cambodia in 1960 and 1961, in relation to the Sambor site, I readily admit that I shared with them the expectation that this was a job worth doing.

From the late 1950s onwards an enormous amount of exploratory work was undertaken in connection with the Pa Mong and Sambor sites as well as in relation to Cambodia's Great Lake and the Mekong's many tributaries. In terms of the major goal of actually beginning the construction of major dams, nothing was achieved. Like so many other plans formulated before or at the beginning of the Second Indochina War, the vision of a transformation of the Mekong developed within the Mekong Committee came to nothing as the war grew in intensity. In 1965, the Johnson Administration mounted a final effort to make development of the Mekong Basin a quid pro quo for North Vietnam to abandon its bid to gain control over the American-backed Republic of Vietnam in the south. This proposal never appeared likely to gain acceptance from America's tenacious opponents. So, by the mid-1960s, hopes of exploiting the Mekong economically had faded as political and military turbulence in the countries along its course offered only sombre promises for the future. It was to be many years before plans for the economic exploitation of the Mekong and its major tributaries could once again be considered against a background of regional peace and stability.

11

War, Victory and Defeat
along the Mekong

. . . this river of evil memory
Colin Thubron's reflections on the Mekong during the Vietnam War, in
Behind the Wall: A Journey through China, *London, 1987*

In the space of fifteen years, from 1966 to 1981, the character of the three countries of former French Indochina that bordered the Lower Mekong changed dramatically. Many of the changes were tragic, almost all were irrevocable. In Cambodia, Laos and Vietnam the bitter years of the Second Indochina War ushered in a period of deeply flawed peace before, in the case of Cambodia and Vietnam, former comrades-in-arms became sworn enemies. The communist victories of 1975 were the prelude to a series of events far different from those most observers had predicted as likely to occur. It was not just that the names of cities and countries changed, so that in a unified Socialist Republic of Vietnam Saigon was renamed Ho Chi Minh City, while Cambodia became Democratic Kampuchea. The changes that took place were much more fundamental than those associated with nomenclature. And in the case of Cambodia what took place was scarcely believable.

The bloodbath that many had thought likely to follow a communist victory in Vietnam never took place. Certainly, there was retribution. Of a million persons singled out for 're-education' because of their links to the defeated regime, more than 100 000 endured harsh conditions as they were locked away for long

periods in remote and unhealthy labour camps. There they were
expected to reflect on their 'sins', absorb Marxist thought, and
open new areas for agriculture. Yet it seems unquestionably the
case that the 30 000 or 40 000 Lao sent for re-education—a
dramatically higher proportion of the population—suffered even
harsher treatment at the hands of the victors than those who
were interned in Vietnam. It was as if the Lao communists were
determined to show that their country's legendary reputation for
gentleness and an easygoing approach to life no longer had a
place in the new, ideologically oriented scheme of things. But
neither in Vietnam nor in Laos did anything take place to match
the tyranny and slaughter that overtook the population of Democratic Kampuchea once Cambodia fell to the Khmer Rouge in
1975 and the victors began their radical restructuring of society.

Much ink has been spilt in a search for the point at which
the multiple tragedies of the Second Indochina War and its
aftermath might have been avoided. This chapter is not an
attempt to offer an answer to that question. Rather it tries to
capture some of the sights, sounds and smells of a region along
the Mekong that from 1966 onwards seemed set on an ever-
descending path towards tragedy and destruction. It is a chapter
about people as much as events, for like so many others who
found their lives linked to the Indochinese region, I formed
friendships with men and women who later paid a high price for
being Cambodian or Vietnamese.

As the human costs of the years of war grew ever greater, it
became increasingly clear that the grand plans drawn up by the
Mekong Committee for the construction of major dams on the
river simply could not be put into practice. The Mekong Committee continued to exist, a shell of an organisation, with three
of its member countries, Cambodia, Laos and South Vietnam,
talking of plans that they knew had no hope of realisation. Some
limited construction took place on tributaries of the Mekong,
but the main course of the river continued to flow unchecked
by any man-made obstacle. For, by the early 1970s, large sections
of the river in Cambodia and Laos had passed out of the control
of governments in Phnom Penh and Vientiane. And in the
Mekong Delta of South Vietnam the best the anti-communist
forces could do was to ensure that the main urban centres
remained in the hands of the Saigon government. Two decades

were to pass before discussion of schemes to develop the Mekong's economic potential could take place on a realistic basis.

By 1966 the Second Indochina War, the Vietnam War, dominated life along the Lower Mekong. But it was a domination that took many different forms. Most dramatic were the battles fought along the watercourses and in the paddy fields of the Mekong Delta. These made news, but just as fundamental was the transformation of Saigon into a city marked by an ever greater degree of tawdriness, a response to the presence in Vietnam of hundreds of thousands of foreign, mostly American, troops. Bars and brothels, the latter claiming a more elevated status as 'massage parlours', sprang up along streets heaped with uncleared garbage which lay stinking in the tropical heat. In some places this garbage filled the gutters only inches away from blackmarket stalls crammed with liquor (Chivas Regal in abundance), torch batteries, shaving cream, insect repellent, and even American army-issue underpants still in their Department of Defense wrappings. All these were the product of the massive theft that was taking place on the wharves or of the thriving abuse of the service commissaries. And to emphasise that decadence and death went hand in hand, execution stakes were erected in the open space close to Saigon's Central Market for use when black market currency dealers were from time to time despatched by firing squad.

Saigon had never been an innocent city, but by now it struggled to retain even a few vestiges of its former charm. In contrast, Phnom Penh when I returned there in 1966 seemed little changed from the city I had first seen in 1959. There were the same clean, tree-shaded streets, the same clusters of Buddhist monks who late each morning emerged from their university in a burst of yellow and orange like a field of flowers suddenly coming into bloom. The same royal elephants could be seen in their stables or processing slowly on their morning exercise—a sign still warned passers-by: 'Beware the naughty elephant'. But this lack of physical change was only part, a not terribly important part, of the Cambodian picture.

What had changed in Cambodia was not immediately apparent to a short-term visitor, for it was change that had occurred in the political atmosphere. The superficially gay and carefree atmosphere of life under Sihanouk in the early 1960s had been replaced by a sense of apprehension. With the war in Vietnam growing in intensity, the prince's policy of appeasing the Vietnamese communists seemed to carry with it ever greater risks to Cambodia's survival free from conflict. What was still not apparent was the extent to which Cambodia's status as 'an oasis of peace'—to use Sihanouk's often repeated words—was about to be threatened from within as well as by the dangers of the Vietnam War spilling over the border between the two countries.

What was it like to be a Cambodian in Phnom Penh or a Vietnamese in Saigon? There were many answers to the question. For the elite in both cities, access to wealth and power initially provided a cocoon of privilege that enabled them to disregard the inconveniences of war or economic decline. For the poor, the costs of the war being fought around them may have seemed little more harsh than their normal disadvantaged place within society. To be poor in Saigon was better than being poor in the Mekong Delta, where control passed out of government hands when night fell, so that a peasant's life was a constant struggle to balance existence between two masters. In Phnom Penh, so long as the countryside remained at peace, the difficulties of being poor in the city could always be ameliorated by returning to the villages from which most low-earning workers had come. It was a return to a life of bare subsistence for many, but for most until the end of the 1960s it was subsistence in peace.

It was often from those in between, the men and women who were neither rich nor poor, that I learnt most about the meaning of the war that was being fought in Vietnam and which threatened to overtake Cambodia. In Saigon I heard a view of the war that was anathema to the Saigon regime and its American backers. This was the view of Duong Sanh, Director of the National Library, a title that sounds much grander than it was in practice. Aged I would think in his early forties when I first met him in 1963, by 1966 he had a deeply pessimistic view of Vietnam's present and future, and mostly sad memories about its past. Shorter even than most of his compatriots, his slight frame was made to seem still more insubstantial by his tendency to stoop as he faced the world with a perpetually worried frown. Although he was a member of the Catholic Church and believed communism to be evil, he told me that he had come to want 'peace at any price'. He deplored the moral decay of his fellow citizens as more and more were ready to prostitute themselves, both literally and figuratively, to gain financial reward from the American presence in Vietnam. This condemnation was accompanied by a wry grimace as he immediately afterwards volunteered to change my American dollars into local currency at the black market rate of exchange.

There were hundreds, indeed thousands, of Duong Sanhs in Saigon. Spared to a large extent the brutalities of life in the countryside and never a focus of international attention as were the generals and politicians, their plight was no less poignant because it was not the stuff of headlines. They were men and women who had reached adulthood during the First Indochina War and had become civil servants in the South Vietnamese administration once the French had left. Educated in French as well as Vietnamese, at one level many in this group were *dépaysé*, never quite sure where they belonged and harbouring a sense that it might be France. For Duong Sanh it eventually was, for after encountering him over several visits in the late 1960s and early 1970s, progressively more mournful on each occasion, I was greeted by him in a corridor of the Bibliothèque Nationale in Paris in 1974. He had found a way to leave, with his wife and young son, and was happy to occupy a minor post in that great library, bringing books from the stacks to the main reading rooms.

He had lived through the shattering experience of the Tet offensive when, at the time of the Vietnamese New Year in late January and early February 1968, North Vietnamese regulars and Vietcong guerrilla forces fought their way into central Saigon to win the staggering propaganda victory that set in train America's slow but certain decision to exit a war it knew it could not win. In a testimony both to the strategic importance of the Mekong Delta and to the failure of American and South Vietnamese efforts to impose their will on that region, many of the Vietcong forces that marched on Saigon came from nearby delta regions such as Long An Province. The cost to the communist forces of mounting the Tet offensive was staggering, leading those who relied on military analysis alone to announce that it was a communist defeat. In a couple of weeks of fighting, the local communist forces suffered a loss of men from which they never recovered and increasingly their places were taken by northern regulars who travelled down to the south along the Ho Chi Minh Trail. But the loss of so many southern communist troops did not mean that the delta was pacified. When the dust of the Tet offensive had settled, the Saigon government could still only claim that it had reasserted control over the major population centres of the delta, even though the cost of doing so involved widespread destruction of some urban centres. Few in Vietnam at the time would ever forget an American officer's comment about the delta settlement of Ben Tre that 'it was necessary to destroy the town in order to save it'. In the villages throughout the delta it was a different story as the communist infrastructure steadily reimposed its authority over peasants who had few, if any, means of gaining the military and civil assistance that could have ensured their security.

Life in these Mekong Delta towns, such as My Tho, Long Xuyen and Rach Gia, could appear deceptively secure, even after the Tet offensive, in the daytime at least. But the true state of security was revealed by the fact that travel by road beyond their outskirts was often impossible without a heavily armed escort. At night it was frequently not possible at all, unless, of course, 'arrangements' had been made between the local South Vietnamese province chief and the local communists. Taken for a night-time drive outside Rach Gia, in December 1969, in the company of a band of retired South Vietnamese army generals, including Tran Van Don, one of the men who mounted the coup that deposed President Ngo Dinh Diem in 1963, I consoled myself with the thought that arrangements indeed must have been made for us to be making this apparently foolhardy trip. I certainly did not find time to reflect on the fact that I was near the site of Oc Eo, the place where archeologists have shown that there was an important trading settlement linked to the Mekong at the very beginning of the river's proto-history.

In Cambodia my view of 'ordinary life' was shaped by an extraordinary commentator, a Catholic priest, Father Paulus Tep Im Sotha, one of the first Cambodians to be ordained by his church. His mother's ancestry had been both French and Vietnamese, but with a Khmer father he identified himself completely with the Cambodian community. As a foreigner who had once been part of an embassy, I knew other Cambodians who were of a higher social status—minor princes who were repositories of almost endless gossip about the sprawling, extended royal family, an army colonel, and senior officials who, so long as they enjoyed Sihanouk's approval, wielded great power. And from these men I learnt much that was important to an understanding of Cambodian politics. But no one matched the insights this priest provided. Compared with the overwhelmingly Buddhist affiliation of most of his compatriots, he was shepherd to a tiny flock of ethnic Cambodian Catholics, probably no more than 4000 in total. Yet he enjoyed links with all levels of society and was able to analyse political and social developments from the basis of having had a rigorous education, first at a seminary in France and then under the guidance of the Dominicans at the Angelicum University in Rome. Though he moved with ease within the Cambodian community, not all of his religious colleagues were so accepting. On several occasions, when I asked French priests to help me locate Tep Im, both in Phnom Penh and Battambang, they were less than helpful. When I mentioned these rebuffs to him he laughed off the slight, remarking that French priests no less than French officials still found it difficult to come to terms with the end of the colonial era.

Tall for a Cambodian, perhaps reflecting his French grand-parent, and athletic in appearance with a frank but disarming manner, Tep Im became a friend. This caused us both amusement since our friendship bridged not only a gap between East and West but also between a dedicated servant of his church and a lapsed Australian Protestant. To add interest to our frequent discussions, our meetings took place in the Eglise Hoalong, the Catholic church on the banks of the Tonle Sap River, just upstream from where it met the main course of the Mekong and on the site of what had once been a Dutch trading factory in the seventeenth century.

The Cambodian world I came to know through Tep Im had little to do with the flamboyant excesses of Sihanouk's court, but much to do with a growing sense of disquiet bordering on alienation among both Phnom Penh's political class and those in the capital that could very loosely be described as 'middle class', men and women who were teachers or worked in government ministries. Perceptively, as hindsight showed, and in a judgment that was not widely shared in the mid-1960s, he argued that, appearances to the contrary, life in rural Cambodia was marked by slowly growing peasant discontent. He did not predict Sihanouk's future overthrow, nor the emergence of the radical Cambodian revolutionary movement led by Pol Pot which was finally to take control of the country in 1975, but as the 1960s drew to a close he increasingly came to fear that dreadful and possibly catastrophic prospects lay ahead. Yet nothing prepared him for the events that followed hard upon Sihanouk's ousting from power in March 1970, when a series of massacres along the Mekong added a new and bloody chapter to the river's history.

By April 1970, the Lon Nol regime that had assumed power after the March coup against Sihanouk was engaged in a rapidly expanding war against a still small number of leftist Cambodian opponents. These radical revolutionaries were supported by a much larger number of communist Vietnamese regulars. The anti-Vietnamese feeling that had contributed to the decision to depose Sihanouk was now exacerbated by an awareness that Vietnamese were responsible for the mounting deaths and casualties being inflicted on Lon Nol's ill-trained troops. Underlying distrust and antagonism towards Vietnamese, which was and is so much part of almost every Cambodian's worldview, began to spill out into ugly incidents in Phnom Penh. Random violence was directed against long-term Vietnamese residents who had no possible connection with the communist forces opposing the struggling Lon Nol regime.

No one has ever been able to provide a full account of all the violence directed against the Vietnamese living in Cambodia in this period shortly after Sihanouk was deposed. What is clear is that there was more than one massacre, beginning in April as the dam of ill-feeling against Vietnamese burst. But there is still no certainty about exactly what caused the first clear case of brutal mass killings when, in mid-April, residents of Neak Luong, the major ferry point across the Mekong on the road from Phnom Penh to Saigon, reported scores of Vietnamese bodies floating down the river. They had been shot and many had their hands tied behind their backs. As best as can be determined, the victims came from an ethnic Vietnamese village on an island a little to the north of Neak Luong, a town that was later to be the site of one of the worst instances of civilians being killed by mistake in the whole course of Cambodia's terrible civil war.

Later in April, with violence continuing into May, it was the turn of the Vietnamese community in Phnom Penh to suffer at the hands of the Cambodian army and police. Over a period of a few days elements from these forces rounded up more than a thousand Vietnamese males from the region of Chrui Changvar, a peninsula bounded by the Mekong and the Tonle Sap Rivers, where a large number of Phnom Penh's Vietnamese residents lived. Some of the men, along with women and children, were gunned down on the spot, others were forced on to barges to be shot there in relays over several days, their bodies disposed of by being thrown into the water. For more than a week bloated, decomposing bodies floated down the Mekong or were snagged by tree roots and washed on to sandbars to provide a lingering, ghastly testimony to the mindless killing. Along the river banks there was a sickening stench of rotting human flesh.

Even with his links to the Vietnamese and French Catholic priests who had ministered to many of the massacred Vietnamese, Tep Im could do little more than confirm the facts of the event when I talked to him later in the year. He had been in Phnom Penh when the killings took place, and like so many others he had seen the bodies floating in the river. The massacre had taken place after he had been translated from his position as a parish priest in Phnom Penh to become the Vatican's Apostolic Prefect based in Battambang, Cambodia's second largest city in the country's northwest. Now Monsignor Tep Im, it was there that I met him in December 1970. He spoke despairingly of the incompetence of those who now controlled Phnom Penh and with deep sorrow of the events of the preceding April and May. He saw the massacres as the result of local factors compounded by anger on the part of the military at their losses in combat with the North Vietnamese. To these immediate causes he joined the long history of difficult and often brutal relations between Vietnamese and Cambodians. Claims that there could be real amity between the two communities, he observed, were some-times made for political reasons. But sadly, he observed, the facts were clear and otherwise. The two communities lived apart, including in their religious life. There had been no Vietnamese among his parishioners in Phnom Penh.

Shortly after the massacre, he had been approached by Yem Sambaur, a key figure in the new power structure that had replaced Sihanouk. The regime was 'embarrassed' by what had taken place, Yem Sambaur told him, and wanted his advice on how to account for what had happened to the South Vietnamese government whose troops were fighting alongside the Phnom Penh forces. Tep Im counselled frankness, not believing that this advice would be followed. He was right. The official line from the Phnom Penh regime was that the killings were the work of the 'Vietcong'.

I was not to see Tep Im again, but for the next two years we stayed in correspondence. Just before I flew back to Phnom Penh he asked if I could send him a copy of the *New English Bible*, for he was determined to translate this into Cambodian to replace the existing translation prepared by American Protestant evangelicals, which he regarded as excessively literal. I was able to do so and he thanked me for this. The last letter I received from him spoke of how, at the end of each day, he tried to translate some passages, however short, using a Latin, French and English Bible to guide him towards the preparation of a Cambodian version. Nearly seven years were to pass before I finally learnt what his fate had been once the Pol Pot regime came to power.

Cambodia's full-scale involvement in the Second Indochina War in 1970 was the beginning of a long and bitter period of tragedy. It was tragedy that continued after the guns fell silent in April 1975. Hundreds of kilometres upstream from the site of Phnom Penh's massacre, the Kingdom of Laos had also been in the grip of war during the 1960s and early 1970s. But this was a hidden war mostly waged well away from the major towns on the Mekong. Yet just as the massacre of Vietnamese in Phnom Penh was inextricably linked to the Mekong, so was the Lao capital, Vientiane, sited on the banks of the great river, an integral part of the American efforts to prevent the triumph of communism in the countries of what had once been French Indochina.

Hidden from the American public and their legislators, the American military and the Central Intelligence Agency had been sending bombers over Laos from as early as 1964. Their bombing raids had the dual purpose of aiding a 'secret army' of

Despite their commitment to a revolutionary communist cause, the Pathet Lao issued bank notes during the Second Indochina War showing the Buddhist That Luang stupa as a decorative symbol. Apart from the stupa, the main upper picture shows various Lao ethnic groups shopping in a cooperative store, while the lower picture depicts Lao revolutionaries shooting down 'imperialist' American aircraft.

anti-communist troops recruited among Hmong hill people and of stopping the flow of men and supplies down the Ho Chi Minh Trail. Part of this effort, which was ultimately unsuccessful despite the vast amount of ordnance dropped throughout Laos, was coordinated by an American base on the outskirts of Vientiane. Known as 'Silver City', or simply as 'Kilometre 6', it was home to intelligence officers and pilots whose presence in the Lao

Efforts by the Lao communist government after 1975 to restrict the practice of Buddhism in Laos failed. Today Buddhism is thriving, with many Lao such as these in Luang Prabang entering the monkhood.

Left Buddha images stored at Wat Xieng Thong, Luang Prabang. Wat Xieng Thong, the grandest of Luang Prabang's Buddhist pagodas, was founded in 1560 and was under royal patronage until the removal of the Lao monarchy in 1975.

Below The Mekong with the former royal palace viewed from Mount Phousi in Luang Prabang. The palace now serves as a museum.

A fishing village at the edge of Cambodia's Great Lake. The future of villages such as this is under threat as the Great Lake is increasingly being affected by negative environmental developments.

Some of the most spectacular scenery on the Mekong is in the
region above Luang Prabang. These great limestone cliffs are
at the point where the Nam Ou River meets the Mekong
opposite the sacred Pak Ou Caves.

Above A Buddhist *wat* on the Mekong near Kompong Cham, Cambodia, with the river swollen to maximum height during flood time.

Below The Mekong at the tri-border region of Burma, Laos and Thailand, now frequently and wrongly termed the 'Golden Triangle'. Thai territory is in the foreground, with Lao territory on the right bank of the river. The land in the left middle ground is in Burma.

The massive Chinese suspension bridge at Jinghong seen under construction in 1998. It was completed in 1999.

Chinese tourists dressed in the wedding finery of the Dai people of the Jinghong region. Once an isolated region with a majority Dai population, Jinghong has become a popular tourist destination for Han Chinese.

The French explorers camped beside the Mekong at Keng Chan (modern Chiang Khan). This illustration from a sketch by Delaporte was published in the official record of the French Expedition. (Courtesy of Hordern House Rare Books)

Tang dynasty pagodas at Dali in western Yunnan Province just outside the walled city of Dali. Set against the dramatic background of the Cangshan mountains, they stand today in a setting little changed from the time when Garnier and his party saw them in 1868.

Sunset on the Mekong above Kratie.

capital fuelled the city's reputation for tropical decadence. The names of the bars that doubled as meeting places for commercial sex remain legendary among those whose memories stretch back to Laos before the communist victory in 1975. The 'Purple Porpoise' and the 'White Rose' offered all of the delights, and more, that are the staple of sex shows along Bangkok's Patpong Road today. But most renowned of all was Madame Lulu's 'Le Rendezvous des Amis', which was celebrated for its offerings of warm beer and oral sex.

The contrast between this routinely available debauchery in Vientiane and the calm of the royal capital further up the river could not have been more striking. Right to the end of the war, Luang Prabang remained a genuine oasis of calm, to the point where opposing Royal Lao Government and Pathet Lao communist forces facing each other across the Nam Ou River, the major tributary that flows into the Mekong not far from Luang Prabang, declared an informal cease-fire at the time of the Lao New Year celebrations. They did this so that the king could come the short distance upstream from Luang Prabang to visit the Buddhist sanctuaries at the Pak Ou caves opposite the confluence of the two rivers. Yet this apparently lackadaisical approach to warfare was not later translated into a gentle peace for those who had fought on the government side or who were deemed to be class enemies. The years of relentless American bombing shaped the attitudes of the communist victors and once the war was finally over in 1975 they insisted on punishment for those they had defeated. And, as we shall see, the Lao royal family was no exception.

12

Tragedies of Peace

For thirteen years they had my body but never my soul.

A former Royal Lao Army officer describing his re-education camp experience; Pakse, Laos, January 1997

It was a time when men were brutal, like wild animals.

Interview with a Cambodian refugee; Sa Keo camp, Thailand, April 1980

The harsh re-education campaigns put in place by the new communist governments of Vietnam and Laos, and in the case of Vietnam the imposition on the south of the country of an unsympathetic band of northern cadres, seem mild when compared to the events that followed the victory of the Khmer Rouge forces in Cambodia. The war fought in Cambodia before the Khmer Rouge entered Phnom Penh on 17 April 1975 was marked by extraordinary savagery, with routine mutilation of enemy bodies and instances of cannibalism. Part of this savagery was linked directly to the Mekong. The key river-crossing town of Neak Luong was constantly a target for the Khmer Rouge, for if they captured it they could prevent vital suppplies being brought by road from Saigon to Phnom Penh. Overrun by the Khmer Rouge in early May 1970, it was recaptured by South Vietnamese forces later in the month and was to remain in government hands until the final days of the war. But before it finally fell to the Khmer Rouge it suffered terrible casualties as the result of a bombing error. On 7 August 1973, a B-52 bomber failed to follow proper procedures in launching its payload and an entire stick of bombs fell on the hapless town. One hundred and twenty civilians died as a result. The American pilot was later fined $700 for his mistake.

Even before Neak Luong finally fell, passage along the Mekong from South Vietnam to Phnom Penh had become highly dangerous. While Phnom Penh troops were able to hold on to Neak Luong, there were other sections along the river from which the Khmer Rouge were able to launch attacks on ships ready to run the gauntlet from South Vietnamese territory to Phnom Penh. With road supply to Phnom Penh impossible by 1974, whether from South Vietnam or from Cambodia's own deepwater port of Kompong Som, and with a limitation on what could be flown into Pochentong airport, supplying Cambodia's capital by river became ever more important. By the end of 1974, some 90 per cent of Phnom Penh's supplies were reaching it by ships travelling up the Mekong.

The English journalist Jon Swain has provided a dramatic account of what it was like to travel from Saigon to Phnom Penh by river in his book *River of Time*. With much of the river bank in the hands of the Khmer Rouge, every voyage was a highly dangerous affair. Each ship that made the trip risked an ambush from shore artillery which was inevitably sited along the areas where the most damage could be inflicted. At the time Swain made his journey in 1974 several ships and barges had already been sunk by the Khmer Rouge and the fact that his and other ships made the journey through to Phnom Penh was a tribute to courage and to the high rewards waiting for crews prepared to take their chances in flag-of-convenience rustbuckets. But in January 1975 the river was closed for good. The voyage had become impossible and in the final weeks of the war Phnom Penh, swollen by hundreds of thousands of refugees from the countryside, waited for the Khmer Rouge to arrive. Stocks of every kind dwindled and rockets rained down indiscriminately on the city in a deadly confusion of siren-like sounds and thudding explosions.

What happened when Phnom Penh fell to the Khmer Rouge has been described many times: the sudden unreal silence as the guns fell silent, the mass evacuation of the city, the executions both in the capital and in the provinces of politicians and soldiers who had fought for the doomed Khmer Republic. And not only politicians and soldiers, for Paulus Tep Im Sotha, who had initially resisted the urgings of his parishioners that he flee from Battambang into Thailand, was among those killed shortly after the Khmer Rouge gained control of Cambodia. He had celebrated mass for the last time on 13 April and offered general absolution to the congregation. Father François Ponchaud in his book *The Cathedral of the Rice Paddy* quotes an eye witness who attended the mass and heard Tep Im say, 'It is the last time that I bless you. I remit your sins, you who are present and those who did not come.' He was still in Battambang when the Khmer Rouge took control of the city on the same day they marched into Phnom Penh. As accounts of Khmer Rouge killings began to multiply, Tep Im finally decided that he should try to reach Thailand, but he was stopped as he drove towards the border and after being held for a few days was taken to a spot near Sisophon and shot in the back by a Khmer Rouge soldier with an AK-47.

In the space of a week Phnom Penh became something approaching a ghost town. Cleared of its swollen population, it was home to the Khmer Rouge leadership and a population numbering no more than twenty thousand, probably one hundredth of those who were in the city when the Khmer Rouge marched in on 17 April 1975. What was life like during the Pol Pot years in the largely deserted city that once had been renowned as one of the most attractive in Asia? There are a limited number of testimonies, ranging from Sihanouk's self-obsessed account of his house arrest in the royal palace, to the harrowing memoirs of the very few who survived the inhuman conditions of Tuol Sleng, the extermination centre through which upwards of 15 000 Cambodians went to brutal torture and death. I heard my first detailed testimony of what it was like to live in Phnom Penh during those years from an unexpected source. In 1980 I was working as a consultant to the United Nations High Commissioner for Refugees in Khao I Dang, the vast refugee camp near the Thai–Cambodian border established at the end of 1979. It had became home to more than 90 000 Cambodians

One of the many tragedies of peace was the outflow of refugees
from Cambodia in 1979–80, in the face of the Vietnamese
invasion of their country and the onset of near famine
conditions. In this photograph the refugees are seen waiting for
rice to be distributed near the Thai–Cambodian border.

who had succeeded in crossing into Thailand after the fall of the
Pol Pot regime and in the face of a threat of famine. I thought
it unlikely that I would meet anyone whom I had known
previously before war came to Cambodia. By this time I knew
that Tep Im was dead, as were other friends—Colonel Kim Kosal
who was executed as the Khmer Rouge entered Phnom Penh,
and Prince Sisowath Entaravong who was driven out of the
Cambodian capital with his wife, never to be seen again.

Then, as I was walking through the lines of small, fragile huts
made of bamboo and palm-fronds in which the refugees were
housed, with the pervasive smells of human sweat, excrement
and marijuana so characteristic of the camp, I suddenly heard a
voice call out my name. And there, sitting in his tiny, cramped
hut was Ping Ling, someone I had known in happier days in

Phnom Penh. More than an acquaintance but less than a close
friend, Ping Ling was an ethnic Chinese who was part of a circle
of Cambodians in Phnom Penh whom I had first come to know
in 1959. He had been present at bibulous evenings I had spent
with that circle of Cambodians in 1966 on houseboats moored
at Takmau, downstream from the Cambodian capital. These were
evenings enlivened by the presence of copious quantities of Black
Label Johnnie Walker and girls from one of Phnom Penh's many
nightclubs. No greater contrast could exist than finding Ping Ling
in Khao I Dang. Always thin, his flesh now barely covered his
bones and I could count every one of his ribs. But he was
otherwise in good health, and in good heart too, for he had
relatives in Australia and arrangements were already in hand for
him to join them.

An engineer by training, he had an extraordinary tale to tell.
When the Khmer Rouge forced most of Phnom Penh's population
out of the capital at the point of a gun, he had been among
those who had been driven north and east, across the Tonle Sap
River at Kompong Luong, just north of Phnom Penh, towards
Kompong Cham Province. Like so many others he quickly found
that his new masters required him to work ceaselessly from dawn
to dusk planting rice in one of the vast state farms that were so
characteristically, and ultimately so unsuccessfully, part of the
Khmer Rouge's hope of turning the entire country into a highly
productive agricultural unit. How he managed to survive this
period he did not know, for by education and ethnic identity he
was a prime target for death. This was a time when to be a
prosperous Chinese or to possess education was to be at terrible
risk. And so, for two months, he laboured in the fields, quite
literally keeping his head down, hiding his hands which until
then had not been roughened by manual work from those who
now had the power of life or death over him.

Then, in a fashion that still puzzled him as he told his story,
he was suddenly plucked from his work unit as someone who
had been identified as an engineer and who could provide the
expertise the Khmer Rouge leadership in Phnom Penh required
in order to keep the city functioning. It was one thing to clear
the city of most of its inhabitants, another to ensure that
electricity generators worked, that refrigeration was available, and

that a basic pool of vehicles was there for the use of the Khmer Rouge leadership.

He had been constantly afraid, Ping Ling told me, for he could never stop thinking of the consequences of failing to ensure that the machinery which he tended continued to work. Surely, I asked him, he must have faced problems being asked to work on machinery with which he was not familiar? This, indeed, was the case, he said, but he was fortunate in the origin of the machinery he had to deal with. He was familiar with items from the United States and France, and in the case of machinery from the Soviet Union or China he usually found that it was simple in its mechanical conception. Although he experienced some bad moments—many more than he cared to remember—he was always able to succeed in repairing or maintaining the machines to which he was directed. Nevertheless, this period was a nightmare that had lasted three years. He had not personally seen people killed after the early weeks of the exodus from Phnom Penh, but he was aware of people vanishing from the barrack-like accommodation he had shared in the capital. They would be present in the morning, but fail to return in the evening. His guards always spoke of these people having been sent 'to attend a seminar'.

The vast and terrible experience of which Ping Ling was a tiny part still defies complete understanding. Analysts can provide a range of answers as to why a group of Cambodians who were fervent followers of what they understood to be Maoist thought presided over the death through execution, forced labour and starvation of up to two million of their compatriots. Disgust at the corruption of Sihanouk's regime and its successor under Lon Nol certainly was important, as was fear their control over Cambodia might suddenly be wrested from the Khmer Rouge by 'counter-revolutionary forces'. For the followers drawn from the lowest and most impoverished levels of Cambodian society, the opportunity to lord it over those who had once considered themselves their betters also played a part. But ultimately the enormity of the leaders' policies defeats rational analysis. To talk to former Khmer Rouge soldiers, as I did in 1980 in the Sa Keo refugee camp not far from the Thai border with Cambodia, did little to resolve one's bafflement. Young men barely out of their teens would speak with blank faces about their part in executions, without remorse for what they clearly saw as a routine duty.

There should no mistake about who were the victims of the Pol Pot regime. Contrary to the views offered by Western sympathisers while the regime was still in power between 1975 and early 1979—and even more shockingly after Pol Pot's regime had been overturned—the Cambodians who suffered were not 'only' members of the Phnom Penh bourgeoisie. Those linked to the former Lon Nol regime or classified as 'educated' may have been among the more prominent early victims, but before the Vietnamese finally drove the Khmer Rouge out of Phnom Penh in January 1979 the reign of terror that had lasted nearly four years had become quite classless in its choice of who should die, as Pol Pot held up the ancient glory of the Angkorian empire as a model for what the Cambodian people could achieve.

Perhaps easier to understand, or at least to describe, was the city the Khmer Rouge left behind when they were forced from Phnom Penh. It had never quite become the 'phantom city returning little by little to the forest' that Father François Ponchaud conjured up in his important book, *Cambodia: Year Zero*, which provided one of the first accounts of what was happening in Pol Pot's Cambodia for readers in the Western world. But Phnom Penh as the Khmer Rouge left it was a changed place indeed from how it had been while Cambodia was still at peace. I saw it in 1981, twenty months after the fall of the Pol Pot regime. In January 1979, he and his closest associates had hurriedly fled the city as Vietnamese troops moved swiftly up Highway 1 from Neak Luong and across the Mekong from the positions they had taken on the river's left bank.

Despite the population's having rapidly increased in size, from perhaps twenty thousand at the time of the Vietnamese invasion in 1979 to around 300 000 when I made my visit, much of the city was still uninhabited. Some buildings were simply shells, their charred interiors showing that they had been destroyed by fire. This was the case with the building that had once been the Hôtel Raja. Other buildings still showed evidence of the use the Khmer Rouge had made of them. The building that had housed the Cambodian Archives, in which I had spent so many hot, sweaty hours in 1966, had been used as a pig sty. The records that remained were in terrible disarray, and it was clear that others had been destroyed. Still others lay rotting in the rain of the wet season. Elsewhere in the city whole blocks of buildings, houses and apartments remained empty, for reasons that no one seemed able or ready to explain.

Many of the buildings that were occupied sheltered squatters living in unrelieved squalor, lacking power or piped water, and subsisting on diets that left thousands of children suffering from malnutrition. The building on the Boulevard Norodom that had once been the Australian Embassy chancery was sheltering ten families, and a pig was tethered in the driveway where I had once parked my car. Like so many others, these squatters had moved into Phnom Penh from the countryside to a life that for them was better than the dangers still to be found in the countryside. These dangers included armed clashes between Vietnamese troops protecting the interests of their newly installed protégé government and the still determined forces of the defeated Khmer Rouge. Even more dangerous were the ubiquitous land mines which then as now wreaked a regular toll of life and limb. Near the centre of the city whole streets were lined with abandoned cars, some heaped one upon the other. The National Bank building had been partially destroyed by explosives as part of Pol Pot's rejection of Western capitalism, and in the gutters banknotes from the Lon Nol regime, which had been defeated six years before, still blew about in defiance of the extremes of Phnom Penh's wet and dry seasons.

The royal palace and the Silver Pagoda by the river had remarkably escaped destruction. So too had the National Museum. No one has explained why this should have been so, since both in the capital and in the provinces the Khmer Rouge had deliberately destroyed or vandalised Buddhist pagodas without concern for religion or history. Perhaps most striking of all, for it took a moment for me to realise what had happened, Catholic churches, including the cathedral near the main railway station, had simply disappeared. Not a stone remained of the cathedral, nor of the major church in the former Chinese quarter of the city which had been sited in Decko Damdin Street opposite the apartment block where I had lived in 1959. In their place coconut palms had been planted amid the scruffy patches of grass and bare ground where the cathedral and the church had once stood. And as if to offer a final comment on the knowledge I had already gained some years before of Monsignor Tep Im's death, the Eglise Hoalong had been demolished also.

Seeing all this, I found myself thinking of something Tep Im had told me at one of our first meetings in 1966. Despite the fact that the small flock to which he ministered were ethnic Cambodians, the Catholic Church was viewed by many, probably most, of his countrymen as an irrevocably foreign institution. In fact, it was known colloquially as the *sasana barang*, the religion of the foreigners. In their desire to be rid all foreign influences from the start of their rule, the abolition of the visible symbols of the Catholic religion had led to the Khmer Rouge's total removal of these churches.

Only a short distance from the capital the task of identifying and exhuming mass grave sites was going on. At Choeung Ek, the 'killing fields' for prisoners who had been held in Tuol Sleng, located about fifteen kilometres southwest of Phnom Penh, some eighty grave sites had been opened up and between three and

The terrible legacy of the Pol Pot regime was evident in the many thousands of skulls and bones exhumed after the defeat of the Khmer Rouge regime in 1979. This mass grave is at Choeung Ek near Phnom Penh.

four thousand bodies exhumed. There were still fifty more graves to be tackled at this one location. The skulls of the exhumed skeletons lay row upon row near the now empty graves, some with still rotting cloth wound around their eye sockets. Whole groups of skulls showed that the victims had been battered to death, their craniums split like walnuts. The smell of decay and corruption hung over the site and I knew that when I wrote up my diary the next morning I would not have adequate words to match what I had seen. What, after all, does one say after looking at the two hundredth, or two thousandth, shattered skull? In the event, I could do little more than write some inadequate words about 'the banality of death'.

There were other tragedies along the Lower Mekong, in Laos and in Vietnam, but nothing comparable to what occurred in Cambodia. The coming to power of a communist government in Laos in 1975 had never threatened the religious monuments of Vientiane or Luang Prabang, or of the major river towns in the south of the country such as Savannakhet and Pakse. For a time an effort was made to discourage Buddhism, so the teaching of religion in primary schools was banned, as was the traditional giving of alms in the form of food to monks each morning. But, whatever else they could change, the Lao communist leaders could not do away with the deep commitment of the population to Buddhism. Less than two years after the ban on alms-giving was instituted the decision was reversed. And at no stage was there an attempt to ban attendance at the myriad Buddhist pagodas throughout the country.

The policy of condemning tens of thousands to re-education, which has already been mentioned, was a harsh measure. This was certainly the case for the former colonel whom I met in Pakse in 1997 and whose re-education lasted from 1975 until 1988. For some the experience was less harsh, though quite how to characterise the forced relocation of Vientiane's bar girls and prostitutes on an island in the Mekong so that they could learn useful domestic arts is hard to know. The greatest symbolic break with the past in the early years after the communist victory—a break that has concerned and intrigued Western observers for two decades—involved the abolition of the Lao monarchy and the subsequent disappearance of the king and other members of the royal family after 1975. If today the broad outline of events is clear, there are still unanswered questions about this issue.

As the war in Laos drew to a close, the Lao king remained in the peaceful surroundings of his palace by the Mekong in Luang Prabang. Savang Vathanna had inherited the throne in 1959, but he had never been crowned. Usually diffident in manner, he could be forceful on occasion, such as when he told Sihanouk in 1961 that he was Laos's 'Public Enemy Number One'; the Lao king delivered himself of this condemnation after the Cambodian leader had gratuitously offered his own plans for a settlement of the Lao civil war. Savang Vathanna was happiest when tending the fruit trees in his riverside orchard at Pak Xuang, not far from his palace. When, at the end of the long drawn out war in Laos, it became clear that he had no real role to play in the new administration that the communists established in 1975 he abdicated his throne.

His hopes of spending the rest of his life in peaceful obscurity at his orchard were quickly dashed as the country's new leadership ordered him out of the Luang Prabang palace but forbade him to go to Pak Xuang. Until 1977 he remained in a private house in the royal city, not far from Wat Xieng Thong, the grandest of Luang Prabang's many Buddhist pagodas. Then, in the wake of fears that the Thai military, in concert with the CIA and disaffected groups within Laos, were planning to incite a rebellion against the communist leadership, Savang Vathanna, his son the former crown prince, and other members of the royal family were hurriedly removed from Luang Prabang to enforced internal exile in Sam Neua Province in the northeast of Laos, not far from the country's border with Vietnam. There, in circumstances that are still uncertain, the king, his queen and his son all died.

Christopher Kremmer, in his book *Stalking the Elephant Kings*, has probably gone as far as anyone will ever be able to in piecing together an account of the royal family's last days in the harsh conditions to which they were subjected. Their end does not seem to have been dramatic, if Kremmer's informants are correct in what they told him. The crown prince was the first to die, of dysentery. His death was followed by those of his parents, first the queen and then his father some months later. Poor diet, malaria and despair all probably played their part in the case of

the older pair. For whatever reason, the communist leadership of
Laos has never officially acknowledged these deaths, this despite
the fact that no less a person than Kaysone Phomvihane, the
Secretary-General of the Lao Communist Party, admitted in Paris
in 1989 that the king and queen were dead, the king of malaria
in 1984, the queen at an unspecified time from 'natural causes'.

Saigon, now renamed Ho Chi Minh City, emerged in the years
immediately after the end of the Vietnam War with remarkably little physical change. The colonial-era buildings that gave
the place its distinctive character still stood in the centre of the
city untouched by anything like the madness that had occurred
in Phnom Penh. In 1981 what was immediately apparent to a
visitor who had known the city before was the absence of the
chaotic traffic of yesteryear in this early period of communist
rule. It was not hard to see other changes, from the police drafted
down from the north in their ill-fitting uniforms, to the drabness
of daily dress, particularly among the women on the street. Except
on Sunday, when fashion consciousness triumphed over communist austerity, or in private homes, there were almost no women
to be seen wearing the distinctive and graceful *ao dai*.

Yet beneath the clear signs that this was a city being ruled by
a very different government, it was not hard to detect remnants
of attitudes that harked back to the recent pre-communist past.
Perhaps the most obvious, one that has been remarked on by many
who visited at this time, was the determination of the city's
inhabitants to continue calling it Saigon. In doing so they
enshrined the feeling of distinctiveness that cut across political
boundaries. It was not surprising that Madame Nguyen Phuoc
Dai, the former South Vietnamese lawyer, senator and renowned
owner of the Bibliothèque Restaurant, insisted that the city's name
was Saigon. In a city where standards of service and cuisine had
sharply declined, a visit to Madame Dai's was almost de rigueur in
the early 1980s, not least because she was ready to give free rein
to her feelings about rule from the north. But to hear the city
called Saigon by Dr Duong Quyen Hoa was another matter.

Dr Hoa had been the Minister for Health in the southern
Provisional Revolutionary Government while the Vietnam War
still raged. A pediatrics specialist, she had gone into the local

maquis in 1968. When I met her in 1981 in a house full of beautiful antique furniture and porcelain, she consistently spoke of the city as Saigon and she was dressed in an *ao dai* of the finest silk. But more significantly, she was vehement in her criticism of the way in which the government in Hanoi was treating those who had fought on its behalf in the south. 'We have been recolonised by the north,' she told me. The members of the Provisional Revolutionary Government had been discarded by a northern-dominated regime which formulated plans for Saigon, and southern Vietnam generally, with little if any regard for local conditions. As for Vietnam's Soviet friends, Dr Hoa said that like most southerners, indeed like most Vietnamese, she tolerated them for the moment because they were needed. But they too would only be transients on the Vietnamese stage.

Whatever Dr Hoa's feelings about Hanoi's errors, she was clearly not suffering materially, and I felt that I gained a more representative assessment of life in Saigon from Phuong, a Vietnamese who had studied in Australia and now worked for the city government, earning what was then the equivalent of US$14 a month. He confirmed the tensions between northerners and southerners, a situation marked by the northerners' arrogance and their doubts about the extent of revolutionary zeal among Saigon's population. With a wry smile, Phuong observed that the northerners had good reason to have these doubts, not least because the population of greater Saigon, including Cholon, still counted upwards of 800 000 ethnic Chinese who had never identified their interests with any state, communist or otherwise. Phuong's comment rang true, for only the week before in Hanoi the Vietnamese Foreign Minister, Nguyen Co Thach, had told me the government was going to 'break' Chinese control of commerce in the south. They did not do so then, and nearly twenty years later they still have not done so. The Chinese merchants are still there, and Thach is dead.

As for Saigon's ethnic Vietnamese population, Phuong continued, of course there was dissatisfaction. You did not have to have held an important position in the pre-liberation government to dislike many of the changes that had taken place. But to think this was a sign that dissatisfaction would be translated into any serious action was absurd. Southerners, in any event, loved to grumble, and too many foreign journalists who were now visiting

Saigon were ready to look at life in the city and wonder how 'nice people' like him could put up with the conditions that existed, and which were obviously less attractive than what could be found in the West. So much was unsatisfactory, he noted wryly, but it was far from insupportable. And, he concluded rather tentatively, even someone as apolitical as he was found the fact that the whole of Vietnam was now governed by a Vietnamese regime was important.

Two memories of this visit stand out for the way in which they summon up images of the 'old Saigon'. They come from a Sunday when the streets were suddenly transformed by the appearance of women in their *ao dai*, in great contrast to the drab clothes of the workaday week. In the square by the colonial rococo post office and the Catholic cathedral a professional photographer plied his trade. As a thirtyish woman in her best *ao dai* posed before him, a group of Russian sailors came into the square and surrounded her, wanting to be photographed with her. Young and for the moment carefree, they reminded me of the groups of other young men, Americans who, in the early 1960s before Saigon lost most of its charm, waited to be photographed in similar fashion.

Then, as evening fell, I ventured down to the Majestic Hotel, the hotel in which I had stayed more than twenty years before on my way to Phnom Penh. It had been renamed the Cuu Long Hotel, the 'Nine Dragons', its new name coming from the words used by the Vietnamese for the Mekong where it flows through the delta. The street in which it stood had changed its name too. What Pierre Billotey had known as the rue Catinat, and which I had encountered as 'Freedom Street' in 1959, had become 'General Uprising Street'. It was clearly not a name that held much meaning for the young men and women who had gathered in the piano bar to hear an accomplished performer play a medley of tunes from the thirties and forties. With one's eyes half closed the scene could have come from an old movie, set in some French colonial possession, perhaps with Bogart and Bergman as the stars. It would be nice to record that the pianist played 'As Time Goes By'. But although this was not so, he did play 'September Song'.

III

Present Imperfect, Future Uncertain

13

The Mekong at Peace:
Dams, Plans and
Controversies I

. . . since Manwan was completed . . . misinformation has been developed as an art form, often amounting to the irresponsible reporting of gross inaccuracies.

> *E. C. Chapman and He Daming, writing about Chinese dams on the*
> *Mekong in 1996*

The rivers are full of a prodigious quantity of fish of different kinds . . .

> *Father Giovanni Filippo de Marini, describing the Mekong and its*
> *tributaries in* Histoire nouvelle et curieuse des Royaumes du
> Tunquin et du Laos, *Paris, 1666*

With only minor respite in the mid-1950s, conflict raged around the Lower Mekong from the period almost immediately after the Second World War until 1975. Hostilities were reignited in the latter part of 1977. But this time the increasingly bloody clashes, instead of pitting Southeast Asians against an external 'imperialist' enemy, were taking place between Cambodia and Vietnam, supposed fraternal allies. For all their apparent identity of purpose against common enemies during the Second Indochina War, the Pol Pot regime and the triumphant Vietnamese government in Hanoi rapidly came into conflict once that war ended. Central to the conflict was the claim Pol Pot's regime made to the southern area of Vietnam around the Mekong Delta that had once formed part of the ancient Cambodian empire.

For Cambodians of all political persuasions this region is still known as Kampuchea Krom or 'Lower Cambodia'.

After what can only be described as insane Cambodian prov-ocations, given the disproportionate size of the adversaries, and involving attacks of savage brutality on Vietnamese villagers, Vietnam finally reacted. It began its invasion of Cambodia on Christmas Day 1978 and by early January 1979 had driven the Pol Pot regime out of Phnom Penh. And still there was no true peace in Cambodia as forces backed by Thailand and the United States, and including the troops of the Khmer Rouge as their most important element, sought to remove the occupying Vietnamese and the government they had installed in Phnom Penh. It was these generally low level, but no less deadly, continuing hostilities in Cambodia that became the fundamental impediment to any hopes that were held of implementing a comprehensive plan for mainland Southeast Asia's economic development. By the late 1980s, there was a growing hope that plans for major development work linked to the Mekong could once more be realistically considered. With Cambodia's political problems resolved, however imperfectly, in the early 1990s, the way seemed open to pursue these plans and the economic possibilities that were seen as associated with the river and the regions surrounding it.

After the years between 1978 and 1994 when the original Mekong Committee established in 1957 had existed largely in an interim capacity, a new body came into being in April 1995: the Mekong River Commission, with Cambodia, Laos, Thailand and Vietnam as its members. Burma, consistent with its pattern of holding the outside world at bay, chose not to join the Commission. Nor, much more importantly, did China join. In this latter case, it was clear then as now that China had no intention of allowing its own plans for the Mekong to be affected by the interests of other riparian states. By the time the Mekong Commission had come into being, there were other players already actively involved in plans for the river and the region surrounding it. Increasingly, there was discussion of the 'Greater Mekong Sub-Region', as the World Bank, the Asian Development Bank, individual countries and non-governmental organisations (NGOs) vied to make their contribution to transforming the landscape of an area that had been neglected for so long. To read of developments in progress or planned in relation to the Mekong and its surroundings nowadays is to find oneself negotiating a thicket of organisations and their acronyms. To look at one newsletter of the Mekong River Commission (MRC) alone is to encounter references to EIAs, WUP, GEF, GWP, NMCs and the GMA—a listing that is not exhaustive. Spelling the terms out we have: Environmental Impact Assessments; Water Utilisation Program; Global Environment Facility; Global Environment Water Utilisation Program Project; National Mekong Committees; Greater Mekong Area.

Well before this surge of activity in the 1990s, change of a fundamental kind had been taking place along the course of the river in China, with some of this change the subject of great controversy. Because of the greater opportunity of access to the countries of the Lower Mekong, even allowing for the problems that had beset Cambodia, knowledge of what had been happening in those countries was widespread. Moreover, and in great contrast to China, no major works had taken place on the lower reaches of the Mekong after it flows out of China. Certainly, so far as knowledge of developments occurring along the river is concerned, some areas were either difficult or impossible of access. This was the case, for instance, with the region close to the important temple complex of Wat Phu in southern Laos, described in an earlier chapter. Access to Wat Phu was impossible until the end of the 1980s. And in Cambodia the northeastern river towns of Kratie and Stung Treng remained largely inaccessible until the United Nations transitional administration was in place in the early 1990s. But even when Laos was closed to foreign visitors, large sections of the Mekong where it forms the border between Laos and Thailand could be observed from the right (Thai) bank. The situation had surreal characteristics. In the mid-1980s it was possible to stand and look across the Mekong to the Lao side of the river from locations such as Chiang Saen and Chiang Khong and see absolutely no sign of human activity. Fearful of foreign interference, the secretive Lao authorities had simply moved the population of river towns such as Huay Xai to interior locations, leaving only empty buildings to be observed from the opposite bank of the river.

The situation was very different in China, including in the regions of Tibet lying alongside the uppermost sections of the Mekong. Reliable information about developments along the 1600 kilometres of the Mekong's course where it flows through eastern Tibet is difficult to obtain, and has been ever since the Chinese invasion of 1950. Apart from the rugged and sometimes inaccessible terrain of the high gorges through which the Mekong runs, there is the Chinese government's concern to restrict access to what are still regarded as sensitive areas in this far from fully integrated autonomous region. Nevertheless, the restricted information that is available is not reassuring. There are apparently reliable reports of large-scale deforestation in eastern Tibet, as hillsides have been stripped of timber which is then floated down the Mekong to Yunnan. The wild nature of the river in this region means that there is considerable wastage of logs which become waterlogged or are badly damaged as the force of the water throws them against rocky obstacles. More importantly, this deforestation is leading to major erosion along the river's course, a development that is ultimately of concern to all downstream locations along the Mekong. Exiled Tibetan groups led by the Dalai Lama have called for a complete rethinking of the way in which management of the Mekong in its upper reaches might be approached, but only the most convinced of optimists would place much hope in this approach ever being implemented.

It is only since the mid-1980s that outsiders have been able to gather information about developments in the extreme south of Yunnan Province, in the area around Jinghong, the town that marked the point where the French explorers finally turned away from the river in 1867 to travel northwards into China. When Lagrée's party reached Jinghong they were aware that they were passing through the Sip Song Panna, the collection of small principalities that still enjoyed a measure of independence from their more powerful neighbours. With China in control of this region from the early twentieth century, the name of the region has been sinicised to become Xishuangbanna. Just as much of Tibet has not been open to foreign visitors until recently, so the Xishuangbanna was off-limits until the mid-1980s. Largely neglected until the Communist Revolution of 1949, this area of Yunnan has been steadily incorporated into Peking's plans to develop its links with the countries joining its southern border. In accordance with a traditional concern to ensure that its interests were understood and respected by the countries on its periphery, China saw the expansion of trade and commercial links with Laos, Thailand and Burma as being of great importance. And southern Yunnan was vital to this vision, since road links could be constructed from this province into the neighbouring states.

What this meant for Jinghong was the transformation of a small, isolated town with a largely non-Han population into a Chinese city. Steadily, particularly since the mid-1970s, the Dai minority people of Jinghong—close linguistic relatives of the Thai and Lao—have been submerged beneath an influx of Han Chinese. Bluntly functional Chinese architecture has replaced the traditional wooden buildings of the Dai people, buildings with their characteristic peacock decorations that would have looked perfectly at home in the villages of northern Thailand or of Laos. And as early as 1960 a bridge was built across the Mekong at Jinghong to aid communication with regions further south. By the 1990s Jinghong was acquiring an identity as a holiday town for Han Chinese who came to observe the 'quaint' dress and customs of the Dai at 'cultural shows', eat local delicacies and sing in karaoke bars.

The effects of this tourist invasion and the strong elements of cultural chauvinism that are involved are stories in themselves to be told later, but in terms of changes to the Mekong the most notable development since the 1980s has been the commencement of a long-term program of dam building along the river in Yunnan Province. At first glance it may seem surprising that this program has not received anything like the attention that has been paid to the Three Gorges Dam project on the Yangtze River. Yet from various points of view this is, perhaps, not too difficult to understand. In contrast to the Yangtze the Mekong, despite its great size, is a much less well-known river. Flowing through or past no fewer than six countries, the interruptions to its course made by rapids and cascades have meant that it has never played the role of being a unifying river in one country, as is the case with the Yangtze, or indeed the Nile in Egypt. And notwithstanding optimistic Chinese plans to navigate the river during its high water months as far south as Vientiane, it has never been a major route for transport. The record of failures and disappointments as the French attempted to use the river for uninterrupted navigation has already been noted. In China itself, and with the exception of Jinghong—a relatively minor settlement by any standard—there are no towns of consequence along the Mekong's upper course.

The fact that the Mekong still remains poorly known by comparison with other great rivers does not mean there is no concern about China's dam-building program. This concern is felt both by foreign environmentalists and by the governments of countries downstream from China who wonder about the long-term effects of the program. In the case of the environmentalists, and as the experience of the Three Gorges project has shown, China has an almost infinite capacity to disregard external criticism, particularly non-governmental criticism, that does not suit its interests. As for the governments, Laos, Thailand, Cambodia and Vietnam have been notably cautious in making public their concerns about Chinese actions and what these might mean for the future health of the Mekong. For all of them, China is perceived as an impossibly large presence whose power is such that to question its actions and motives is to risk unquantifiable damage. As a country that can only be judged by its actions, there seems no way that its Southeast Asian neighbours can influence a program on which it has embarked if China chooses to act contrary to their perceived interests. The water politics involved here bring into sharp relief the lack of parity that exists between China and the countries of the Lower Mekong, a situation perhaps even more striking than other cases of a lack of parity throughout the world. If we cast the issue in terms of population size alone, Vietnam and Thailand, the two largest of the downstream countries, each have a population less than one-tenth the size of China's.

China began its dam-building program on the Mekong in 1984 at Manwan, a location a little more than a hundred kilometres south of the city of Dali in western Yunnan Province. Completed in 1993, the Manwan Dam is a high wall dam, with a waterhead level of ninety-nine metres, constructed to take advantage of the gorges through which the Mekong flows for most of its course through Yunnan. Manwan's primary purpose is to provide hydro-electric power for the rapidly growing industrial developments in the area around Kunming, Yunnan

Province's capital. And in this regard it has been very successful, with a capacity to generate 1500 megawatts. Major power shortages in Yunnan have largely been overcome since Manwan's generators came on line. As is inevitable with such large-scale constructions, there were human costs, even in an area that is by Chinese standards lightly settled. Flooding some 24 square kilometres, the dam displaced the inhabitants of 96 villages to a total of perhaps 25 000 people, most of whom were members of minority groups rather than Han Chinese.

Construction of a second dam at Dachaoshan, downriver from Manwan, began in 1996, and it is expected that two more dams will be under construction before 2010. One will be located a little upstream from Jinghong, while the other, at Xiaowan, upstream from Manwan, is to be an immense reservoir with an active storage capacity of 990 million cubic metres and a waterhead of 248 metres. Some sense of the latter's size is gained from the estimate that its pond will stretch back 169 kilometres from the dam wall. Beyond that date a further three dams are under consideration; it is possible that as many as another seven or eight might eventually be constructed on the Mekong where it runs through China.

While the principal purpose of these Chinese dams is to provide hydro power for use in Yunnan and nearby provinces, and possibly for eventual external markets in Laos, Thailand and Burma, other benefits are claimed for them. In particular the 'cascade' of dams will, it is said, be valuable in 'evening out' the flow of the Mekong, so that it will no longer fluctuate so dramatically between high and low water levels according to the seasons. Although Manwan, and Dachaoshan and Jinghong when built, will, according to the Chinese, have a negligible effect on the amount of water flowing down the Mekong, the completion of the massive dam at Xiaowan will greatly increase the amount that will flow down during the dry season. Moreover, Chinese sources point out, of the water that flows down the Mekong no more than 20 per cent (sometimes the figure cited is 16 per cent) comes from China. While this is correct, it is a prime example of the problems associated with raw statistics. Only 20 per cent of the *total* volume of the water that flows down the Mekong comes from China, but at the Lao capital of Vientiane, well downstream from China's border, the percentage is very different.

The Upper Mekong in Yunnan Province, showing the location of Chinese dams already built, under construction or planned.

For at Vientiane it is still the case that about 60 per cent of the water in the Mekong has its origins in China. And there is growing concern in Laos that, whether attributable to the Chinese dam-building program or not, dry season water levels have been lower in recent years than was the case two or three decades ago. In the case of the already completed dam at Manwan, there is clear evidence that there were major interruptions to water flow in the course of the dam's construction, at one time causing the cancellation of an important water festival in Luang Prabang.

The key questions raised by the Chinese dam-building program are obvious enough. Will the alterations to the Mekong's flow resulting from the dams have a serious effect on the fish catches in the regions of the river downstream from China? And, linked to this concern, will the reduced wet season flow of the Mekong, and its converse, an increased flow in the dry season, have a negative impact on the functioning of Cambodia's Great Lake as a prime breeding ground for the fish that make up such a large proportion of that country's protein intake? Most broadly of all, what sort of river could the Mekong become if the reassuring answers given by the proponents of China's dam-building program prove not to be correct? For at present much of the dry season agriculture of subsistence communities living along the Mekong depends on horticultural planting along the river's banks as the waters subside at the end of the wet season.

The questions may be straightforward, but the answers, and there are many and often contradictory answers, most certainly are not. There is no doubt that some of the suggestions made about the effects already being sustained because of the construction of the dam at Manwan are, as the Australian geographer Ted Chapman has stated, 'gross inaccuracies'. Yet even if the construction of the Manwan Dam has not so far had all, or even any, of the effects critics ascribe to it, negative changes are already occurring along the course of the Mekong and these cannot be ignored. Reports, many of them anecdotal, point to declining fish catches along much of the river, from the areas where the Mekong flows below the border between China and Laos down to the Mekong Delta. In relation to some species there is simply no doubt that a long-term decline in numbers has occurred and that it began well before construction of the first Chinese dam, as a result of overfishing. The giant freshwater catfish (*Pangasianodon gigas*), which can weigh up to 300 kilograms, is caught increasingly rarely in Laos and Thailand, and may have reached a point where it will be fished out in a matter of years. The same fate is all too prospectively possible for the freshwater dolphins (Irrawaddy dolphins), whose habitat above and below the Khone Falls has rendered them particularly vulnerable to the lawless elements that have been living in these areas over the past two decades. Today there are perhaps two hundred of the dolphins left, many of their number having been killed by high-powered rifles or by dynamite, both for 'sport' and for the oil that can be extracted from their carcasses, or as the result of gill net fishing.

These two species have attracted attention because of their size and exotic character, and their now precarious prospects for survival. Longer term, the fisheries of the Mekong and its tributaries are dependent on species which are less dramatic in size but which are even more essential for the diet of the populations in the region. It has been estimated that the value of the fish catch in the Lower Mekong Basin is no less than US$800 million annually and that in terms of weight the catch amounts to around one million tonnes per year. Despite the efforts that have been made, and continue to be made, through programs supported by the Mekong River Commission and the Asian Development Bank, there is still much that is not known about the fish that are taken from the Mekong and the tributaries that flow into it.

Experts have calculated that there are no fewer than 1200 different indigenous species of fish in the Mekong, but knowledge of the extent to which some are migratory and others are not is still being accumulated. What we do know is that where tributaries of the Mekong have been dammed, as is the case with the Pak Mun Dam on the Mun River near Ubon in Thailand, fish catches have declined dramatically and possibly irrevocably. And while the causes may be an issue for dispute, the fishermen of the Mekong Delta have no doubt that they are now catching smaller numbers than once was the case. They blame fertiliser run-off, increased irrigation drawing water from the river, and rising salination as tidal effects reach further up the delta from the South China Sea. In this respect, the fact that silt is no longer adding to the extension of the delta's coastline, as it once did, is suggestive of quite serious changes to the river's ecology. But these fishermen also ask whether there might be other factors involved that are yet to be identified.

Against this background, one has to look with some scepticism at a Mekong River Commission pronouncement in July 1998 that 'Yes, The Fish Is Still There'.

This is not how Cambodia's *prahok* fishermen see the situation. *Prahok* is a fermented fish condiment that is as essential to Cambodian cuisine as the better known *nuoc mam* is to the cooking of Vietnam. Near to Phnom Penh it is made from the young fish that surge down the Tonle Sap River from the Great Lake early in the dry season. Over the last few years the number of fish caught by *prahok* fishermen has declined sharply. The causes for this decline are many, and certainly include the more frequent use of fine mesh nets further up the river and in the Great Lake itself. But the fishermen are also convinced that other factors are involved, including the deforestation of the areas around the lake that are subject to flooding at high water for it was in these flooded forests that much of the annual fish-breeding cycle took place. At the same time, periods of drought in the last years of the 1990s have contributed to lower water levels in the Mekong, and this too has adversely affected fish breeding.

The same complaints about lower catches can be heard in the fishing villages of the Great Lake itself, both those on the margins of the lake and those that float on it. At first glance the complaints seem puzzling, for to wander through these rough and ready settlements with their populations a mix of Cambodians, Chinese and Vietnamese, and with their distinctly frontier character, is to be constantly aware of fish. All activity seems to revolve about them. Large fish are taken from boats to be thrown on great blocks of ice before being sent to market. From other boats piles of small fish are shovelled into large baskets before being dumped into trucks for later processing into *prahok*. But, the fishermen say, the pervasive sight and smell of fish is misleading. For whatever reason, catches are declining. Or, as one fishermen put it to me as I stood by the Great Lake in 1998, how much longer would Cambodians be able to quote their old proverb, 'Wherever there's water there's fish'?

To counter the perception of negative future developments, the Chinese reiterate that only 16–20 per cent of the Mekong's volume comes from China, so that it would be wrong to be alarmist about the dams they are building. Moreover, they say, they will be carrying out research into the effects of the dams both above and below the Chinese border with Laos in order to determine what, if any, adverse effects might result from their actions. In the latter case, research will involve representatives from the downstream countries as well as Chinese experts. These studies are due to be completed by 2000. It is obvious, but no less essential, to note that this research will be finished long after the Manwan Dam was completed in 1993 and with the Dachaoshan Dam approaching completion.

Official expressions of concern about the possible impact of the Chinese dams by representatives of the downstream countries have been muted, but even on first meeting senior Lao and Cambodian officials are ready to speak in worried terms about China's actions. Although careful not to accuse the Chinese of bad faith when I met him in Vientiane in 1998, Dr Kithong Vongsay, the Chairman of the Lao National Mekong Committee, told me of the worries he and his colleagues had about the dams. He knew that the Chinese were insisting that the dams would not have a damaging effect on downstream countries through which the Mekong flows, but he still had not seen convincing evidence that this would be the case. And why, he asked, had China chosen not to become a member of the Mekong River Commission? Chinese officials had told him that they still had to study the agreement concluded between Cambodia, Laos, Thailand and Vietnam, but they had already had several years to do that. All in all, the question of what the building of dams in China might do to the lower reaches of the Mekong was a matter for concern and he well understood why his counterparts in Cambodia and Vietnam held deep concerns for the possibility that the dams might have long-term and major negative effects on fish catches.

As Dr Kithong outlined his scepticism about the Chinese dams, I sensed that he spoke more in sorrow than in anger. But when he came to talk of another Chinese proposal there was no doubting his passionate feelings. The Chinese, he said, had repeatedly urged upon the Lao government the desirability of blasting a channel along the Mekong's course that would allow sizeable boats to travel from Yunnan Province down to Vientiane throughout the year. This was something that he vehemently opposed. The fact that the Chinese had already undertaken river clearing on the Mekong north of Laos's border with China was a matter of concern in itself. Clearing away rocks and sandbars could lead to increased river flow and with it erosion, but to contemplate blasting a channel through the sections of the Mekong that ran through the rugged gorges between Ban Huay Xai in the north and Vientiane in the south was simply unthinkable. There was no telling what such a plan would mean for pollution or for fish catches, he said. With vivid memories of travelling through the natural grandeur of the Mekong as it runs between the gorges above Luang Prabang, I could only reflect on another of the costs of such a plan. If tourism is to continue as one of Laos's important ways of earning foreign exchange, the prospect of a radical alteration to the Mekong and its surroundings as the result of blasting a navigation channel can only be deeply disturbing.

The concerns I heard expressed in Vientiane about China's dams were echoed in Phnom Penh by Dr Mak Moreth, the Minister for the Environment, when I travelled on from Laos to Cambodia. He began his comments by stressing that he was not anti-Chinese, but went on to express deep concern about the dams in Yunnan *and* plans under discussion for possible dams on the Mekong in Cambodia itself. It was all very well for the Chinese to enumerate what they claimed were the benefits that would result from their dam-building program—the greening of China, increasing dry season flow and the minimising of sediment—but this was a list seen from a Chinese point of view. The greening of China was a Chinese not a Southeast Asian benefit, and sediment discharge both historically and in contemporary terms was a *benefit* to downstream countries, not a negative. Most worryingly of all, the suggestion that the Chinese dams would increase the dry season flow of the Mekong—the 'evening out' of water flow between the wet and dry seasons referred to earlier in this chapter—could well mean a disaster for Cambodia's Great Lake. It has been calculated that during Cambodia's wet season some 60 per cent of the water that brings the lake to its maximum size results from the flood waters that come down the Mekong and then turn north, reversing the flow of the Tonle Sap River. To discount this major contribution to the Great Lake's unique ecosystem is cavalier and worse, he argued.

Mak Moreth's concern for the future of the Great Lake was no surprise, though the strength of his conviction as he outlined his worries were a salutary reminder of just how important this issue is to Cambodians. And, as he emphasised, detailed research knowledge of the lake is still not available. Indeed, in December 1998, the Mekong River Commission's newsletter hailed a month-long hydrographic survey of the lake as 'the first' to be undertaken. This, of course, is not the case, though it is all too typical of the hyperbole that seems to be the common coin of many of the announcements and comments made by bodies whose raison d'être is linked to the Mekong.

Surveys of various kinds have been made over the years, including serious studies undertaken when Cambodia was still under French control before the Second World War. Such studies have provided information on the 700 commercially important fish found in the lake and, through recent aerial photography, confirmation of the decline of woodland around the lake and the continuing increase in the amount of settlement in marginal agricultural areas on the lake's periphery. Both of these trends will have an impact on the most worrying possibility of all—the prospect of an irreversible change in the depth of the lake due to a rapid increase in unwanted sedimentation. Cambodia's King Sihanouk may have been showing his own readiness to indulge in overstatement when he spoke of his worry that in the near future it would be possible to wade across the lake as the result of rapidly falling water levels due to increased sedimentation, but the cause of his concern is real nonetheless. Although much more rigorous scientific research will be needed before firm conclusions can be made about what is happening to the lake, there is no denying the extent to which it is a unique resource that is endangered.

Visiting the towns of the Mekong Delta in Vietnam, it is hard to think that this is a region with major social problems and a range of environmental concerns. To see the markets at My Tho or Can Tho and the bustle on these towns' waterfronts is to marvel at the transformation that nearly twenty-five years of peace have brought about. New buildings have changed the physical appearance of these towns almost beyond recognition from how I saw them while the Vietnam War still raged. But the picture of prevailing prosperity is deceptive. Although the delta produces 40 per cent of Vietnam's agricultural output and is able to export over a million and a half tonnes of rice annually, it is a region that has serious social and environmental problems. Some of these problems are directly linked back to the period of the Second Indochina War. Deliberate deforestation in the Plain of Reeds area to deny its being used by the communist forces has had the long-term result of producing acid soils, so that, during the wet season, water washing over these soils runs into the delta's myriad canals and creeks with negative effects on both agriculture and fishing.

Increasing salinity is another major problem. With an expanding population and increasing drawing off of water for irrigation, as much as one and a half million hectares of the delta, with a population of over five million people, are affected by salinity intrusion. This problem has steadily grown worse with the impact of salination now stretching as far as sixty kilometres upstream from the coastline. These are problems that exist in a region where, despite its agricultural productivity, there is substantial unemployment and a growing incidence of poverty. Even on the basis of the government's figures, more than 15 per cent of the delta's population live in poverty; the real percentage is certainly higher. The social problems of the Mekong Delta that made it such a rich ground for recruits to the Communist Party in earlier decades have still not disappeared.

14

The Mekong at Peace:
Dams, Plans and
Controversies II

Save a fish and kill a baby!

*A mock slogan for environmentalists said to have been suggested by an
irate Lao official in response to protests about Lao plans for dams on the
Mekong's tributaries—possibly apocryphal*

While the future impact of the Chinese dams on the Mekong
itself is a ground for controversy, it is the dams already
built or being planned on the river's tributaries in Laos, Thailand
and Cambodia that have ignited the fiercest environmental
debate. And it is in relation to these tributary dams that Thailand's growing environmentalist movement has become so heavily
involved, not just for dams within Thailand itself but also for
those contemplated for Laos. Citing the arguments involved in
the ongoing debate between those who favour the building of
dams and those who oppose them is easy enough. Reaching a
conclusion about where right and truth lie is frequently a very
different matter.

A starting point for any analysis is a recognition that there is
now a body of evidence that raises serious and fundamental
questions about the desirability of building large dams, particularly, but by no means solely, in underdeveloped countries. By far
the best known advocate of this position is Patrick McCully in
his 1996 book, *Silenced Rivers*. The comprehensive evidence he
and others put forward as opponents of large dams cannot simply
be ignored as the product of unthinking commitment to unrealis-

able environmental goals. It is patently the case that claims for the benefits of large-scale dams have often been grossly overstated. And it is equally true that there have been repeated examples of dams being built that have carried with them high and irreversible social costs. The 'clean' generation of electricity through hydro-electric power, one of the most compelling arguments advanced by the advocates for building big dams, is, to take a vitally important example, a far from straightforward issue. I needn't attempt to rehearse all of McCully's arguments, but he advances convincing evidence that relatively rapid silting of dams can quickly diminish their effectiveness for generating hydro power. And he shows that the issue of combatting 'global warming' is not just a matter of replacing the use of fossil fuels by hydro power, since large dams can create ecological situations in which destroyed wetlands can generate increased carbon dioxide emissions. Perhaps most striking for the non-specialist is the evidence showing that the construction of large dams has almost routinely led to population displacement with attendant major social disruption.

The record of what has happened in the course of and following the construction of large dams in areas away from the Mekong is largely, if not universally, bleak. Even with the questionable figures supplied by the Chinese government, construction of dams in China between 1950 and 1989 is said to have resulted in the displacement of more than 10 million people—McCully cites unofficial figures from a Chinese critic suggesting the true figure could be in excess of 50 million. Other estimates which McCully provides of the numbers who have been forced to relocate because of the construction of large dams include: the Sardar Sarovar project in India, which has resulted in the displacement of 320 000 people; the Tarbela Dam in Pakistan, with a displacement of 96 000 people; and, away from Asia, the Akosombo Dam in Ghana, where 84 000 people were displaced. And it is worth remembering that when, in the 1960s, there were plans to build a dam at Pa Mong on the Mekong above Vientiane, there was a recognition that this could lead to the displacement of no fewer than 250 000 persons living in the projected catchment area. At the time this project was conceived, its proponents appear to have thought that the costs of such a massive relocation of population, with all its attendant social costs, were both necessary and acceptable. The possibility of building a dam at Pa Mong was briefly considered again at the beginning of the 1990s before being rejected.

In terms of the figures just recorded, the numbers who have been displaced from dams built on the Mekong's tributaries, or who are projected to be displaced, seem small indeed. So too do the numbers of those whose livelihood has been or might be affected by dam building. Take the case of the Pak Mun Dam built under the auspices of the Electricity Generating Authority of Thailand (EGAT) and funded by the World Bank. Construction of this dam on the Mun River not far from where it flows into the Mekong, and located near the important Thai provincial centre of Ubon, began in 1991 and was completed in 1994. In the process of building the dam, more than 200 households were displaced, suggesting a total of around 1000 persons who had to move from their established villages. Some argue that the figure for those displaced should be much higher, once those living close to the dam's margins are taken into account. Still, Pak Mun was described in a World Bank report in 1998 as being 'in a class by itself' and as having had a 'satisfactory resettlement outcome'.

A coalition of Thai NGOs vigorously dispute these conclusions. As a result of their interviews with those who have been displaced, the NGOs claim that in most cases the compensation these people received was insufficient to allow them to purchase alternative farming land away from the area flooded by the dam. Even more importantly, the completed Pak Mun Dam has drastically reduced the opportunities for fishing in the Mun River, and so eliminated a food source that was vitally important to those living by it. Claimed to be a 'run of the river' dam—that is, a dam that does not impede the continual flow of water below the dam wall—Pak Mun has not proved to be so in fact. In the dry season water ceases to flow downstream of the dam in anything like the quantities that existed before the dam's construction and sometimes stops altogether. As a result, fish catches have declined sharply both below and above the dam, by as much as 70 per cent. Efforts to overcome the interruption of fish movement caused by the dam through the construction of a fish ladder have been a near complete failure, as local fish have shown a distinct reluctance to emulate the feats of salmon in other parts of the world.

With additional difficulties for displacees in finding work in areas away from their former homes and the impossibility of using the Mun River for water transport below the dam for much of the year, the picture that emerges of the results of the Pak Mun Dam is bleak. The social costs that have been incurred scarcely seem to justify the meagre 136MW of hydro power that the dam generates. Tellingly, and following the protests that the Pak Mun Dam has sparked, the Thai government has stated that it will not build any additional dams for the generation of electricity. In making this decision in 1995, it did so with the knowledge that plans were already in train to acquire additional electricity generated by hydro power elsewhere, from Laos.

There is no doubt where the Lao government stands on the need to build dams that can sell hydro power to Thailand and provide electricity to the country's rural regions. As a desperately poor country—one of the world's poorest, with a per capita annual income of less than US$300—it has few ways to earn foreign exchange. A pointer to the limitations of the Lao economy is the fact that the sale of aircraft overflight rights represents one of the more important components of the country's foreign exchange earnings. Without significant alternative energy sources such as coal, and given Laos's topography with major Mekong tributaries running through mountainous areas, the generation of electricity through hydro power has obvious attractions. Indeed, the best estimates are that tributaries of the Mekong in Laos contribute no less than 60 per cent of the water flowing into the Lower Mekong, providing the country with theoretical potential to generate in excess of 18 000MW. Some indication of the Lao government's commitment to hydro power generation is provided by noting that four projects are currently under construction and a further eleven projects are being assessed for their environmental effects.

Laos has been selling hydro power to Thailand since the 1970s, following the completion of the Nam Ngum Dam which was built with Japanese and American assistance at a site a little to the north of the capital, Vientiane. Much more recently, work was completed on the Theun Hinboun Dam at the end of 1998. This dam in central Laos also has as its primary purpose the sale of electricity to Thailand. Like the Pak Mun Dam in Thailand, Theun Hinboun has come under heavy criticism from environmental groups, and for many of the same reasons. While the Asian Development Bank (ADB) has publicly congratulated itself for 'having backed a winner', and stated that 'there is little for the environmental lobby to criticise in Theun Hinboun', this messsage has been sharply rejected by the dam's critics. They point to complaints from people living downstream of the dam that fish catches have declined by as much as 70 per cent. Agricultural land has been affected both above and below the dam, critics say, while they also claim that fragile ecosystems are now under threat. In response to these criticisms, a Special Review Mission from the ADB visited the areas affected by the dam's construction at the end of 1998. The mission's report acknowledged the validity of some of the complaints directed against Theun Hinboun and made what would appear to be a classic bureaucratic response. Negative impacts from the dam are now to be identified so that compensation and mitigation may be provided. It is difficult not to conclude that this is another case of those who supported the building of the dam having been ready simply to disregard views that did not accord with their own.

It is against this background of deep division between the proponents of dams as an answer to Laos's formidable economic problems and the passionate beliefs of conservationists to the contrary that debate has been joined over the projected Nam Theun 2 Dam. Planned for an area not far distant from the Theun Hinboun Dam, Nam Theun 2 is projected to be on a much larger scale. Whereas Theun Hinboun's generating capacity is put at 210MW, Nam Theun 2, if built, will generate 680MW. As of June 1999 no decision has been reached as to whether the consortium consisting of Australian, French and Thai firms in association with the Lao goverment will, in fact, go ahead. The key to a positive decision lies with the World Bank, and with that body's awareness of past criticism of its support for big dams it has still not indicated that it is ready to provide the guarantee of covering sovereign risk without which commercial banks by and large have been reluctant to provide funding.

A few statistics give a sense of the scale of the Nam Theun 2 project. The dam wall itself would not be particularly large:

44 metres high and 315 metres wide. But the topography of the proposed site of the dam would allow it to deliver water to a power station 350 metres below the dam itself. Nevertheless, despite the relatively small size of the dam head its construction would lead to the flooding of over 450 square kilometres and the displacement of some 5000 villagers, most of them members of ethnic minority groups. This flooding would also affect the adjoining Nakai Nam Theun National Biodiversity Area. Originally projected to cost US$800 million when plans for Nam Theun 2 were first drawn up in 1989, the most recent estimates are for a final cost of US$1.5 billion.

Opposition to Nam Theun 2 has focused on three main issues. For some critics, the very fact that a dam is involved is the essential basis for opposition. These critics draw their support from the long record of negative impacts that large dams have had throughout the world. Other critics argue that there *are* alternatives to relying solely on hydro power for the generation of cheap electricity. One such would be the combining of hydro power with gas turbines. Yet other critics, particularly concerned with the disruptive social costs of dams such as Nam Theun 2, call for approaches that will draw on the strength of local communities to manage their own development. Partly informing this last suggestion is concern that the Lao government is ready to take advantage of building dams to implement its announced policy of resettling all of the country's shifting cultivators in permanent locations by 2000. Against all discussion of alternatives, the point has to be made that from the Lao government's perspective there is little reason to consider other possibilities unless these can produce foreign exchange.

With the collapse of the Thai economy in 1997 another, and extremely important, factor has entered the debate over whether or not Nam Theun 2 should be built. When the first estimates of likely returns to Laos from selling electricity to Thailand were made in 1991, the expectation was that it would provide an annual income credit of US$176 million. Estimates made seven years later suggested that this figure was highly inflated and that a more realistic figure would be US$38 million annually. Of course, until the dam is built all of these estimates remain theoretical, and just as importantly the whole question of whether or not Thailand will want to buy electricity generated by Nam

Theun 2 remains uncertain. As Thailand's economic crisis began to bite in late 1997, the electricity generating authority EGAT settled on a new development plan to replace earlier optimistic projections of electricity requirements. At the same time EGAT cancelled an existing agreement to buy electricity from Nam Theun 2 on the basis that it would not be completed by 2000.

So, will Nam Theun 2 be built, and should it be? Writing in June 1999, the odds still seem to be in favour of eventual approval being given for the dam to go ahead. The most persuasive reason for its doing so is the lack of obvious alternatives that can provide Laos with the foreign earnings it so desperately needs at a time when its economy has been battered by the Asian economic crisis. As an index of Laos's problems, the value of its currency, the kip, declined by 50 per cent over 1998 alone. Against this background, Nam Theun 2's supporters argue that when completed the dam will have the capacity to reduce poverty both on a national level and in the area of the dam itself. In this regard, the Lao government and the consortium do not deny that there will be some negative consequences for those who have to be resettled. But in taking account of these consequences both parties have pledged funds to ensure that resettled villagers will eventually be better off than previously. Plans have been drawn up for fishing in the dam's reservoir, for managed timber harvesting and for the development of a tourist industry. Yet none of the unquestionably well-meaning plans to which I have just referred mean that reaching a positive decision in relation to Nam Theun 2 is an easy call, not least because the proof of who is right or wrong will only come when the project has been completed. And, worryingly, it is difficult to be sure that there will not be long periods between the commencement of work on the dam and its completion during which the displaced population is left in limbo; moved from their existing locations but not yet provided with the promised resettlement areas that are supposed to benefit from the construction of the dam. Or, to put the question another way, what do people who at present rely on fishing do when there is no opportunity for them to fish?

Of course, there will always be some observers who can never be persuaded that benefits will outweigh negative consequences so far as Nam Theun 2 is concerned. And, equally, supporters of the project can be rigid in rejecting alternative views. Because of the World Bank's link to the project, and the bank's less than glowing record in its support for building large dams elsewhere in the world, Nam Theun 2 has become a major focus for NGO criticism; while other hydro projects in the south of Laos have attracted much less attention, as well as having proceeded with inadequate environmental assessment in great contrast to the exhaustive studies devoted to Nam Theun 2. Even for doubters such as myself, it is not easy to disregard the arguments in the dam's favour that come from its Lao advocates.

It did not take long in talking to Houmphone Bouliyaphonh, the Director-General of the Electricity Department in the Lao Ministry of Industry and Handicrafts, in 1998, to hear his strongly held views about the critics of Nam Theun 2. It was a little like hearing Margaret Thatcher's affirmation that 'there is no alternative'. What were the Lao to do?, he asked rhetorically. He accepted that some, if not all, of those who criticised Lao reliance on hydro power were genuinely concerned for the people of his country, but he found it difficult to understand why these critics could not accept that the government held the same concerns. And, in particular, he deplored the fact that some of the most vocal critics of the plans for Nam Theun 2 had not accepted invitations to hear the Lao point of view. Nevertheless, he said, they still wrote their vigorous condemnations of the government's plans.

In the end, what one thinks about the Lao government's plans to rely on hydro-electricity as their major foreign exchange earner comes down to personal judgments about possibilities and alternatives. Given the errors of the past, whether in Southeast Asia or elsewhere, there is every reason to approach the issue of building dams on the Mekong's tributaries with healthy scepticism. But that scepticism must not be allowed to obscure the possibility that precautions can be taken to minimise the negative impacts that inevitably accompany large-scale infrastructure projects. To argue otherwise is to adopt the position that the future is not open; that it is not possible to learn from the past. There is a risk that in opposing a project such as Nam Theun 2 some, at least, of its critics are placing their own concept of 'development' ahead of the concepts held by the Lao themselves. Certainly, in the straitened economic circumstances of Laos itself, and of the region as a whole, it is difficult to see viable alternatives that are available to the government of Laos as it searches for ways to improve the lot of its population. All this said, there is no argument against the need for the strictest oversight of the Nam Theun 2 project if, finally, it goes ahead. Most critically of all, the final test of the desirability of building the dam relates to questions of benefit. Improving Laos's balance of payments by selling electricity to Thailand will only be of value if improvement in the country's economic situation is genuinely of benefit to the population as a whole. And the fact that those who will be displaced if the dam is built are members of the wider population must never be forgotten.

That a need for strict oversight is necessary thoughout the Mekong Basin is given further emphasis by brief reference to two other projects involving the river and its tributaries. These are far from the only other projects that demand attention, but they are worth mentioning since they are of a kind that has largely been overlooked by outside observers lacking a direct interest in developments involving the Mekong. The first is the Kok-Ing-Nan Water Diversion Project. This is a plan to dam the Kok, Ing and Nan Rivers, tributaries of the Mekong in northeast Thailand, so as to divert their water to the Chao Phraya River, the river that flows past Bangkok. The plan envisages the diversion of 2200 million cubic metres (MCM) from the tributaries each year. Whether this project will actually go ahead is unclear at the time of writing, but it has already excited opposition from villagers who currently depend on these rivers for agriculture and fishing. Serious concern has also been expressed by Cambodia's Minister of the Environment, Dr Mak Moreth, who has put forward the understandable view that his country must be concerned about any plan that reduces the flow of water down the Mekong's mainstream.

Yet in Cambodia itself projects are being discussed that raise their own questions about negative consequences. Among these is the Prek Thnot project, a plan to build a major dam on the Prek Thnot River which flows into the Bassac, the second and western arm of the Mekong after it splits in two below Phnom Penh. Projected to cost around US$200 million, the dam, in Kompong Speu Province west of Phnom Penh, has been identified as one of the Phnom Penh government's top priorities. The project's origins predate the civil war that broke out in 1970 and led to the Khmer Rouge coming to power in 1975. As a regular visitor to Cambodia in the 1960s, I was conscious of the work being undertaken in relation to this planned dam by the Snowy Mountains Engineering Corporation, the Australian company formed as an engineering consultancy after the completion of the massive Snowy Mountains Scheme in the 1950s. With the onset of the civil war, work on the dam that had begun in 1969 was abandoned in 1973.

Now the revival of the project is under way, and with it the familiar emergence of controversy between its supporters and opponents. Conceived as taking advantage of the massive outflow of water from the Cardamom Range in western Cambodia during the wet season, Prek Thnot would be Cambodia's first large dam, with a reservoir covering 256 square kilometres and leading to the displacement of an estimated 17 700 people. Interestingly, it appears that opinion is divided among NGOs as to the project's benefits, or lack of them. Some apparently see a dam as providing opportunities for developing a freshwater fishing industry. Others argue that much of the area around the planned area of the dam's reservoir is currently desperately short of water every dry season, a situation that could be rectified by the construction of a major dam. The other side of this particular coin is the concern held by critics of the scheme concerning the resettlement that will be required for so many people, the adequacy of their access to land and the fertility of the land available. Once again, one set of apparent imperatives confronts another. As with so many other projects the choices are difficult and the future is uncertain.

15

Bridges over Troubled Waters and Lands: Present Imperfect, Future Uncertain

> . . . an economically prosperous, socially just and environmentally sound Mekong River Basin.
>
> *The Mekong River Commission's 'new vision' for the Basin, as recorded in the Commission's newsletter, December 1998*

There are few more telling reflections of the changes taking place along the Mekong than the bridges that have been constructed, or are currently being built, across its broad waters. These are not the first to be thrown across the Mekong. As recorded in an earlier chapter, since the early centuries of the present era there has been a bridge, in fact several bridges, across the river where its course runs through western Yunnan Province in China. Most were minor affairs, but the bridge that now spans the Mekong near the site of the Old Burma Road is the direct descendant of these earliest man-made crossings. And, again as noted before, the Chinese government built a bridge across the Mekong at Jinghong nearly forty years ago, in 1960. So bridges, in themselves, are not new. What is new is the scale of these new bridges and, most importantly, the fact that all but one of these bridges are on the Lower Mekong.

Until 1994, no bridges had ever been built across the lower mainstream course of the Mekong. In the 1960s, it is true, the Japanese government funded the construction of a bridge across the Tonle Sap River at Phnom Penh to link the northern part of that city with the Chrui Changvar Peninsula, the site of the notorious massacre of Vietnamese in 1970. During Cambodia's bloody civil war, Vietnamese frogmen sappers fighting with the Cambodian revolutionaries destroyed the bridge, and it was not rebuilt until the early 1990s. It was only in 1994 that a bridge was finally constructed across the Lower Mekong's mainstream. This was the so-called Friendship Bridge, funded by the Australian government, which links the northern Thai town of Nong Khai with the left, Lao, bank of the Mekong, a few kilometres from the Vietnamese capital, Vientiane.

Since that time there has been an acceleration of plans and construction. The Australian government is funding another bridge at My Thuan in the Mekong Delta, while the Japanese government is paying for the construction of bridges at Kompong Cham, in Cambodia, and at Pakse, in Laos. Other bridges are either under consideration or set to be constructed at Can Tho in Vietnam, at Neak Luong, the main ferry crossing on the road between Phnom Penh and Ho Chi Minh City, at Savannakhet in Laos and between Chiang Khong in Thailand and Huay Xai in Laos. Meanwhile, further up the river at Jinghong, the Chinese have completed the construction of a massive suspension bridge that will ultimately facilitate the passage of heavy transport crossing the Mekong to travel down the expanding road system being directed towards Burma, Laos and Thailand.

There is no doubt this surge in bridge building will eventually have a major effect on the way in which goods move around southern China and through the countries of mainland Southeast Asia. Long delays at ferry crossings will be eliminated, so that it almost seems churlish to note that not all of the results of the construction that has taken place or is in process have automatically been viewed as positive in character. Take the case of the My Thuan bridge across a major arm of the Mekong in southern Vietnam, which will be completed by the end of 2000. It is the biggest single aid project that has ever been funded by the Australian government, which is meeting two-thirds of the total outlay, at a cost of more than US$39 million. When completed the bridge will be 1.5 kilometres long, with the main span 660 metres in length.

At present the expanse of water over which this bridge is being constructed is serviced by a fleet of vehicle ferries. Each day these ferries move more than twenty thousand people and some

Large vehicle-carrying ferries of the type seen here and still used at the My Thuan river crossing, will be replaced by the My Thuan bridge due to be completed in 2000.

four thousand tonnes of freight. When I crossed over, in June 1998, no fewer than six ferries were shuttling backwards and forwards to service the busy route leading from Ho Chi Minh City down to the major delta centre of Can Tho. They presented an impressive sight, jockeying for position at the wharves on either side of the river, where shouting ferryhands directed, cajoled and bullied the never-ending mass of vehicles on and off the ferries. Cars, trucks and buses competed for places, along with innumerable bicycles and foot passengers. Somehow or other, order came out of apparent chaos. But though the ferries were remarkably effective, it was abundantly apparent that a bridge would make this crossing easier and quicker. What I saw left me readily understanding why the Vietnamese government was so keen that Australia should make the construction of the My Thuan bridge its major aid contribution to Vietnam. And there is no doubt that greater ease of transportation will be important in allowing the delta's farmers and fishermen to ship perishable goods to Ho Chi Minh City more quickly and reliably.

And yet not everyone is convinced that the bridge is what is needed at My Thuan. Indeed, while the members of the present Australian government were in opposition before 1996, their spokesman on foreign affairs, Alexander Downer, the present Foreign Minister, was highly critical of the proposal to build the bridge, arguing that there were much better ways in which Australia could assist Vietnam than by commiting virtually all of its available aid funds for Vietnam to this single project. He questioned the rationale of the then Australian Labor Party government that the bridge would be both a valuable contribution in itself and another opportunity to show, as had been done with the Friendship Bridge linking Thailand and Laos, that Australian companies had the skills to undertake major infrastructure projects. Rather, Alexander Downer suggested, money should be spent on many small-scale projects spread over a wider geographical region.

As Peter Mares, an Australian journalist who has written in detail on this issue, points out, not all of the considerations that exercised Downer's and his party's minds when discussing the projected bridge in opposition related to the bridge as such. The conservative parties in Australian politics were suspicious of the importance their political opponents attached to developing close links with Vietnam despite that country's continuing poor record on many human rights issues. This said, Downer was by no means alone in arguing that funds could be better spent than on this one major project. This was also the view of Australian NGOs who queried the desirability of placing all, or virtually all, aid eggs in one basket. But perhaps most strikingly of all, the desirability of building a bridge was questioned by one of Vietnam's most respected academics and a former National Assembly member, the Vice-Rector of Can Tho University, Professor Vo Tong Xuan.

An agricultural expert who has not been afraid to offer views on Vietnam's economic development that do not always accord with those held by the leadership in Hanoi, Xuan's criticisms are the more persuasive because he acknowledges that the bridge will indeed bring some benefits. The problem, as he identifies it, is that there could be better ways of spending the large sums of money being committed to this single project. Xuan argues that more benefit would have flowed to the farmers of the Mekong Delta if a series of smaller bridges, capable of carrying vehicular traffic, had been constructed. These could have provided transport links between the villages of the region that currently depend on narrow footbridges across the creeks and canals that abound in the delta. If this had been done, Xuan has argued, it would have helped to stimulate regional development rather than promoting ever greater use of the road leading to Ho Chi Minh City. Additionally, since transporting rice by truck rather than by boat to Ho Chi Minh City will be more expensive, and will add to the traffic congestion that already exists, Professor Xuan believes that a better choice would have been to spend Australian aid on improving port facilities in the delta itself. To do so would make it possible to ship exports abroad directly from the rice-producing region.

There is more than a little irony in the fact that the original decision to construct the My Thuan bridge in the Mekong Delta was promoted in part on the basis that Australia could point to the success already achieved as the result of building the Friendship Bridge linking Thailand and Laos. From an engineering point of view, of course, the Friendship Bridge is undoubtedly a success, stretching as it does more than a kilometre across the Mekong, with a sufficient width to accommodate both vehicular and, eventually, rail traffic. And, as intended, construction of the bridge has demonstrated the capacity of Australian companies to complete a major infrastructure project in Southeast Asia. This demonstration has been a matter of criticism from some NGOs, which argue that linking aid with such commercial considerations distorts the way that assessments are made of the desirability or otherwise of aid projects.

But there is a more immediate and less abstract problem associated with the bridge. The problem lies in the bridge's utilisation, or more correctly its far from satisfactory utilisation. For once the bridge was opened in 1994 it became clear that the Lao government was worried that unrestricted use of the bridge could lead to an erosion of its control over the state. With this in mind, it has severely limited the bridge's use by foreign private passenger vehicles. Individuals are not allowed to walk across the bridge and must make use of a crowded shuttle bus service, which only operates in daylight hours. The number of trucks that may use the bridge for commercial purposes remains severely circum-scribed. And the bridge is closed to all traffic at night. All these restrictions are justified in the minds of the Lao authorities as a way of preventing 'spiritual pollution' from neighbouring Thai-land. Given that Thai television transmissions are readily received in Laos, it seems a largely empty, and irritating, gesture.

Nevertheless, and despite the actions of the Lao government and the criticism the My Thuan bridge has provoked, the clear fact is that the infrastructure of the countries of mainland South-east Asia lying beside the Mekong is undergoing a major transformation. The bridges across the river are part of a massive change, much of which will further diminish the already limited role the Mekong has as a means of transport for goods and passengers. One notable example of this transformation is taking place along Route 13 in southern Laos, the road that leads from Pakse to the Lao–Cambodian border down which I travelled to see the Khone Falls. The old narrow French-built road is being replaced by a modern highway. When completed in 2000, as part of a larger upgrading program that will reach as far as Vientiane, the attrac-tion of using the Mekong for more than local traffic or for tourism in southern Laos will largely disappear. Traffic will move up and down the newly upgraded highway along a north–south axis to be joined by other traffic crossing the Mekong at the bridges at Pakse and Savannakhet from destinations to the east and west.

Concentration on major infrastructure developments and their shortcomings carries with it the risk of overlooking the fundamental social and political problems of the countries within the Mekong Basin. Yet these problems are very real, and in some cases apparently intractable, at least in the short term, so that the uncertain future for the Mekong itself is mirrored in the wider world of the countries through which it flows. Of all the countries along the river's course, only one, Thailand, can claim to be a democracy. This seems a proper judgment despite the presence of persistent social and political inequalities and the uncertainty that still attaches to the role of the armed forces, which have in the past been ready to stage coups to protect their position. But the fact that Thailand, since the 1970s, has slowly moved along a path towards greater democracy has not meant, as already recorded, that the country has avoided major environmental problems. The devastating floods that have been a consequence of unrestricted logging are one instance of this fact, as are the multiple problems that have followed upon the construction of the Pak Mun Dam.

In Burma, power has been held by a self-perpetuating military junta since 1962. Ruthless in maintaining its control over the population, as shown by its savage suppression of student protests in 1988, which involved the deaths of thousands of protesters in Rangoon, the Burmese leadership gives no indication of a readiness to change its ways. Certainly, the policy of 'constructive engagement' that the members of the Association of Southeast Asian Nations (ASEAN) relied on to bring change in the country, when they admitted Burma to membership of that body in 1997, has so far had little if any effect. Fortunately, so far as the Mekong's future is concerned, Burma's links to the river are relatively limited. It is elsewhere in this unhappy country that environmental degradation, particularly of forests, is rampant.

In China, Laos and Vietnam, communist parties control the government and dictate the policies of the state. Of course, communism as a political and economic theory has little relevance in these countries, except as a way of describing the determination of those who hold power to ensure that it does not pass to others. Or it can be appealed to as a theory when justifying interference in market mechanisms if these are feared likely to undermine the party's political control. The extent to which economic policies have been liberalised in both China and Vietnam, and to a lesser extent in Laos, is remarkable when compared with the quite recent past. But it is salutary to remember that economic liberalisation has not meant that these countries are ready to have any truck with democracy. Neither has it meant that these governments have embraced concepts of the rule of law or of social and political justice which are, in theory at least, part and parcel of life in Western democracies. All these facts need to be kept in mind when judgments are made about the capacity of the governments linked to the Mekong to act as wise custodians of the river in the future.

The same comment applies to Cambodia. It is difficult to know what political description should be given to this Southeast Asian state which, more than any other, has suffered so grievously as the result of domestically imposed tyranny. Its modern history has lurched from one tragic experience to another, with the most recent example being the July 1997 putsch that entrenched Hun Sen and his Cambodian People's Party in power. The elections of the following year could never be 'free and fair' given the control he and his party had over most of the military and civil apparatus of the country. That control has been maintained in circumstances that have led to the development of a culture of impunity, a situation in which many senior former members of the Khmer Rouge live free and unpunished and the killers of opposition politicians have never been brought to trial. The same culture of impunity has meant that illegal logging, with resultant environmental damage to the Mekong, has also largely gone unpunished by the government in Phnom Penh.

So, all of the countries along the course of the Mekong face political, social and environmental problems of a serious, even profound, character. In concentrating in previous chapters on the actual or potential problems associated with developments on the river and its tributaries, I have only touched lightly on the issue of pollution. Yet here is a problem that increasingly afflicts the Mekong's health. I knew of the massive discharge of untreated sewage and chemicals into the Mekong at Phnom Penh, and of the pollution from fertilisers that are an increasing bane for farmers and fishermen in the Mekong Delta. But, before I travelled there, I scarcely expected to hear that pollution now afflicts Lake Erhai, the major lake in western Yunnan set beside the city of Dali and a vast natural reservoir whose waters finally flow into the Mekong. On reflection this was a notably naive view, given my knowlege of the long-standing evidence of China's readiness to use its rivers, major and minor, as a means to carry off industrial waste and polluting substances of every kind.

Visiting Dali in 1998 was a form of pilgrimage, a personal tribute to the French explorers led by Francis Garnier who had reached this walled city one hundred and thirty years before and then had been frustrated in their final attempt to see the upper reaches of the Mekong. Standing looking at my guide book in the middle of the city, I was surprised to hear a voice asking in perfectly modulated English whether I needed any help. And so

I met 'Mr Wang', the name he said I could use in speaking to him. He was a man in his late sixties or early seventies, with the height of a northerner, a thick thatch of grey hair and an erect carriage. On a bustling market day, with Dali thronged by members of the Bai ethnic minority in their distinctive clothing, Mr Wang stood out in the crowd.

Without my asking, he explained his near-faultless use of English. Many years ago he had taught the language in Peking, but then came the Great Proletarian Cultural Revolution and he was sent to work in the countryside at Dali. When that 'madness' dissipated, he had decided to stay on in this provincial city he had come to like, though he feared that its character was about to change. Because of tourism? I ventured. Ah, yes, he responded, but not so much because of foreigners like you. It was his compatriots who were his cause for concern. For, he continued, they are—and here for the first time he searched for an English word—so often 'vulgar'. It was a comment I was to remember only a short time later when I visited Jinghong in Yunnan's deep south.

Unprompted, Mr Wang went on to talk about the changes he feared would take place in Dali when, as would happen soon, it would be linked with Kunming, Yunnan's provincial capital, by a modern highway. As I had travelled from Kunming to Dali, I had seen this new highway being built parallel to the older road my bus travelled on. The expectation was that, once the highway was completed, the eleven-hour journey I had experienced would be reduced to half that time. And these were not the only changes that were a cause for concern, Mr Wang observed. Lake Erhai, no matter how clear and sparkling it was looking in the spring sunshine, was no longer the lake he had come to know thirty years earlier. Now, it is heavily polluted with sewage and agricultural run-off. As a result, fish stocks have declined sharply, a situation made more serious by the tendency of local fishermen to overfish in an effort to compensate for their smaller catches. He would be surprised, he told me, if I saw many cormorants being used to fish on the lake when I went there later in the day. Once this had been a widely used way to catch fish, but not any more. With fish becoming scarce this traditional method was too slow and unrewarding. He was right. In more than four hours spent travelling on the lake, I did not see a single example of a cormorant being used by the many fishing boats I passed.

Mr Wang's comments about his compatriots' tendency to be 'vulgar' tourists was in my mind as I waited to fly from Kunming to Jinghong. I was aware that Jinghong was a prime domestic tourist destination, receiving more than a million Chinese visitors each year. But I was surprised to hear a critical view of the city's tourist character expressed vigorously even before I boarded my aircraft. The commentary came from a fellow passenger who spoke to me, as we waited in the departure lounge, at Kunming Airport, after she saw that I was reading a book in English. I had noticed this woman because she and her daughter, a child of about four years of age, were wearing clothes that looked as though they came from somewhere other than China. What I had not at first noticed was the cast of the mother's and child's features, which were quite different from those of the other, Chinese, passengers waiting for their flights. Had I ever been to Jinghong before, she asked? As I had not, and since this was originally her home, she was happy to tell me something about it. 'Marie', as she asked me to call her if I ever wrote anything about our conversation, was a member of the Dai ethnic minority. Married to an American, she was taking her young daughter to meet the child's Dai grandparents. She hoped I would record what she told me, but she would prefer that I didn't use her real name. Perhaps, she said, this was a case of being over-cautious, but while she would soon be leaving China again her parents still had their lives to lead in Jinghong. For this reason, it might not be wise to use her real name.

What I would see in Jinghong, Marie told me, was a city that had almost totally lost its character as a centre of the Dai people. I would find a tourist strip, and if I looked behind the recently constructed buildings housing cafes and bars, with their half-hearted approximation of traditional Dai architecture, I would see the last remaining cluster of the wooden buildings that had once made up the city before the Han Chinese flooded in. I would find new hotels just completed or being built. When I went to the National Minorities Park I would encounter Chinese tourists dressing up in Dai costumes and posing to be photo-graphed in front of a stupa built in the local style. It had no real religious significance and was just another prop to create the illusion of authenticity. Perhaps, too, I would see the tourists throwing water at each other, because the Chinese tour operators encourage their charges to behave as if every day is the same as

A view of Jinghong, once a Dai settlement and now a Chinese tourist centre; nondescript modern buildings have replaced the traditional local architecture.

the period of the Dai New Year, when water fights are part of the celebrations. Worst of all, I would see paintings for sale in tourist shops showing Dai women bathing topless in the Mekong. This was not a practice, Marie assured me, that was part and parcel of her people's behaviour but rather a Han Chinese fantasy. Like Mr Wang in Dali, she now searched for a word. They think, she finally said, we are quaint.

With the exception of the water fights, all that Marie predicted I would see was there when I reached Jinghong. It was depressing and very hot. The contrast, I found, lay in the countryside, only a short distance from the city. Travelling by local bus to Ganlanba, a small settlement on the Mekong twenty-five kilometres downstream from Jinghong, I was translated into a different, Southeast Asian, world. The palm trees that had looked out of place against the background of the ugly architecture of Jinghong now seemed to fulfil their proper function around the Dai houses of the villages I passed through. With only minor architectural changes, the Buddhist pagodas at Ganlanba could have been in Laos or northern Thailand, as could the Buddhist monks and novices whom I saw.

Only later, when I read an article by Grant Evans, an Australian anthropologist who has studied the Dai for nearly a decade, did I learn that consideration is being given to further expanding tourist facilities in the Jinghong region. Plans have already been drawn up for a theme park, featuring ethnic minority peoples, in a ten square kilometre area south of Jinghong. In addition to showing off the minority groups to visiting Han Chinese, the park would include a racecourse and an 'elephant performance area'. To cap these plans, Evans records, there is talk of building what the Chinese developers have called a 'Southeast Asian Paradise' along the 'River Danube of the Orient'—in other words, the Mekong.

Plans comparable to those contemplated for Jinghong are not unknown further down the river. Before the collapse of the Thai economy, and in a prospective deal that seemed to contravene all the tenets of Laos's socialist government, permission was given to a Thai consortium to build a massive golf and gambling resort on the islands in the Mekong just above the Khone Falls. The size of the planned resort—which now seems most unlikely ever to be built given the downturn of the Thai economy— was mind boggling, involving a 2000 room hotel, an 18-hole golf course and two casinos. To service this resort the development plans called for the construction of an airport large enough to accept Boeing 737 aircraft. That permission was ever given for this development is an index of Laos's economic problems and of the extent to which corruption can still thrive in a supposedly austere, socialist state. For it is hard to disregard the fact that the Lao Prime Minister, Khamtay Siphandone, comes from the area where the resort was going to be built at a cost of US$300 million, while his elder brother is reported to have been a close friend of the Thai developer who had been planning the project.

The examples of the major political, social and environmental problems that afflict the countries of the Mekong Basin that have been recorded so far in this book are only some of the more apparent examples in a catalogue of disadvantage that would stretch to many more pages. Not all the countries linked to the Mekong face the same problems, and when problems are shared these are not necessarily shared at the same level of threat or difficulty. By their very size the economies of China and Vietnam have the potential to produce more positive results in the longer term than is the case for Laos and Cambodia. So, while social and environmental problems abound in China, it seems proper to conclude that it is better placed than the poorest of its Southeast Asian neighbours to meet and eventually over-come the challenges it faces, should it be determined to do so. There is little evidence for the moment that this is the case. And so far as the Mekong is concerned, this may mean that China's pursuit of economic growth through industrial development occurs at the expense of the downstream countries, as dams continue to be built to generate hydro power that will fuel industry in Yunnan and further afield.

In terms of economic need, Cambodia and Laos are set to be cast in the role of mendicants for years to come. And of these two countries, Cambodia already faces the risk of ecological disaster, a disaster that could have the gravest effects on the Mekong and its tributaries. When, in early 1999, the Asian Development Bank drew up a report on Cambodia's economy for consideration at an international donors' meeting, it was deeply negative in tone, concluding that if the current pace of deforestation taking place in Cambodia were maintained the country would be logged out in five years' time. The accompa-nying cost in terms of sediment flowing into the Great Lake and affecting the flow of the Mekong itself can readily be imagined.

These are problems facing a country in which it is now estimated that each day another hundred men contract the HIV virus. Indeed, this is another region-wide issue that cannot be ignored. Even allowing for the serious efforts that Thailand has made to deal with the AIDS epidemic, the countries of the Mekong Basin, most certainly including Burma, face a public health challenge of almost incalculable size and cost from this modern plague.

So, the 'vision' of the Mekong region's future held by the Mekong River Commission and quoted at the beginning of this chapter is likely to prove elusive for many years to come. To make this judgment is not to discount the good that has been and is being done in a multitude of small projects along the course of the Mekong: the work being undertaken to assist flood mitigation; the research into fish breeding cycles; the efforts to conserve and resuscitate wetlands. But in terms of the wider picture only a supreme optimist could feel confident that the problems of the present will be readily overcome or could think of the Mekong's future without a heavy measure of foreboding. It will be many years before economic prosperity, social justice and a sound environment are the unchallenged characteristics of the countries of the Mekong Basin.

There is room for one further cautionary comment in relation to the Mekong's future. It is a point made cogently by Philip Hirsch, an Australian researcher who is one of the leading experts on the Mekong's development prospects. Who, he asks, controls the Mekong's development agenda? The implication of this question is clear, for in so many ways it often seems, and certainly is sometimes the case, that decisions are made in connection with the river and its region that take little if any account of the interests of the people who rely on the Mekong and its tributaries for their livelihood. More broadly, there are issues to be considered relating to sovereignty. Is it desirable, in the longer term, for dams to be built with the intention that they will bring profits to private companies as well as to the state? The answers to questions such as these are not simple, but the questions need to be asked.

And these are questions that go to the very heart of the continuing controversy over what constitutes 'development', and who should pay for it. As the future of the Nam Theun 2 project remains unresolved, there is, once again, evidence that World Bank decisions have the capacity to excite strong negative reactions, as the result, it would seem, of insufficient attention being given to the fundamental issue of who will benefit from another major project in China. This time the proposal is for the resettlement of 58 000 farmers who currently live in the poor northwestern Chinese province of Qinghai—an undertaking conceived as a poverty-alleviation project and costing a projected US$160 million. The World Bank's possible support for this scheme has come under sharp criticism as it has become clear that the farmers will be resettled in an area that is the traditional home of ethnic Tibetans. By contrast, the social disruption that would accompany the construction of the Nam Theun 2 Dam is relatively small. The issues involved, nevertheless, are no less real.

Epilogue

Without doubt, no other river, over such a length, has a more singular or remarkable character.

Francis Garnier, second-in-command of the French Mekong Expedition, 1866–68

A nd still there is the river, the Great River, the Mother of the Waters, running its immense course from Tibet to the South China Sea. We finally know the location of the Mekong's source, since the French explorer and writer, Michel Peissel, and his companions settled its exact position in September 1994. At an altitude of 4975 metres, at the head of the Rupsa-la Pass in eastern Tibet, they found that the river rose at latitude 33 degrees 16 minutes 534 North and longitude 93 degrees 52 minutes 929 East. Few travellers will share this sight of the Mekong's beginnings in the windswept, treeless landscape of upland Tibet. But there is much that can be seen along the river from its mouths on the South China Sea to the point at which it flows out of China. Beyond that point, the Chinese government remains reluctant to allow a traveller to use the waterway to move downstream from Jinghong into northern Laos, but there is no difficulty in viewing the Mekong at various points along its course in Yunnan. No longer the unknown river that Francis Garnier saw in the 1860s, what the Mekong lacks in mystery at the end of the twentieth century is more than compensated for by its variety and its grandeur.

To travel on and by the Mekong in its delta is to wonder at the extraordinary expenditure of human energy that has tamed the watery land. For the delta to have become Vietnam's rice basket is a testimony to centuries of tireless canal digging and drainage work, undertakings that still continue today. Even now, when flying above the delta at the height of the wet season, it almost seems that the battle with the river has been lost, for with water covering the paddy fields the countryside below looks more like a giant inland sea than a region that will yield two rice crops each year.

Further north, at Phnom Penh, the modern traveller encounters a city with a split personality. Wealth and poverty sit side by side. Although many new buildings have been constructed over the past decade, with others restored after the madness of the Pol Pot years, there is much of the inner city that looks unchanged since the early 1990s when a kind of peace returned to Cambodia. Streets in what was once the Chinese quarter are more like rutted country roads than the thoroughfares of a capital. Their surfaces are decaying into dust or mud; their gutters are clogged with garbage. And in the central post office square the repainted colonial building looks directly across at the still burnt-out ruin of what was once my favourite restaurant, 'La Taverne', run by the ebullient Monsieur Mignon. But much sadder still are the amputees who wait by the palace or the museum to beg from tourists. For they, most poignantly of all, are the human legacy of Cambodia's wretched past.

Beyond the Cambodian capital, the countryside along the river's banks reflects a different world. Despite its burgeoning population, Cambodia remains a lightly settled country, very different in this respect from Vietnam. Instead of villages grouped one after another along the various arms of the river in the delta, there are long stretches without signs of settlement. With the country on either side still monotonously flat, distance is defined by the tall trunks of the sugar palm trees. Then, conforming to no obvious pattern, the presence of a Buddhist pagoda will mark the existence of a riverside village. Rising above the fragile wooden huts which surround them, these places of worship appear exotic at a distance. Too often, on closer inspection, one finds they are crudely constructed in concrete, totally lacking in the grace that can still be found in the rare older *wats* that have survived from the nineteenth century. The most visible sense of life comes from the craft that pass up and down the river: wood-burning ferries built decades ago and still functioning, barges moving slowly downstream with dun-coloured lateen sails, slim canoes, though nowadays often powered by noisy outboard motors rather than by oars or paddles.

Beyond Kompong Cham, a riverside town which once was the pride of a local French administration that had grown fat on the revenues of the nearby rubber plantations, the traveller enters a region that is even more lightly settled than before. After passing the red cliffs of Krauchmar, the boat winds through a wilder landscape where jungle cover frequently reaches right down to the river's banks. Even today this is a remote area for most Cambodians. And the sense of remoteness still hangs heavy about the riverside settlement of Kratie, the last point on the Mekong that can be reached without having to overcome the barrier to easy navigation posed by the presence of rapids. Not far distant to the east of the river are the upland regions inhabited by hill peoples whose way of life is very different from that of the lowland Cambodians. Treated as outsiders and worse over many centuries, these hill people became prime recruits for the Khmer Rouge during the years of the civil war.

It was just a little to the north of Kratie, at Sambor, that the French explorers came to fear that their dream of a Mekong open to commercial navigation was probably just that, a dream. More recently, Sambor was where Cambodia's long-time leader, Prince and King Sihanouk, decreed that a stupa containing the ashes of a distant ancestor, Princess Nucheat Khatr Vorpheak, was to be kept in proper repair. At some time in the nineteenth century—no one seems to be sure of the exact date—this princess was taken by a great crocodile, only to have her body miraculously recovered. More than a hundred years later Sihanouk communed with her spirit, seeking guidance on issues of foreign policy.

Once in Laos, after having passed Stung Treng and the Khone Falls, the path of the river alternates between stretches of deep, wide water and rapids that remain an impediment to easy navigation. Accounts by nineteenth century European travellers of their passage through the recurring rapids abound with descriptions of boats and rafts tossed by churning water, or swamped as their craft were drawn down into the raging whirlpools. Perhaps this experience was what made times spent in settlements beside the calm sections of the river so attractive. The French explorers were only the first of a series of foreign travellers who found contentment at Bassac, the modern Champassak, though contentment it will be remembered was not enough for the members of the expedition's escort.

While the French controlled Laos, Champassak was the seat of the prince whose family had traditionally ruled this region. Today, Champassak is a minor settlement at a ferry crossing, a jumping-off point for visits to the Angkorian-period temples at Wat Phu. With its decaying pagodas and a few wooden Chinese shophouses, two villas built in the European style are the only reminders of a very different past. The last ruler of this region was Prince Boun Oum, a man whose name was briefly associated with Laos's complex politics in the 1960s. He was a foreign correspondent's delight, a fat, grey-haired old man, fond of wine and spirits, seldom far from the comforting presence of his household of young women. Yet for all the readiness of the Western world to see him as an Asian buffoon, he was something more, a man bypassed by time who honoured his traditional ceremonial obligations as he saw his way of life slip away. Like so many of the Lao elite he left his country in 1974 before the communists took power and ended his days in France, where he died in 1978. Not so his brother, Boun Houm, whom I found was still living at Champassak in one of the settlement's pink-painted villas when I stopped there in early 1997. A feeble old man in his eighties, he barely knew who or where he was, but the faded photographs on the walls of his house spoke of another and happier time. The Lao authorities seemed quite relaxed about leaving him to spend his dotage amid the remnants of a world and a way of life that had vanished forever.

A little further up the river, at Pakse, is Boun Oum's legacy to his country, the palace he began constructing in 1968. It was never completed before he went into exile and it has now become the Champassak Palace Hotel. It is a building of quite staggering awfulness, from any architectural point of view, a kind of Southeast Asian 'wedding cake' in external appearance with red and gold decoration in the public rooms. Now owned by a Thai commercial group, it is chiefly a glorified brothel for Thai businessmen who drive the short distance into Laos from Thailand to patronise the mainly Vietnamese prostitutes who ply their trade there. On my last visit in 1998 it had also recently been the venue for a 'graduation ceremony'. The public areas of the hotel displayed hundreds of colour photographs of Lao dignitaries being awarded 'degrees' by a fly-by-night American diploma mill. Despite my asking, I could not find an answer to the question of who paid for this curiously unexpected extravaganza.

Ascending the river past Savannakhet, the largest town in southern Laos, a traveller finally reaches Vientiane, the country's capital. Were it not for two or three of its Buddhist pagodas and the great That Luang stupa, modern Vientiane would scarcely be worthy of mention. Capital it may be, but it has an overwhelmingly provincial air. Seeming more a town than a city, Vientiane is set on a flat river plain, dusty in the dry season and muddy in the wet. Visitors inclined to romantic explanations might say that it has never recovered from the sack of 1828, as they look for the hotel where Jerry Westerby, John le Carré's 'honourable schoolboy', stayed after the Circus ordered him to leave Saigon. It still exists, though no longer under its former name—the Constellation Hotel. Perhaps there is romance of a kind here, for its manager has emerged resilient from re-reduction camp to run the hotel. For the rest, even the backpackers are puzzled by the problem of what to do in this sleepy capital. There is slim reward to be found in the Revolutionary Museum, even when the staff elect to honour its proclaimed opening hours.

Continue north from Vientiane on the Mekong and the story is very different. For this is the section of the river that rewards a traveller with striking memories. Beyond the flat plains of Vientiane, the Mekong runs through thickly forested gorges that narrow its width. Jagged rocks rise up on either side of the river as a threat to a careless boatman or a craft thrown out of control by a whirlpool. At other times the rocks give way to giant sandbanks, which according to the time of the year can rise as high as ten metres above the level of the river. It is through this dramatic landscape that the traveller comes to Luang Prabang, the jewel of all the settlements along the Mekong.

With its setting on the river amid the hills and mountains

that rise behind it, the pagodas and tree-shaded streets and lanes of the old section of the city offer a sense of calm unmatched in mainland Southeast Asia. This is a feeling reinforced in December and January when Luang Prabang experiences its coolest months and morning mists hang heavy over the city and the river. Protected as a World Heritage site, there are still reasons to wonder whether Luang Prabang and its unique character are not on the brink of disturbing change. The road linking Luang Prabang with Vientiane is steadily being improved, which ultimately will mean that more traffic will reach the former royal capital. Already the airport has been upgraded, so there is the prospect of international flights coming directly to Luang Prabang, eliminating the necessity to travel first to Vientiane. And further strain will come from the completion of a road link between Luang Prabang and the northwestern Lao town of Muang Xay (Oudomxay). The latter is already a popular tourist destination for visitors from China. With what has happened to Jinghong to reflect on, the thought of a heavy Chinese tourist invasion of Luang Prabang is sad to contemplate.

Luang Prabang and the Buddhist shrines at the Pak Ou caves a little further upstream are a high point, for many *the* high point, of travel on the Mekong. Laos may no longer have a king, and the royal palace in Luang Prabang is a forlorn reminder of that earlier time, but the country's Buddhist past lives on in a profoundly Buddhist present. And nowhere is this more apparent than in the former royal capital, where monks in their robes are a constant feature of daily life. Yet there are plenty of ways in which the fact of change is brought home to a visitor. Travel further upstream from the Pak Ou caves and the great limestone cliffs that face them, where the Nam Ou River joins the Mekong, and you come to Pak Beng, a grubby settlement frequented by timber-getters and, some say, by drug-runners. This is no Asian arcady, but more a combination of work camp and truck stop along a road gouged out of the hillside which rises sharply from the river's banks. Many of the foreign travellers who stop briefly at Pak Beng do not reach it on a slow-moving boat that allows them to drink in the constantly changing sights along the river. They come instead in noisy 'longtail' boats, light skiffs that race up and downstream in a flurry of spray as their passengers crouch one behind the other, their heads encased in crash helmets. And this is the face of contemporary tourism.

Pak Beng is a reminder that the Lower Mekong has never been a wild river, untouched by human contact. It has always been a river for work, for travel and fishing, and not infrequently for war. Now, with the construction of the Chinese dams under way, let alone the wishes the Chinese have expressed to blast a channel through the Lao gorges, for the first time in its history questions are being raised about the possibility of fundamental alterations to the Mekong's character. Will a change in its flow affect the river's fish, whether in Laos, Cambodia or Vietnam? What will be the effect of a continuing program to build dams on its tributaries—for the river itself and for the people who must be moved so the dams may be built? Are the effects of pollution in its many forms reversible? Even to see reason to ask such questions is to admit that all is far from well with the mightiest river in Southeast Asia.

Like other travellers, I treasure my own special memories of the Mekong. What I find striking is how closely they accord with the memories and reflections of those who travelled on and by it before me. They too marvelled at the spectacular rush of water at the Khone Falls. And they remarked on the extraordinary contrasts of the river where it flows wide and deep for long stretches before being suddenly interrupted by rapids. I have found myself echoing their pleasure in the cool misty mornings of Luang Prabang and sharing their discomfort in the heat of high summer. Much of the wildlife that Father da Cruz described when he travelled on the river in the sixteenth century has vanished, but the kingfishers that were so often mentioned in nineteenth century descriptions are still there, darting down from the trees with a halcyon flash to pluck a fish from the water. And I have been struck, as have so many before me, by the changes in colour of the waters of the Mekong. At Jinghong the river is rich orange-red as it runs through the surrounding laterite hills. Further downstream at low water it appears dark green. At noon it will be blue and silver; in the late afternoon a regal purple. As Francis Garnier rightly said, it is a singular and remarkable river.

Sources, Notes and Acknowledgements

The material in this book reflects an acquaintance with the Mekong River that began in 1959. Over the past forty years I have lived beside the Mekong in Cambodia for two sustained periods and have been a regular visitor to that country. Additionally, over many years, I have visited Saigon for extended periods and travelled on, by and above the Mekong in Vietnam, Thailand, Laos and China. The book also reflects my own research into the history of the countries of the former French Indochina, in relation to both the nineteenth century and more contemporary periods. Much of this research was carried out in the French Colonial Archives (Archives Nationales de France, Archives d'Outre-Mer), initially in Paris and more recently in Aix-en-Provence, where those archives are now located. At all times the staff of the archives were generous in their assistance. Material in the book also reflects research in the archives held in Phnom Penh and Saigon (Ho Chi Minh City) before 1975. Some of the material in the book is drawn from personal journals I have kept during my periods of work and travel in mainland Southeast Asia. But in a book dealing with nearly two millennia of history I have, of course, needed to rely on the work of other writers. While the bibliographic commentary that follows, chapter by chapter, is not meant to be exhaustive, I hope I have been able to acknowledge those authors whose material has been of principal assistance to me in addition to the explicit references to published work that exist in the text of my book.

Before listing these bibliographic acknowledgements, I am glad

to record personal debts of gratitude associated with my interest
in the Mekong that go back many years as well as thanks more
immediately related to the present book. I was more than
fortunate in having Francis Stuart as my head of mission when
I served in Phnom Penh in 1959–61. As an 'old Asia hand' before
becoming Australian Ambassador to Cambodia, he was tolerant
of my historical interests at the same time as he taught me much
about understanding an exotic political culture and how to write
about it. Later, as a Cornell graduate student, I was fortunate to
enjoy the peerless supervision of Professor O. W. Wolters, whose
guidance three decades ago is, I hope, still reflected in some
measure in the historical sections of this book. During the time
I carried out research in Paris, I benefitted from the friendship
and guidance of Phillipe Devillers and was introduced to the rich
nineteenth century French literature on the exploration of the
Mekong by Ian Feldman, a bookdealer who became a friend.
From the time I spent in Cambodia in 1966, I remain grateful
for the friendship of Prince Sisowath Phandaravong, a friendship
that has lasted for many years. Without the help of Leslie
Fielding, then Chargé d'affaires of the British Embassy, Phnom
Penh, I would not have been able to make what was then my
second visit to the Khone Falls. He, too, remains a generous
friend. In Saigon, in the same year, I was treated with kindness
by Charles Truong Vinh Tong. Later, during the war years in
Vietnam, Senator Le Tan Buu offered me both the hospitality of
his home and the opportunity to travel widely in the Mekong
Delta when to have done so without his help would have been
extremely difficult. When I came to write my first book about
the Mekong, the fact that it saw the light of day owed much to
Robert J. Meyers, at that time publisher of *The New Republic*.

In connection with the writing of this book, I am again
indebted to friends who took the trouble to read and comment
on various drafts. I have already thanked them personally. At the
level of professional assistance, I must thank Aileen and John
Forsyth, travel agents extraordinaire. No matter what part of the
Mekong I wanted to visit, however out of the way, it was never
beyond their ability to provide me with guides and the means
to travel on the river. In Bangkok, Denis Gray, Bureau Chief of
the Associated Press, added to a friendship of many years by
bringing me up-to-date with current environmental issues associ-

ated with the Mekong and its tributaries. In both Vientiane and Phnom Penh I was given every assistance by the staffs of the Australian Embassies, so enabling me to interview senior Lao and Cambodian officials. Their help made a real difference and I am suitably grateful. In terms of the issues—academic, historical and contemporary—discussed in the book, I record my sincere thanks to Ted Chapman, Sue Downie, Pamela Gutman, Peter Hinton, Philip Hirsch and Bob Stensholt. Their professional comments were of great assistance. Most particularly, I am grateful for the detailed commentary on a draft of my manuscript which, once again, David Chandler provided. We met in Phnom Penh nearly forty years ago and have remained friends and *compagnons de route* in the study of Cambodia ever since. Finally, my thanks go to my editor Lynne Frolich and my publisher, Patrick Gallagher. This is the fourth book Patrick and I have worked on together, a testimony to friendship as well as to his admirable capacity to encourage an author to do his best. As with the commentary that follows on the source materials I have used, my thanks to those I have just mentioned does not mean that they would necessarily endorse all that I have written. As is always the case, I alone am responsible for the judgements made and the inter-pretations offered in this book.

Chapter I Monuments, Tombs and a Great River

More detailed information on Doudart de Lagrée and Francis Garnier may be found in my *River Road to China: The Search for the Source of the Mekong, 1866–73* (London and New York, 1975; new edition, Singapore and Sydney, 1996; New York, 1999). A detailed French account of the Mekong expedition is contained in Jean-Pierre Gomane's *L'Exploration du Mékong: La mission Ernest Doudart de Lagrée—Francis Garnier (1866–1868)* (Paris, 1994). Gomane's book also contains a useful summary of the Mekong Basin's geography, and biographical notes on the expedition's explorers. Accessible information on the Mekong's geography is included in *The Mekong: A River and its People* (Bangkok, 1991), by John Hoskin and Allen W. Hopkins. This book contains excellent photographs taken along the river. More detailed bibli-ographic references to Lagrée, Garnier and Henri Mouhot are provided in Chapters 4, 5 and 6. As an example of the Mekong's being referred to as an area of danger among American Vietnam War veterans, see James Lee Burke, *Cadillac Jukebox* (London, 1996). A fascinating collection of photographs and prints of the Mekong and its environs, most dating from the early decades of the twentieth century but including earlier periods, is *The Basin of the Mekong River: Images of the Past*, compiled by Bernard Gay (Paris, 1996).

Chapter 2   A River gives Birth to an Empire

Somerset Maugham's account of his first visit to the Angkor ruins is contained in *The Gentleman in the Parlour: A Record of a Journey from Rangoon to Haiphong* (London, 1930). The best introduction to the early history of Cambodia is David Chandler, *A History of Cambodia* (2nd edition, Boulder, Colorado, 1993). In this book Chandler draws on the vast body of research carried out by several generations of French scholars including, most notably, George Coedès, Louis Finot, Bernard-Philippe Groslier and Claude Jacques. More recently, there is a very helpful account of Angkorian Cambodia in Ian Mabbett and David Chandler, *The Khmers* (Oxford, 1995). A summary of Louis Mallaret's research at Oc Eo was published in *L'Archéologie du Delta du Mékong*, 4 volumes (Paris, 1959–63). Michael Vickery has published his account of early Cambodian history as *Society, Economics, and Politics in Pre-Angkor Cambodia: The 7th–8th Centuries* (Tokyo, 1998). In addition to the challenging arguments Vickery advances in this book, he provides a detailed bibliography for works on early Cambodian history. The comment on life in the Mekong Delta in the 1820s comes from Phan Huy Chu's 'Description of the Institutions of all the Dynasties' in a modern Vietnamese translation (Hanoi, 1960–61). George Groslier's evocation of Wat Phu is taken from his *A l'ombre d'Angkor* (Paris, 1916). Chou Ta-kuan's account of thirteenth century Cambodia is contained in *The Customs of Cambodia* (2nd edition, Bangkok, 1992). The reference to Marco Polo's passage past Lake Erhai comes from Ronald Latham's translation of *The Travels of Marco Polo* (London, 1958). Among the many studies of Angkor that include rich photographic treatment of the temples is Claude Jacques, *Angkor* (French edition, Paris, 1990; English edition, Cologne, 1999). The grandest of all the Angkorian temples, Angkor Wat, is the subject of a major recent study by Eleanor Mannikka, *Angkor Wat: Time, Space and Kingship* (Honolulu, 1996; Sydney, 1997).

Chapter 3   Priests, Freebooters and Merchants

The quotation from Tomé Pires is taken from *The Suma Oriental of Tomé Pires*, edited and translated by A. Cortesão (London, 1944). An account of Albuquerque's attack on Malacca may be found in Hugh Clifford, *Further India: The Story of Exploration from the Earliest Times in Burma, Malaya, Siam and Indo-China* (London, 1904; new edition, Bangkok, 1990), and the quotation from van Linschoten is taken from the same book. The expansion of the Spanish and Portuguese overseas is described in J. H. Parry, *The Spanish Seaborne Empire* (London, 1966), and C. R. Boxer, *The Portuguese Seaborne Empire* (London, 1969). Valuable summaries of Iberian activity, including descriptions Portuguese and Spanish authors offered of Angkor, are provided in Donald F. Lach, *Asia in the Making of Europe* (Chicago, 1965–77), particularly in Book III. Of great interest for developments in Cambodia during the sixteenth century involving the Portuguese and Spanish is B.-P. Groslier and C. R. Boxer, *Angkor et le Cambodge au XVIe Siècle d'après les Sources Portugaises et Espagnols* (Paris, 1958). Extracts from van Wuysthoff's account of his journey up the Mekong are included in Paul Lévy, 'Deux relations de voyage au Laos au XVIIe siècle', in *Présence du Royaume Lao*, a special issue of *France-Asie* edited by René de Berval (Saigon, 1959). The same source provides the account of the Mekong given by Father Leria, which is taken from Father Giovanni Filippo Marini's *New and Curious History of the Kingdoms of Tunquing and Laos* (first published in Italian in 1663). Given the obscurity of many of the Portuguese and Spanish texts dealing with the countries along the Mekong, it is worth noting the availability in English of a modern translation of Gabriel Quiroga de San Antonio's *A Brief and Truthful Relation of Events in the Kingdom of Cambodia* (Bangkok, 1998). First published in Spanish at Valladolid in 1604, the title is somewhat misleading, since much of the book does not deal with Cambodia. It is, nevertheless, of considerable interest and includes material relating to the exploits of Diego de Veloso and Blas Ruiz. Li Tana, *Nguyen Cochinchina: Southern Vietnam in the Seventeenth and Eighteenth Centuries* (Ithaca, NY, 1998) fills a gap in the history of this region, including the Mekong Delta. An older, Vietnamese source dealing with the delta and translated into French in 1863 is G. Aubaret, *Histoire et Description de la Basse Cochinchine (Pays de Gia-Dinh)* (Paris, 1863). Condor's *The Modern Traveller* which deals with the Mekong was published in London in 1830 and was part of a remarkable 30-volume collection, *'Description, Geographical, Historical, and Topographical, of the Various Countries of the Globe'*. As always with issues in Southeast Asian history, valuable synthesis of the period described in this chapter may be found in D. G. E. Hall, *A History of South-East Asia* (4th edition, London, 1981).

Chapter 4   Filling in the Blanks on the Map

Martin Stuart-Fox, *A History of Laos* (Cambridge, 1997) provides the first modern, comprehensive history of Laos. Boxer's and Groslier's *Angkor et le Cambodge*, already cited, gives details on visits to Angkor by Europeans in the seventeenth and eighteenth centuries. On McLeod's journey to the Mekong, see Clifford's *Further India*. Father Bouillevaux described his visit to Angkor in *Voyage dans l'Indo-Chine 1846–1856* (Paris, 1858). Henri Mouhot's account of his explorations, including his visit to Angkor, was published posthumously in 1864 as *Travels in Siam, Cambodia and Laos, 1858–1860*, London. The book may be consulted in a modern reprint edition with an Introduction by Michael Smithies (Singapore, 1992). Smithies has also written an extended essay on Mouhot in Victor T. King, ed., *Explorers of South-East Asia: Six Lives* (Kuala Lumpur, 1995).

Chapters 5 and 6   The Mekong Explored

Both Jean-Pierre Gomane's and my own book on the Mekong expedition (see the references for Chapter 1 above) provide detailed bibliographies for the account related in these chapters. Special mention should be made of the official record of the expedition produced under Francis Garnier's direction and with Garnier as the principal author, but with contributions from other members, notably Delaporte, Joubert and Thorel. Comprising two volumes of text and two folio volumes of maps and plates, the short title of this bibliographic rarity is *Voyage d'Exploration en*

Indo-Chine effectué pendant les années 1866, 1867 et 1868 (Paris, 1873). A posthumous version of Garnier's own more informal account of the expedition was published in Paris in 1885 as *Voyage d'Exploration en Indo-Chine*. This book and Garnier's articles originally published in *Le Tour du Monde* form the basis for English language editions of the nineteenth century material: *Travels in Cambodia and Part of Laos* and *Further Travels in Laos and Yunnan* (Bangkok, 1996). Many of the plates from the 1873 edition of the expedition's report are reproduced in an accompanying volume, *A Pictorial Journey on the Old Mekong: Cambodia, Laos and Yunnan* (Bangkok, 1998). An extended biographical esssay on Francis Garnier's life is my 'Francis Garnier (1839–1873): Explorer of the Mekong River' in King, *Explorers of South-East Asia*. Louis de Carné's account of the expedition, *Travels in Indo-China and the Chinese Empire* (London, 1872), is available in a modern edition, *Travels on the Mekong: Cambodia, Laos and Yunnan* (Bangkok, 1995).

Chapter 7 Gunboats and 'Conquered Hearts'

The events discussed in this chapter should be read against the broader background of colonial endeavour as outlined in studies such as: David Chandler, *A History of Cambodia*; David Wyatt, *Thailand: A Short History* (New Haven, 1984); Le Thanh Khoi, *Le Vietnam* (Paris, 1955); Martin Stuart-Fox, *A History of Laos*; Milton Osborne, *The French Presence in Cochinchina and Cambodia* (Ithaca, NY, 1969). Jules Harmand's accounts of his travels, originally published in *Le Tour du Monde*, have now appeared in an English translation as *Laos and the Hilltribes of Indochina* (Bangkok, 1997). His comments on the populations of Cambodia are taken from manuscript sources in the French colonial archives, Aix-en-Provence. Paul-Marie Néïs, like Harmand, published his material in *Le Tour du Monde*. An English translation of his articles in that magazine is *Travels in Upper Laos and Siam* (Bangkok, 1997). His account of his illness is, again, held in the archives at Aix-en-Provence. A modern reprint of Pavie's account of his role in Laos is available as *Au Pays des Millions Eléphants et du Parasol Blanc (à la Conquête des Coeurs)*, with an introductory essay on Pavie's life by Loïc-René Vilbert (Rennes, 1995). The Pavie mission's explorations are recorded in *Mission Pavie: Indochine*

1879–1895, 10 volumes (Paris, 1898–1919). A critical British view of France's expansion into the countries of Indochina is James George Scott, *France and Tongking* (London, 1885). A modern survey of this period focusing on developments affecting Siam is Patrick Tuck, *The French Wolf and the Siamese Lamb: The French Threat to Siamese Independence* (Bangkok, 1995). Archibald R. Colquhoun's reference to his crossing the Mekong is contained in *Across Chryse, Being the Narrative of a Journey of Exploration through the South China Borderlands from Canton to Mandalay*, 2 volumes (London 1883). G. E. 'Chinese' Morrison writes of crossing the Mekong in *An Australian in China* (London, 1895). For a modern retracement of Morrison's travel in China, see Angus McDonald, *The Five Foot Road: In Search of a Vanished China* (Sydney, 1995). Prince Henry of Orleans expresses his doubts about navigating the Mekong in *Around Tonkin and Siam* (London, 1894).

Chapter 8   Navigating the Mekong

On Reveillère and his long association with Indochina, see Volume 2 of Georges Taboulet's monumental study, *La Geste Française en Indochine* (Paris, 1956). The details of d'Arfeuille's and Rheinhart's survey are contained in documents consulted in the archives at Aix-en-Provence. Luc Lacroze, *Les Grands Pionniers du Mékong: Une Cinquantaine d'Années d'Aventures, 1884–1935* (Paris, 1996) provides much of the detail on which I rely in this chapter. I gladly acknowledge the importance of his research. H. Warington Smyth's comments on Simon's achievements are contained in his *Five Years in Siam, From 1891 to 1896*, 2 volumes (London, 1898). Marthe Bassenne's memoirs have been published in an English translation as *In Laos and Siam* (Bangkok, 1995). The account of Peter Hauff's shipment of teak logs down the Mekong is contained in Fleur Brofos Asmussen, *Lao Roots: Fragments of a Nordic–Lao Family Saga* (Bangkok, 1997).

Chapter 9   Fear and Fascination

Pierre Billotey's account of his travels was published in 1929. It is representative of a literary school that enthused over France's colonial endeavour and followed in the footsteps of admiring descriptions of earlier decades, such as A. Masson, *Hanoi Pendant la Période Héroïque* (Hanoi, 1929). For French relations with the Cambodian court, see Alain Forest, *Le Cambodge et la Colonisation Française: Histoire d'une Colonisation sans Heurts (1897–1920)* (Paris, 1980), and John Tully, *Cambodia Under the Tricolour: King Sisowath and the 'Mission Civilisatrice' 1904–1927* (Melbourne, 1996). The Vietnamese view of this period was naturally very different and is well reflected in David Marr, *Vietnamese Anticolonialism* (Berkeley, 1971). For a non-French view of the interwar colonial period, see H. Franck, *East of Siam: Ramblings in the Five Divisions of French Indochina* (New York, 1926). Norman Lewis described his visit to Laos in *A Dragon Apparent* (London, 1951). On André Malraux and his activities in Indochina, see Walter Langlois, *André Malraux: The Indochina Adventure* (New York, 1966). This a book that contrasts very favourably with the account of Malraux in Cambodia and Vietnam to be found in Axel Madsen, *Malraux: A Biography* (London, 1977). A more balanced recent biography is C. Cate, *André Malraux: A Biography* (New York, 1997). Pierre Brocheux has published a major study of the Mekong Delta, which is now available in translation as *The Mekong Delta: Ecology, Economy, and Revolution, 1860–1960* (Madison, Wisconsin, 1995). Grant Evans' essay, 'The Transformation of Jinghong,' in Grant Evans, ed., *Where China Meets Southeast Asia* (Singapore, forthcoming) provides historical background on Jinghong, including the reference to William Dodd's visit in 1919 recorded in Dodd's *The Tai Race: Elder Brother to the Chinese* (Cedar Rapids, Iowa, 1923).

Chapter 10   War, Failed Peace and Plans for the Mekong

There is an enormous range of material dealing with the First Indochina War. As a summary review of the period, Stanley Karnow's *Vietnam: A History* (revised edition, London, 1991) is reliable and readable. An older but still valuable account is Donald Lancaster *The Emancipation of French Indo-China* (London, 1961). Philippe Deviller's book quoted at the beginning of this chapter was published in Paris in 1953. On Cambodia during the period 1945–54, Chandler's *A History of Cambodia* is, as always, penetrating. For Laos, Martin Stuart-Fox's *History of Laos* should be consulted. Andrew Graham's satirical novel, referred to in this chapter, was published in New York in 1959. This chapter reflects my own residence in Cambodia, 1959–61 and 1966, and my presence in Vietnam at the time of the Battle of Ap Bac. It was reported at the time with great insight by David Halberstam, who includes an account of the battle in *The Making of a Quagmire* (New York, 1964). For the events leading up to the establishment of the Mekong Committee, I am indebted to the opportunity to read a 1995 manuscript by Nguyen Thi Dieu of Temple University, 'Water, War and Peace: The Mekong River and the Struggle for Indochina'. The quotation from the United States National Security Council report at the beginning of this chapter comes from Ms Dieu's work. On the Mekong Committee, I am also very glad to acknowledge the opportunity given me by Abigail Makin to consult her 1997 Griffith University PhD thesis 'The Politics of Regional Cooperation on the Mekong, 1957–1995'.

Chapter 11   War, Victory and Defeat along the Mekong

As well as relying on the general works dealing with Cambodia, Laos and Vietnam already cited, this chapter reflects a series of research visits to Cambodia and South Vietnam between 1966 and 1972, and two periods of acting as a consultant to the United Nations High Commissioner for Refugees in relation to the Cambodian refugee problem in 1980 and 1981, working along the Thai–Cambodian border. I have not previously written in detail of Duong Sanh, but Monsignor Paulus Tep Im Sotha receives extended treatment in my *Before Kampuchea: Preludes to Tragedy* (Sydney, 1979; expanded edition, 1984). More information on Tep Im may be found in François Ponchaud, *The Cathedral of the Rice Paddy* (Paris, 1990). In gathering material concerning Tep Im's death, I remain grateful to Father John Carroll S. J. of the Ateneo de Manila who kindly made enquiries on my behalf with the Sacred Congregation for the Evangelisation of the Peoples in Rome. I was also able to talk with Tep Im's former secretary in Battambang in August 1981, when he confirmed many of the details of Tep Im's last days in 1975. Among the accounts of the massacre of Vietnamese in Cambodia, Denis Warner's *Not Always On Horseback: An Australian Correspondent at War and Peace in Asia, 1961–1993* (Sydney, 1997) is particularly valuable. Cambodia at war is described in a masterly fashion by David Chandler in *The Tragedy of Cambodian History: Politics, War and Revolution Since 1945* (New Haven 1991). Wilfred Deac provides a military perspective in *Road to the Killing Fields: The Cambodian War of 1970–1975* (College Station, Texas, 1997). For an account of the rise to power of the Khmer Rouge, see Ben Kiernan, *How Pol Pot Came to Power* (London, 1985), and David Chandler's biography of Pol Pot, *Brother Number One: A Political Biography of Pol Pot* (Boulder, Colorado, 1992, and Sydney, 1993; revised edition, Boulder, 1999). My biography of Sihanouk, *Sihanouk: Prince of Light, Prince of Darkness* (Sydney, 1994) offers commentary on the atmosphere of life in Phnom Penh while Cambodia's long-term leader held power. The American air war in Laos is vividly descibed in Christopher Robbins, *The Ravens* (New York, 1989).

Chapter 12   Tragedies of Peace

There is now a large literature covering the victory of the Khmer Rouge forces in 1975 and the subsequent Pol Pot years. In this chapter I make specific reference to Deac, *Road to the Killing Fields* (see above), for the bombing of Neak Luong; to Jon Swain's *River of Time* (London, 1995); and to Father François Ponchaud's *Cambodia: Year Zero* (New York, 1978). But any discussion of this period will take account, at least, of David Chandler's and Ben Kiernan's books already cited, plus Kiernan, *The Pol Pot Regime: Race, Power, and Genocide in Cambodia under the Khmer Rouge, 1975–79* (New Haven, 1996); Elizabeth Becker, *When the War Was Over* (New York, 1986); Bernard Hamel, *De Sang et de Larmes* (Paris, 1977); Someth May, *Cambodian Witness* (London, 1986); Karl Jackson, ed., *Cambodia 1975–1978: Rendezvous with Death* (Princeton, 1989). In his recent account of the multiple tragedies of Cambodia's modern history, *Cambodia: Report From a Stricken Land* (New York, 1998), Henry Kamm provides telling portraits of some of the key personalities who acted on their country's political stage. The material available for Laos is much thinner. Martin Stuart-Fox's general history is, as ever, important. It should be noted that his estimate for the number of those sent to re-education camps is, at 30 000, somewhat lower than other estimates. On the events in Laos following 1975, Grant Evans,

Lao Peasants Under Socialism (New Haven, 1990) is important, as is his more recent *The Politics of Ritual and Remembrance: Laos Since 1975* (Chiangmai, 1998). Also valuable is Joanna Scott, *Indo-china's Refugees: Oral Histories from Laos, Cambodia and Vietnam* (Jefferson, North Carolina, 1989). Coverage of developments in Saigon in the period after the communist victory of 1975 is relatively limited, but insight may be gained from passages in Neil L. Jamieson, *Understanding Vietnam* (Berkeley, 1993) and Henry Kamm, *Dragon Ascending: Vietnam and the Vietnamese* (New York, 1996). Of particular note is the commentary on post–1975 developments provided by a former senior North Vietnamese soldier, Colonel Bui Tin, who lived in Saigon after the communist victory. Originally published in Vietnamese, his memoir is avail-able as *Following Ho Chi Minh: Memoirs of a North Vietnamese Colonel,* (London, 1995). A general survey is Louise T. Brown, *War and Aftermath in Vietnam* (London, 1991). My extended conversations took place with Ping Ling in March and April 1980. Ping Ling has written an account of his life under the Khmer Rouge with the title 'Cambodia: 1,360 Days!'. While I had an opportunity to consult this memoir in the early 1980s, my understanding is that it remains unpublished. Full details of my 1980 survey of Cambodian refugees are in my article, 'The Indo-Chinese Refugee Situation: A Kampuchean Case Study', in Charles Price, ed., *Refugees: The Challenge of the Future* (Canberra, 1981). I visited Vietnam and Cambodia in August and September 1981, when the conversations recorded in the present chapter took place. The account of the incarceration and death of the Lao royal family draws principally on Christopher Kremmer's *Stalking the Elephant Kings: In Search of Laos* (Sydney, 1997).

Chapter 13   The Mekong at Peace

Two valuable accounts of the hostilities that developed between Cambodia and Vietnam while Pol Pot held power in Phnom Penh are: Grant Evans and Kelvin Rowley, *Red Brotherhood at War* (revised edition, London, 1990) and Nayan Chanda, *Brother Enemy* (New York, 1986). Some sense of the paranoia of the Pol Pot regime may be gained from my Australian National University Working Paper, *Aggression and Annexation: Kampuchea's Condemnation of Viet-nam* (Canberra, 1979). For this and the following chapter, I have benefitted from two recent collections of essays dealing with a wide range of issues affecting the Mekong itself and the wider 'Mekong Subregion', both published by the Monash University Asia Institute. These are: Bob Stensholt, ed., *Developing the Mekong Subregion* (Melbourne, 1997) and Stensholt, ed., *Development Dilemmas in the Mekong Subregion* (Melbourne, 1996). The quotation from the article by E. C. Chapman and He Daming at the head of this chapter comes from their article in *Development Dilemmas*. For this and the following chapter I have had the opportunity to consult material issued by the Mekong Commission, including its Annual Reports and various newsletters; also material issued by the Asian Development Bank and the World Bank. Chapman and He provide the most detailed, accessible survey of the Chinese dam-building program in their article, 'Downstream Implications of China's Dams on the Lancang Jiang (Upper Mekong) and their Significance for Greater Regional Cooperation, Basin Wide', in Stensholt, ed., *Development Dilemmas*. Gabriel Lafitte's article in the same volume, 'Ethnicity, Identity, and Economy', provides one of the rare assessments of developments on the Mekong in Tibet. On all environmental issues connected with the Mekong, I have found the publication of the Thailand-based NGO TERRA (Towards Ecological Recovery and Regional Alliance), *Watershed*, of great interest. As an organisation with a clearly defined position that is critical of many of the development plans for the Mekong, it raises many issues that deserve consideration. *Watershed* volume 4, no. 3, March–June 1999 is devoted to fishing issues. My comments on fishing in Cambodia reflect visits to that country and the Great Lake, in 1998 and 1999. I visited the Mekong Delta most recently in 1998. Two valuable discussions of general issues associated with the Mekong River are Peter Hinton's essays, 'Is It Possible To "Manage" a River?: Reflections From the Mekong' in Stensholt, ed., *Development Dilemmas* and, 'Where Nothing Is As It Seems: Between South China and Mainland Southeast Asia in the Post-Socialist Era' in Grant Evans, *Where China Meets Southeast Asia*. A report on concerns raised by Australian and Vietnamese researchers in relation to planned dam building on the Mekong may be read in an article by Leigh Dayton in *The Sydney Morning Herald*, 15 June 1996. On the general issue of ecological problems involving the Mekong, there are useful articles by Michael

Richardson in *The Australian* newspaper for 28 April 1997 and *The International Herald Tribune* of 18 January 1999. For a survey article on Cambodia's Great Lake see Joe Cochrane, *The Australian*, 6–7 March 1999. For an overview of environmental problems in Southeast Asia which includes essays dealing with the Mekong River and its region, see Philip Hirsch and Carol Warren, eds, *The Politics of Environment in Southeast Asia* (London, 1998).

Chapter 14   The Mekong at Peace

In relation to issues raised both in this and the previous chapter, I had the opportunity to discuss Mekong issues with the Mekong Commission in Bangkok in May 1998. For a general discussion of dams and development in China and Southeast Asia, see Gavin McCormack, 'Dams and Water in Southeast Asia', *The Asia-Pacific Magazine*, nos. 9 and 10, 1998; and Philip Hirsch, 'Dams, resources and the politics of environment in mainland Southeast Asia,' in *The Politics of Environment* cited above. The full details of Patrick McCully's book are: *Silenced Rivers: The Ecology and Politics of Large Dams* (London, 1996). Issues associated with the Pak Mun Dam in Thailand have been examined in a number of issues of *Watershed*; see in particular volume 4, no. 2, November 1998–February 1999. Similarly, the Theun Hinboun dam has received detailed attention in *Watershed*, volume 4, no. 3, March–June 1999. On the long-running debate generated by plans to build the Nam Theun 2 Dam, I am especially grateful to Sue Downie for having given me the opportunity to read her unpublished 1997 paper, 'Does the proposed Nam Theun hydroelectric project meet a "sustainable development" criteria, in economic, environmental and social terms?'. Andrew Nette reviews the controversy in his article, 'Dams, Bank and the Asian Crisis', *The Asia-Pacific Magazine*, no. 12, September 1998. Philip Hirsch provided one of the earliest examinations of the many environmental and social issues associated with Nam Theun 2 in his monograph study, *Environmental and Social Implications of Nam Theun Dam* (Sydney, 1991).

Chapter 15   Bridges over Troubled Waters and Lands

For discussion of the My Thuan bridge, see Peter Mares, 'Building Bridges in Vietnam', *The Asia-Pacific Magazine*, nos. 9 and 10,

1998. I visited the site of the bridge in June 1998. My comments on the Friendship Bridge reflect my having made use of it in 1997, but the problems I describe still continue and were the subject of discussions I held in Vientiane in 1998. My visits to Dali and Jinghong, which were the subjects of my discussions with 'Mr Wang' and 'Marie', took place in May 1998.

Epilogue

The details of Michel Peissel's location of the source of the Mekong are in his book, *The Last Barbarians: The Discovery of the Source of the Mekong in Tibet* (New York, 1997).

Index